Eating Uganda

From Christianity to Conquest

Acknowledgements

Any book is more of a combined effort than I realised when I started this one. I want to thank Sheelagh Killeen, who worked with me throughout the project; Professor P.K. Tibenderana of Makerere University, Uganda, and the Rev Michael Meech, Methodist minister, for advice on the manuscript; Georgina Rhodes and Richard Proctor of Rhodes and Proctor for the cover design; Breege Cameron for drawing the maps; Dr Helen Szamuely for compiling the index; Andrew Boyd for the interview in Kampala on which the last chapter is based and the Bible Society of Uganda for making his trip possible; Andrew again for the final form of the title and Brenda Ellison for spotting a serious wrong turning with the sub-title. None of the above, of course, are responsible for mistakes that have crept in; those, regretfully, belong to me. I also want to acknowledge a debt to Thomas Pakenham, whose magnificent Scramble for Africa, combining scholarship with colour and pace over a huge canvas, first made me aware of the fascinating Uganda Question.

CP

Eating Uganda

From Christianity to Conquest

Cedric Pulford

ITURI

Copyright © 1999, Cedric Pulford
The moral rights of the author have been asserted

Published 1999 by Ituri Publications
39 Portway
Banbury, Oxon OX16 7QH (UK)

ISBN 0 9536430 0 X

Text set in 11 pt on 13 pt Ehrhardt,
with headings in Gill Sans Bold,
by Book Production Services, London

Printed in Great Britain
by St Edmundsbury Press
Bury St Edmunds, Suffolk

A CIP catalogue record for this book is available from the British Library

Contents

List of Maps

Names and places

The varying uses of the names Buganda and Uganda are at first sight puzzling. It all began with a pronunciation shift: in the country itself it was Buganda, but at the coast it was pronounced Uganda. The early explorers and writers, coming to the country from the coast, naturally continued to call it Uganda. Early in the colonial period, however, the two words ceased to be interchangeable. As now, Buganda came to mean the original kingdom while Uganda referred to the larger colonial protectorate, which took in Bunyoro, Ankole, Toro, Busoga and other areas as well as Buganda.

Like most sub-Saharan languages, Buganda's is to the outsider an initially confusing mass of prefixes. The language itself, for instance, is Luganda. Kiganda is an adjectival form – e.g. Kiganda culture. Plurals are made by prefixes, not by adding S or some other suffix. One citizen of Buganda is a Muganda; together they are Baganda or Waganda. wa- is the coastal (Swahili) form, and ba- is the form used by the Ganda themselves. The early European travellers used wa-. I have not changed these references in quotations, but otherwise I use the preferred ba-style – even though that modern tribe of African leaders who measure their success in Mercedes-Benz cars sound better as the wa-Benzi!

For names, I have tried to keep to the preferred current forms except in quotations, where the original version is kept. The Zambezi river, for instance, was for Dr David Livingstone the Zambesi. Less obviously, Entebbe and Ntebé are the same place.

The title of the book is based on a common African expression: "to eat the country" means to take control of the country. This is the story of how – in the manner of diners who don't plan their meal, who decide on the courses as they go – the British "ate" Uganda.

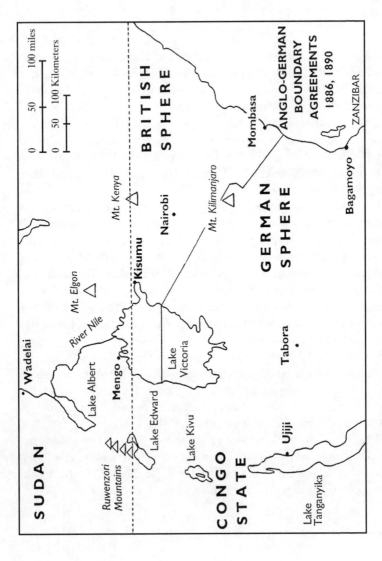

Fig 1 The Great Lakes region in the latter 19th century

North and East

Africa since independence has been a disappointment to its people and to development workers alike, with most countries, more than three decades after independence, afflicted with poverty, exploding populations, corruption, arbitrary rule and crumbling infrastructure. For many Africans living standards are lower than at independence in the 1950s and 1960s.

Yet for a time it seemed that independence would make all things new. On the most charitable reading, it was felt the colonial administrations had neglected their territories. The more common view among African leaders and Western liberals was that colonialism was actually designed to keep dependent territories as vast plantations and mines supplying the so-called mother countries while at the same time providing a captive market for the mother countries' manufactured goods, particularly second-rate ones they chose to dump in the colonies. With independence the future would redeem the past.

Uganda, long before it came to be seen by most Westerners as a rather obscure, politically disturbed country that produced Idi Amin, was one of Britain's most well favoured colonies. Sir Winston Churchill, and the explorer Henry Morton Stanley before him, called it the "Pearl of Africa". In the 1890s the Uganda Question gripped the British nation in the way that more recently the great African famines have done. The all-but-forgotten Uganda Question is well worth revisiting because of what it can tell us about Africa now.

The issues were varied: the abolition of slavery, the protection of Christian missionaries and converts, the expansion of commerce. In two months of 1892, the Foreign Office in London received 174 "resolutions", mostly with many signatures. Religious organisations, particularly the Church Missionary Society, were prominent. Slavery was mentioned in 104 resolutions, commerce in 75 resolutions. Christianity and commerce were never far apart in 19th century Africa.

The question stirring up so much commotion was whether Britain should annex Uganda, a country or properly a series of kingdoms with which it had become progressively involved through the activities of explorers, missionaries and administrators of the private Imperial British East Africa Company. It was a question on which the public, filled with images of David Livingstone's missionary travels and General Gordon's violent death in Khartoum at the hands of Islamic zealots, felt free to have an opinion.

There was plenty to be said on either side of the case. William Gladstone's government was itself divided, with the foreign secretary, Lord Rosebery, in favour of annexation while the prime minister – whose delay in sending relief had probably cost Gordon his life – was against further colonial escapades.

Uganda was well known because two of the heroes of African exploration, John Hanning Speke (1862) and Henry Morton Stanley (1875), had been there and told the world. Buganda, the principal kingdom, was the most sophisticated country in the whole of eastern and southern Africa, yet it lay mysterious and exotic deep in the interior, north of the Great Lake, the Victoria Nyanza, more an inland sea than a lake. On top of all that, Uganda was the source of the Nile, for so long the preoccupation of geographers and explorers.

After the explorers had come the missionaries, and after the missionaries the soldiers in a seemingly inevitable sequence. It, or something like it, had been and was being played out all over Britain's imperial domains. But Buganda was unusual. First, the missionary presence in the remote kingdom had been brought about by one man – Stanley, whose trumpet call for evangelists brought a rapid response from the Church Missionary Society in London. Secondly, the annexation issue was precipitated as much by the need to protect those missionaries and their converts as by the prospects of trade.

What drove the missionaries over much of Africa was the continuing spectre of slavery. Their inspiration was Dr David Livingstone, who had travelled in Africa for more than three decades and publicised the evil traffic in human beings.

Uganda in the late 19th century bristles with controversies that more than a century on retain their power to inflame. It is impossible for an African and a European to perceive the colonisation of the country in the same way, except to the extent that modern Europeans are inclined self-consciously to join the other side.

Even now, Roman Catholic and Protestant authors describing the pivotal event in securing British control over Buganda – the Battle of Mengo in 1892 and its bloody aftermath on Bulingugwe Island – could be writing about different battles.

The three actors upon whom this book is focused – the explorer, Henry Morton Stanley; the missionary, Alexander Mackay; the soldier, Frederick Lugard – are all strong characters where it is difficult to have a middle opinion. Was Stanley a political double-dealer or a Christian pathfinder, a brute with a gun or an inspired leader of men? Was Mackay a selfless servant of Africa, or an arch-imperialist, a true evangelist or a Calvinist bigot? Was Lugard a brilliant soldier-administrator or a bungler, a truth-sayer or a liar?

Obviously I have my own views about all these things, but I have tried to make them not too obvious. The book is not an attempt to rival professional historians over ground already covered; it is about the sheer colour and drama of the clash of two cultures, the African and the European, letting wherever possible the actors speak for themselves. The Uganda story is an astonishing pageant of explorers, missionaries, soldiers, kings and chiefs, porters – the literal beasts of burden. If ever the expression "a cast of thousands" fitted, it is in this story.

Now that Kenya is the powerhouse of East Africa, it is strange to realise that in the 19th century it was simply somewhere one passed through on the way to Buganda. Much of it was barren and peopled by tribes perceived as backward. The souls to be won were to be found in Buganda. So too was the wealth to be taken out in the form of ivory, and to be brought in as manufactured goods. The beginning of the city of Nairobi, Kenya's capital, was accidental. The existing tiny settlement was picked as the headquarters for the

Uganda Railway administration because it was more or less half way between the coast and Lake Victoria, from where steamers completed the journey to Buganda. A town began forming and the Kenya colonial administration at Machakos felt it had to shift so as to be on the railway line.

We naturally think of Uganda as part of East Africa along with Kenya and Tanzania; yet with a different roll of history's dice it might have been an extension of North Africa, an Egyptian, Islamic province instead of a British, Christian colony. It might have looked not eastwards to Mombasa for its route to the world but northwards along the Nile to Khartoum and Cairo. Early European contacts with Buganda came as readily from the north as from the east. Samuel Baker, the first governor of Egypt's Equatorial Province (part of the Sudan) in the 1870s tried but failed to absorb Bunyoro to the south. His successor in Equatoria, Charles Gordon – later the hero of Khartoum – sent emissaries to both Bunyoro and Buganda. He even tried to garrison Buganda but the ruler, Mutesa, captured his troops and they were extricated with difficulty. In 1879, soon after Mackay reached Buganda by the east coast route, a Church Missionary Society party of three arrived from the north along the Nile.

The rise of the Mahdi in the 1880s removed the prospect of Egyptian administration extending south to Bunyoro and Buganda by cutting off the farthest provinces from Cairo and eventually Khartoum. It also blocked the access of European travellers via the Nile. The Mahdi's Islamic fundamentalist movement conquered much of southern Sudan before it took the capital Khartoum in 1885; for a while, it looked poised to reach even Bunyoro and Buganda. In fact, the high tide of Mahdism reached only as far as Equatoria, to the north of Bunyoro, covering some but not all of that province.

In what remained of the province the governor, Emin Pasha, was stranded along with his several hundred Egyptian and northern Sudanese officials, clerks and soldiers. With the blocking of the Nile route and then the fall of Khartoum, he had no source of supplies and had to subsist on whatever could be procured or made locally.

Emin hoped that Equatoria could become a British territory along with Buganda. If this wish had been realised, the tragic history of Sudan in our own time, arising from the domination of the Muslim north over the Christian and animist south, would surely not have happened. The capital of Equatoria before Emin, under pressure from the Mahdists, removed it south to Wadelai was Lado, near modern Juba, the present southern Sudanese capital. If Equatoria had become British, a smaller, Muslim Sudan would have faced a larger, Christian Uganda, or perhaps the Commonwealth country of Equatoria, which would also have taken in other parts of the non-Arab southern Sudan. Reports of continuing slavery in Sudan are a reminder of the enduring, contemporary effects of long-ago political manoeuvres.

Emin was visited by the occasional traveller; he was also able to get letters out to the east coast via Mackay in Buganda. In these ways his plight became known. A relief expedition was organised in London under Stanley. The failure of this expedition (1887-89) was a cause célèbre in its day. It managed not the relief of Emin but his removal, with many of his followers. A couple of years later Lugard began the making of Uganda as a British colonial possession, but by then there could be no question of including Equatoria because there was no Equatoria to include.

The British government's eventual answer to the question should Britain annex Uganda was yes, and Buganda was joined with adjacent kingdoms into a protectorate, declared in 1894. The country spent the next seven decades under British rule, although protectorate status – based on treaties with the indigenous rulers – provided somewhat more local autonomy than a colony would have.

Because the high hopes of Africa's independence generation have not been fulfilled – for reasons that are examined in this book – it is now possible to take a more balanced view of the colonial experience. One of the apparent puzzles is why during the colonial period chiefs and leaders of African society co-operated so fully, happily even, with the foreign masters. Which of us wants to condemn our parents or grandparents as quislings, yet that is what many Africans seem to confront. But Europeans also have emotional journeys to make. If colonialism is to be condemned as wholly evil does that make our parents and grandparents, who were there, evil too?

The historian D.A. Low asked about Buganda in the colonial period, who were the collaborators and who were the resisters, and answered that they were often the same people. Perhaps we are better placed to understand that insight than when Low published it in 1971. Africa remains a fascinating place for those who care to look, listen and feel; a place of many layers with colonial, and indeed neo-colonial, structures and attitudes working alongside far older, indigenous forms which, we now see, never went away.

2

The Great Lake

Much of the Uganda story is about water, in particular the Great Lake, the Victoria Nyanza. The lake, the largest in Africa, 26,000 square miles (67,000 sq km) in size, almost as big as Scotland, nowadays is bordered by three countries: Uganda, Kenya and Tanzania. In Victorian times it found redoubled glory as the long-sought source of the Nile. This flows out the lake and makes its way via Lake Kyoga into Lake Albert at the top (northern) end.

Lake Albert has a most distinctive shape: it is 100 miles (160 km) long and around 20 miles (32 km) wide. On one side is Uganda and on the other side the Republic of Congo (the former Zaire). This formidable body of water is still less than one-twelfth the size of Lake Victoria.

From Lake Albert the Nile flows northwards through the heartland of the one-time Egyptian province of Equatoria. At Khartoum this White Nile is joined by the Blue Nile from the Ethiopian highlands, to form one of the world's mightiest rivers.

Uganda's other great lake is Lake Edward, which again it shares with Congo. The lake is linked to the smaller Lake George by the Kazinga Channel. To the south, beyond the Uganda border, lie Lake Kivu and Lake Tanganyika; beyond those again is Lake Malawi (formerly Lake Nyasa).

Uganda is a country of a stunning beauty made up of rivers, forests and hills. Part of its western boundary runs along the Ruwenzori Mountains, which haunted Victorian writers under their ancient name, the Mountains of the Moon. The Ruwenzori reach 16,765 feet (5,110 metres). The whole country is high up although with a big variation in height: Lake Albert is at 2,030 feet (619 metres), Lake Edward 2,991 feet (912 metres) and Lake Victoria 3,717 feet (1,133 metres) – a fact that the builders of the Uganda Railway from the coast knew too well.

From the beginning Lake Victoria was an obsession with European travellers. Ronald Hardy, in *The Iron Snake*, pictures how the railway builders in the 1890s were at one with earlier travellers in their feelings:

"The Lake was much more than the terminus for a railroad. It had long had a mystical place in the imagination, exciting many of the Great Explorers and those that sent them on their strange and wonderful journeys. An aura of cruelty lay on its southern shore: to these beaches the early Arab slavers had come from Kazeh. It was romantic: only forty years had passed since Speke came to Mwanza and saw for the first time this vastness of water. It was beautiful: behind the tawny beaches the land was exuberant with palms, mangoes and flamboyants. It was malignant: the northern shore was infested by the mosquito, the spirillum tick and the tsetse, and in the groves and islands lived death and desolation. It was unpredictable: it oppressed with its gloom and sullenness and turbidity, it enticed with its colour, it disturbed with its scent of barbarism, it beguiled with its serenity, it frightened with its sudden moods of violence and the electric storms that charged the water with power and turned it black as pitchblende. And, of course, it was the fountain of the Nile … The Lake was no docile basin of water. It was a force: a secret and a mystery: the source of life and fertility."

The lake was also a barrier for Buganda-bound travellers in the sense that a straight line from either Bagamoyo (near Dar es Salaam in present-day Tanzania) or Mombasa (Kenya), which were the main points of departure, runs through the middle of it. The missionary Alexander Mackay sailed across the lake from the Church Missionary Society base at Kagei to reach Buganda for the first time, but most travellers went round it. Earlier travellers followed the routes of most of the explorers, leaving from Bagamoyo and entering Buganda through Karagwe, at the south-west end of the lake. The other way was from Mombasa through Masailand and into Busoga, at the north-east end of the lake.

The choice of the Bagamoyo route was based partly on fear of the Masai, across whose lands the route from Mombasa ran. The fierceness of the nomadic and pastoralist Masai had been much exaggerated by the explorer Joseph Thomson, who may himself have been given a false impression by traders wanting to discourage outsiders. The Masai's seemingly gruesome habit of feeding on their animals' blood helped build a myth has lasted to this day.

Busoga, the territory next to Buganda on the approach through Masailand, was highly sensitive. The Baganda had a belief that a conqueror would emerge from the east (as he did in the form of Captain Frederick Lugard of the Imperial British East Africa Company) so they were extremely suspicious of strangers entering Busoga. When this route became safe for European travellers, it was the shorter and better way. Eventually, the Uganda Railway followed close to the caravan route.

To reach Buganda from the coast a trek of about three months was needed for the journey of approaching 700 miles (1,100 km) through the tribal lands of what are now mainland Tanzania and Kenya. Travellers moved in caravans at a surprisingly slow pace: seven or eight miles (11-13 km) a day was usual. Water, food and fuel-wood were constant preoccupations. Parties picked their routes by the availability of water, and had to stop early to scour the area for food and fuel.

Provisions were paid for with trade goods, of which cloth, wire and beads were especially popular. An eye had to be kept on fashions, however. Frederick Jackson recorded how a vast stock of blue beads, which had accumulated at the Mumia's staging post, became valueless because of a sudden change in fashion (*Early Days in East Africa*).

Journeys relied on human porterage. Many experiments were made with pack animals, especially donkeys, but these did not cope well with the climate, the tsetse fly or the fevers that abounded. Illness was common among the porters, whose standard load was 65 pounds, or 30 kilos – half as heavy again as a suitcase filled to airline maximum weight, which most modern travellers can manage from the trolley as far as the check-in belt. Another reason for the slowness of marches was that sick men travel slowly – except where they were treated like useless pack animals and discarded by the roadside.

It is not easy for modern Westerners to imagine the constant illness that was the experience of the early Europeans in Africa. Fevers were commonplace and frequent, as they still are for many millions of Africans even in the cities. Illness affected not only European travellers but also those in a settled situation. Often it was brought on by hard work. Both Lugard and Père Lourdel, one of the first Roman Catholic missionaries at the Buganda capital, make interesting comments (quoted later) about the connection between fatigue or stress and illness. It is an insight easily missed in modern urban life, but one that could save millions of pounds in doctors' fees and prescriptions.

3

'This Open Sore'

*Livingstone's example * Crossing the continent * Missionary Travels *
Senate House challenge: commerce and Christianity * Exploring the
Zambezi * Heart-sore of slavery * Meeting with Stanley * Livingstone's
last journey * Enduring achievement*

The story of modern Uganda begins, paradoxically, many hundreds of miles to the south with the man who more than any
other brought home to the English-speaking world the evils of the
slave trade throughout Africa. David Livingstone was the inspiration for the first missionary involvement in the country.

He was born to poor parents in Blantyre in central Scotland in
1813. After starting working life in a cotton mill, he eventually qualified as a medical doctor and became ordained. He arrived in Africa
in 1840, aged 26. With only two visits to Britain, he was to spend the
rest of his life – more than three decades – there.

Livingstone, who married the daughter of the famous missionary,
Robert Moffat, spent the first years in South Africa. On various
travels he came face to face with the ghastly reality of slavery, of captured Africans, many of them young boys, wrenched from their
homes and put into yokes as they were marched towards the coast,
of villages burned and deserted after a visit by slave raiders. These
searing experiences caused him to turn away from the life of a settled missionary to take up travel and exploration. Livingstone's
vision was to find viable routes into the interior for legitimate commerce and Christianity. He believed that slavery would only be
ended through the commercial development of Africa, which would
put in place alternative, honest means of making a living.

What remains inspirational about Livingstone's travels is that for
much of the time he travelled solely with African companions and,
having very little money at least in his early years, he enjoyed such
good relations with chiefs that they gave him porters for no payment.

With his family back in Britain, Livingstone set out from Linyanti (in present-day Zimbabwe), with 27 followers of the Makololo people to seek a route to the west coast, a journey by river and land of more than 1,000 miles (1,600 km).

They reached Luanda and got back, but the route did not seem promising, and soon Livingstone – this time with more than 100 Makololo in support – was heading over a similar distance for the east coast. The route lay along the River Zambezi. In November 1855 he became the first European to see the Victoria Falls, or Mosi-oa-Tunya (the Smoke that Thunders) as the local people called it. This expedition ended at Quilimane on the coast, so he had successfully crossed the continent from west to east.

Livingstone returned to Britain in 1856 to a hero's welcome. During this visit of about 15 months he wrote *Missionary Travels and Researches in South Africa*, which was published in 1857. He also made his famous challenge to well-wishers crowding the Senate House, Cambridge: "I go back to Africa to try to make an open path for commerce and Christianity; do you carry on the work which I have begun. I leave it with you!"

Back in Africa, he headed a Zambezi expedition, with the rank of British consul, Quilimane. His family was with him; so too was a young doctor, John Kirk, later the British consul-general in Zanzibar and a major force behind the final suppression of the slave trade in East Africa.

Livingstone now explored the Rivers Zambezi and Shiré, using a portable boat, the Ma-Robert (an African name for Livingstone's wife). During this five-year expedition, he explored Lake Nyasa (now Lake Malawi), and led the Makololo whom he had left near the coast after the crossing of the continent back to their homes at Linyanti. Sometimes the tragedies of the slave trade could be forgotten: this was an Africa of primeval beauty. He counted a herd of 800 elephants. With primeval beauty went primeval tragedy: fever was ever-present, and in 1862 Mrs Livingstone died from a fever at Shupanga on the Zambezi.

Livingstone was back in Britain in 1864, staying for just over a year. He wrote another book, *The Zambesi and its Tributaries*. When he sailed to Africa for the third and final time, it was at the request of the Royal Geographical Society to explore the watershed around

Lakes Nyasa and Tanganyika and to try to unravel the continuing mystery of the source of the Nile.

Livingstone was already 52, even today an advanced age for expeditions and perhaps unwise in the conditions then. His supply of quinine was stolen – a devastating loss in the malarial climate. Nevertheless, he walked doggedly on, exploring Lake Mweru (now shared by Zambia and Congo) and Lake Bangweulu (in modern Zambia). Even his faithful followers became restive at the Doctor's desire to see yet another lake, but Livingstone knew that he was by the headwaters of either the Congo or the Nile, and would not be deterred.

Slavery was all about. He confided to his journal: "I am heartsore, and sick of human blood." He travelled into the country of the Manyema, a tribe much feared by those around them. At that time they were cannibals, and were also used by the Arabs in slave raids. By now more than six years had passed since his return to Africa. He was fever-racked and a living skeleton when he made for Ujiji, an Arab settlement on Lake Tanganyika. He had ordered supplies to be sent there, but they had been stolen.

Livingstone was ill and destitute when Henry Stanley, on an assignment for the New York Herald, found him in Ujiji on October 28, 1871. With Stanley's resupply and his company, Livingstone rallied. They sailed together in a canoe on the lake, then travelled to Unyanyembe. Stanley left with the promise to send supplies and equipment to allow Livingstone to carry out a final task: he wanted to ascertain whether the River Lualapa fed into the Congo or the Nile (it was the Congo). The supplies arrived, but by now he was too ill to continue the work and died at Chitambo's village in Ulala on May 1, 1873. He was 60.

The world rightly saw as his finest epitaph the fact that six of his followers brought the body through many difficulties and obstructions to Zanzibar, from where it was returned to Britain for interment in Westminster Abbey. Livingstone's heart, meanwhile, had been cut out and buried at Chitambo's. The memorial stone in the abbey quotes Livingstone's words about slavery to the New York Herald, the newspaper that sent Stanley to find him: "All I can add in my solitude is, may Heaven's rich blessing come down on every one, American, English, or Turk, who will help to heal this open sore of the world."

After the lionising of Livingstone, it was inevitable that a reaction would follow in later years. His achievements in exploration have been questioned; it has been said he made few converts, that he exposed his wife to the hazards which killed her, that travel in the end became travel for travel's sake. Even if it were all true, Livingstone's enduring achievement is one of witness: of dramatising the evil of the slave trade, of humanity and forbearance, of non-violence and doggedness unto death. Africa certainly says so. Three decades after independence, when other European names had been consigned to history, there was still a town called Livingstone in Zambia and a city called Blantyre in Malawi.

Livingstone also called into being the career of one the giants of African exploration – Henry Stanley. When Stanley met Livingstone he was a journalist who had knocked about here and there, and for whom the expedition was ultimately just another assignment; after what Stanley recognised as a defining experience of his life, he saw himself as an explorer and gave the rest of his life to work in Africa.

When Basil Mathews's *Livingstone the Pathfinder* was published in 1912, a living voice emerged from history: Sir John Kirk. Livingstone's companion on the Zambezi expedition added his recollection to later editions of the book. He spoke of Livingstone's "absolute lack of any sense of fear" (adding that it "amounted almost to a weakness"). This quality, which probably cannot be learned or willed, many times allowed Livingstone to face down hostile tribesmen and to die in God's time, not man's.

Kirk told how Christ Church Cathedral was built on the site of the old slave market in Zanzibar. He said of his old chief: "How happy he would be to see it! ... Perhaps he does."

4

Meeting Mutesa

*Encounter with the kabaka * Stanley's vision * His appeal to
Christendom * Tales of angels * A man of paradoxes * Mutesa's motives
* An advanced kingdom * Universality of the banana plant * Powers of
life and death * Sir S. Baker in Bunyoro * Under siege by Kabarega *
The bible beats the gun*

For us more than a century later, Stanley's words seem to crash
through every racial and ethnic taboo in sight. The Ganda – the
inhabitants of Buganda – were "an extraordinary people, as different from the barbarous pirates of Uvuma, and the wild, mop-headed
men of Eastern Usukuma, as the British in India are from their
Afridi fellow-subjects, or the white Americans of Arkansas from the
semi-civilized Choctaws", he told readers of *Through the Dark
Continent*. Fine if you are a Briton, a white American or a Ganda;
not so hot if you happen to be an Afridi, a Choctaw or from Uvuma
and Usukuma.

At the time of publication in 1878, however, Stanley's words
would have been read in quite the opposite sense. Here was confirmation that in this near-legendary kingdom of Buganda, in the
African interior, were foundations that could be built upon for
Christianity, commerce and civilisation. Few doubted that the three
belonged together, or that the people of the world were strung out
in levels of social evolution, with the goal for all to become like the
great industrial nations of Europe and North America.

When Stanley met Mutesa, the kabaka (king) of Buganda, beside
Lake Victoria on April 5, 1875, he quickly formed a favourable view
of the ruler. The explorer John Hanning Speke a few years before
had found Mutesa wallowing in blood, but for Stanley he was "an
extraordinary monarch", "an intelligent and distinguished prince".
In the evening of their first meeting, Stanley confided to his diary:
"In this man I see the possible fruition of Livingstone's hopes."

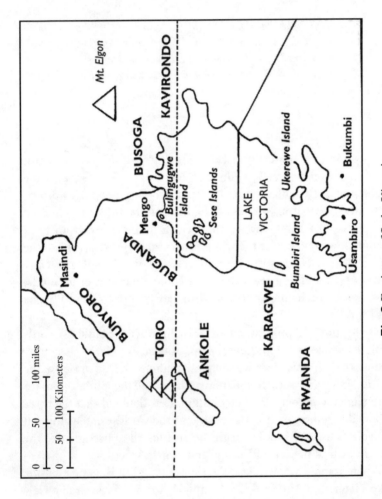

Fig 2 Environs of Lake Victoria

Mutesa was "the light that shall lighten the darkness of this benighted region".

Stanley clearly had no doubts about deciding what was right for Africa and, misplaced as such self-confidence may seem to us, his attitude then was commonplace. He wrote of the kabaka: "My impression of him was that ... I should make a convert of him, and make him useful to Africa." Perhaps Stanley saw what he wanted to see: he needed a charismatic figure as the climax to this stage of his expedition, and he found one. Missionaries later spoke of Mutesa's continued blood orgies, but for Stanley a change of character had been wrought by a visiting Muslim called Muley bin Salim. Unfortunately, this meant Mutesa's conversion to Islam, but Stanley was not deterred. "I shall begin building on the foundation stones laid by Muley bin Salim. I shall destroy his belief in Islam, and teach the doctrines of Jesus of Nazareth."

This was Stanley's second African expedition, following his journey to find Livingstone. He was the prototype explorer-journalist, generating press copy as abundantly as he made discoveries. For this trip the New York Herald, sponsors of Livingstone expedition, had been joined by the Daily Telegraph of London. One of Stanley's tasks was to establish the shape and proportions of the great inland sea of the Victoria Nyanza (lake). Along the northern side of the lake lay Buganda.

Mutesa's scouts found Stanley aboard his big rowing boat, the Lady Alice, named after one of his unsuccessful loves, so that when the expedition was ready to land in Buganda the kabaka and his nobles were waiting in full ceremonial order beside the lake at Usavara. Two to three hundred guns, as Stanley estimated it, were fired in welcome with much drumming and shouting.

It was nearly another mangled meeting for the explorer. He had greeted Livingstone with a banality born of unnecessary precision; now he strode up to a short young man standing beside a great standard, but was told in time that this was not Mutesa but the katikiro. Not knowing what a katikiro was, Stanley bowed and the young man bowed back. Later, Stanley learned that the katikiro was the title of the first minister. He met the ruler after being given the opportunity to bathe, brush up and prepare externally and mentally for the Foremost Person of Equatorial Africa (Stanley's capitals).

Mutesa must have made a very striking figure. He wore a tarboosh (an Islamic-style cap, similar to a fez) and a black robe, with a white shirt belted with gold. Approaching middle age, he was slender and about 6ft 1in (1.85m) tall. Stanley explains that among the Baganda this was not an unusual height. The explorer was just 5ft 5in (1.65m), although heavily built. Stanley described the king as dark red brown in colour, with a "general expression of amiability combined with dignity". When not in council, he gave rein to hearty peals of laughter. He seemed to be interested in the manners and customs of European courts, and wanted to hear about "the wonders of civilization". He understood Swahili, as well as the indigenous Luganda language, and could read and write in Arabic characters.

If Stanley was impressed with Mutesa, the feeling was probably mutual. Stanley impressed by shooting a crocodile at 100 yards (90m). The party soon transferred to the nearby capital, which Stanley in his book introduces in breathless tones. The hill Rubaga! The imperial capital! This was journalistic licence. Although Rubaga was on a large scale, it was a town of straw huts and vegetable gardens set among plantain groves.

The country was described as crescent-shaped beside the lake, 300 miles (480km) long and 60 miles (95km) wide. Including Sese and other islands in the lake, the size was 30,000 square miles (77,700 sq km) with tributaries adding another 10,000 square miles (25,900 sq km). Stanley estimated the population of Buganda proper at 750,000 and the total population including the tributary states as 2,775,000. These figures can be nothing more than "best guesses" by the traveller (and the density of population in the tributary states is curiously higher), although Buganda's allocation of the country into feudal estates must have helped the accuracy of the guesstimates.

At the royal court, Stanley found another European visitor. This was Col Linant de Bellefonds, a member of General Gordon's staff in the Equatorial Province (Equatoria) of the Sudan. Much of the conversation at court was about Christianity. Fortunately for the future of Christian mission in Buganda, the French de Bellefonds was a Protestant. The first missonaries might not have found a footing if Protestants and Roman Catholics had contradicted each other at the start, as happened commonly later on. As it was, Stanley records Mutesa's astonishment that the Frenchman "employed nearly the same words, and delivered the same responses" as Stanley had.

The king learned about Christian doctrines including the Ten Commandments. Stanley prudently added an eleventh commandment: "Honour and respect the Kings, for they are the envoys of God." His evangelical fervour was rewarded when Mutesa ordered Christian prayers every Sunday. Mutesa was still a Muslim, but before Stanley finally left Buganda he converted to Christianity – which the explorer acknowledged was "only nominal".

It was a start. but Stanley, as we have seen, had plans for Mutesa. Before he left the court after a visit of 11 days, he wrote his famous letter to his sponsors, the New York Herald and the Daily Telegraph, appealing for missionaries. It was entrusted to Col Linant de Bellefonds, who would send it on after his return to Equatoria. De Bellefonds was ambushed and killed on the journey back. The letter was found concealed in one of his boots. Seven months after Stanley wrote it, the letter reached England, where its publication in November 1875 caused a sensation.

The appeal, written hurriedly as Stanley acknowledged, was couched in the most high-flown language: "What a field and harvest ripe for the sickle of civilization! Mtesa would give [the missionary] anything he desired – houses, lands, cattle, ivory, &c.; he might call a province his own in one day. It is not the mere preacher, however, that is wanted here. The bishops of Great Britain collected, with all the classic youth of Oxford and Cambridge, would effect nothing by mere talk with the intelligent people of Uganda. It is the practical Christian tutor, who can teach people how to become Christians, cure their diseases, construct dwellings, understand and exemplify agriculture, and turn his hand to anything, like a sailor – this is the man who is wanted. Such an one, if he can be found, would become the saviour of Africa. He must be tied to no church or sect, but profess God and His Son and the moral law ...

"I speak to the Universities Mission at Zanzibar and to the Free Methodists at Mombasa, to the leading philanthropists, and the pious people of England. 'Here, gentlemen, is your opportunity – embrace it!' The people on the shores of the Nyanza call upon you. Obey your own generous instincts, and listen to them ..."

What a stirring call to evangelism and adventure! Stanley may have been writing the job description of an angel rather than a human being, but thousands of young men must have felt they could fill the bill.

The author, meanwhile, continued the exploration of the lake. There were his customary scrapes, including an escape from the dastardly chief of Bumbireh Island, whom he later attacked in revenge. In Ukerewe, he was impressed by King Lukongeh, whom he described as "quite as much influenced by conversations about Europe as Mtesa" and "as eligible a convert to Christianity". The route took the party near what became the Ripon Falls, the boundary between Buganda and Busoga. Here Stanley met Mutesa again.

This time the kabaka was in battle mode. He was about to make war on Uvuma. Stanley put Mutesa's army at 150,000 spears, plus 50,000 women followers and 50,000 children and slaves. Scholars have challenged the figure of 150,000 troops as inconceivably high, just as Stanley years later gave an even less credible figure of 200,000 Wanyankori (Ankori [Ankole] was claimed by Buganda as a dependency) brandishing spears. All agree that the numbers were large. The time needed to assemble the army left plenty of opportunity for talk. At one of these meetings in the camp at Nakaranga, Mutesa remarked that if you wanted knowledge you must talk to the white men to get it, then lobbed in: "Now, Stamlee, tell me and my chiefs what you know of the angels." Stanley was not flummoxed, at least not for long: he described the angels of Michelangelo and Gustav Doré, then, sending for his bible, translated passages about angels from Ezekiel and St John. He knew his bible and pressed it to his aid.

There is no reason to doubt the genuineness of Stanley's Christianity. Nor was it simply an expedient to open Buganda to a European presence. Stanley was, however, a man of the deepest paradoxes, whose personality and actions have puzzled and divided biographers ever since. He was an evangelical Christian who stomped through Africa in shoot-'em-up style. He claimed to fight for food only when he could not trade for it, yet he fought far more than most other explorers, some of whom did not find it necessary to fight at all. He was a Welsh poor-house boy who became a knight of the realm. He was British, then American, then British again. In his later activities directed at Equatoria and Buganda he may have been serving two masters and playing the highest politics, or he may have been rescuing a trapped man for humanity's sake. He was self-taught, yet wrote with the erudition and style of an Oxford scholar. He has been called a suppressed homosexual, but he could look back on heterosexual amours and married for the first time when he was over 50.

At least until his final expedition into Equatoria, Stanley could rightly claim to be the most successful African explorer. He was also one of the most brutal. He was Bula Matari (the "Breaker of Rocks"), a nickname that referred to his road-building exploits in the Congo and also describes his character. Whether he was successful because he was brutal, maintaining discipline, securing provisions, forcing the way through, is a question that still divides commentators. To present-day readers (and to many contemporaries) Stanley's readiness to execute members of his own expeditions for disciplinary offences is shocking. So too are revenge attacks like the one he made on the chief of Bumbireh Island. Stanley saw these actions as setting examples and sending signals. His writings do not suggest that he had any doubts about his actions. A certain sort of evangelical has the happy knack of knowing that God invariably agrees with his own preferences.

Frederick Jackson summed up in *Early Days in East Africa* Stanley's reputation as he found it in Zanzibar: "There, he was regarded as a man of undoubtedly great courage and determination, but self-centred, overbearing, ruthless and a man who would stick at nothing; not quite the hero he was in Europe and America."

Stanley is full of paradoxes, yet in another sense he seems transparent. It is easy, and not necessarily wrong, to see the seeds of the man in his monumentally disadvantaged beginnings. Born illegitimate in 1841, he was named John Rowland. He was abandoned by his mother to the poor-house, and again rejected by her a few years later. In his mid-teens he went to America as a ship's boy and stayed. He took the name Henry Morton Stanley from a great benefactor he found in New Orleans. The benefactor soon died, leaving him friendless again. At Stanley's height, and with this background, you either learn to stick up for yourself or you go under.

Stanley got caught up in the American Civil War, enlisting on the

Confederate side. After capture, he "turned" and served with the Union forces – evidence of opportunism for his critics. He landed on his feet at the New York Herald, where with the most rudimentary education his resourcefulness and a willingness to be away from home (which he hardly had) for months at a time soon took him to the post of a top foreign correspondent. Then he was picked for the choicest assignment of all: to find Livingstone.

Stanley's background seems the perfect crucible for the man he became: self-reliant, serious and tough. All commentators, contemporary and current, agree that Stanley had a will of iron that nothing could break. This gave him the edge on his rivals.

Frank McLynn, in *Hearts of Darkness: The European Exploration of Africa,* finds both practical and psychological motives for African exploration in the 19th century. It was a means of rising socially and financially; it could also be an expression of an "action neurosis" – the need to keep moving. Many explorers had a distaste for urban life and the burgeoning industrialisation of the period. Stanley manifests a "Prospero complex" – seeking a world where one can ignore the personalities of others. Leading expeditions across the expanses of Africa was obviously an inviting activity for a 19th century Prospero, and McLynn points out that Stanley could not accommodate equals. All five Europeans on his first two expeditions died, for instance. Excessive aggression directed to the external world, McLynn notes, is a classic sign of a death drive. (It is not suggested that Stanley brought about the deaths of his companions.) Stanley did not get his wish, if that is what it was, to leave his young bones in Africa, but he was several times on the point of death there. He died in England in his early sixties, racked to the last by the fevers that had been his constant companions in Africa.

Mutesa's prime motive in accepting a European presence that eventually "ate" his country was to obtain goods and, above all, weapons. These he needed to withstand the attacks he feared from the Mahdists to the north. Moreover, the kabaka seems to have had a love of ideas and learning. Buganda combined complex political and social structures with a very low technological base. What was needed for life above the village subsistence level had to come from outside. The Europeans were an even better source of goods than the Arabs, whose presence they balanced. In time the Europeans ceased to be an opportunity and became a threat, but the failure to see a fledgling cuckoo is only too common. In the modern world, there are plenty of present-day countries that have found great powers easier to invite in than to get out. Stanley's *Through the Dark Continent* gives us a detailed sketch of Buganda before the coming of the Europeans. His aim was to awaken England and beyond to the opportunities for trade and Christianity in Buganda. He drew for his readers a picture of an advanced state, under a civilised prince, lacking only the redeeming moral base of religion. Even with these rose-coloured lenses, the information is valuable reportage from one of the first whites to see the country.

Social organisation was evidenced in the scale of the kabaka's dramatically sited hilltop palace at Rubaga. The audience chamber, which was made of a wooden frame and supports covered with straw, was 60ft (18m) long by 18ft (5.5m) wide. It had a gabled roof which at its highest reached to 25ft (7.6m) . The king's compound consisted of many huts, and the whole was surrounded by palisades. The palace was approached by wide avenues cut through the plantain groves.

Construction techniques were of the simplest. Alexander Mackay, who arrived in Buganda in 1878, remarked that wood was fixed together by lashing, not nailing or pegging, while the principle of the lever was unknown. However, the principle of the wheel was understood: banana trees were used as rollers to move logs or canoes, and Stanley noted that Mutesa was planning a wagon or carriage.

Much of the country was of "inexhaustible fertility" with a landscape dotted with hills giving way to higher land of treeless savannah. Stanley, with his reporter's eye for detail, listed the crops: plantain, banana, pawpaw, yams, sweet potato, peas, beans, melons, cucumber, vegetable marrow, manioc (the unattractive root, dangerous unless properly cooked, that was both life and death for African expeditions), tomato, wheat, rice, maize, sesamum, millets and vetches. Not only was the food various but it was also plentiful. So too was pombé (beer) and maramba (banana wine). The great staple in the area was plantains.

The people were elaborately clothed compared with most surrounding tribes. The universal dress was bark cloth, made from strips of tree bark beaten time after time until the required thinness was achieved. This was worn as a clay-coloured robe reaching to the feet. The nobles wore woven cloths obtained from the Arab traders. Many Baganda were tall, as Mutesa was: they often stood more than 6ft 2in (1.88m). The language, Luganda, was not put into written form until the coming of the missionaries, but Stanley noted that the kabaka and many of the nobles could read and write Arabic.

Buganda society is presented in three layers: the kabaka, chiefs and peasants. The treatment is inevitably superficial; the writer spent just days in the country. Even the term "peasant" belongs more to the toilsome lands of Europe than to favoured Buganda where crops virtually leapt fully formed out of the ground. Stanley's archetypal peasant, contentedly at home in his hut surrounded by simple but sufficient household effects, has a decided feel of Merrie England!

Either Stanley was puzzled by the ordinary people of Buganda, or he bent his comments to support his theme of an estimable nation awaiting only the arrival of Christianity: they are said to love cleanliness, neatness and modesty; also to be crafty, fraudful, deceiving, lying and thievish knaves – a range of qualities not usually found together.

Stanley's writing is characterised by enormous energy and range, and when he forgets to be portentous in the high Victorian manner, great clarity. The range of subjects is especially striking: no sooner have we learned in detail about the rank structure of the Buganda royal family than we are offered a list of the various uses of the banana plant, which "in the eyes of the untaught civilized man ... seems to be of no other use than to bear fruit after its kind".

However, the different varieties of banana give the Baganda
(1) their main food,
(2) a "honey-sweet, cider-flavoured" wine and, mixed with millet, beer,
(3) fronds for thatch, bedding, wrappers and covers of everything from a table to a pudding,
(4) stems for fences and as rollers to move heavy logs or canoes,
(5) stalks from which can be made both shields and sun-hats,
(6) pith to be turned into toilet sponges,
(7) cord from the fibres.

Stanley concludes that "besides its cool agreeable shade, the banana-plant will supply a peasant of Uganda with bread, potatoes, dessert, wine, beer, medicine, house and fence, bed, cloth, cooking-pot, table-cloth, parcel-wrapper, thread, cord, rope, sponge, bath, shield, sun-hat, even a canoe – in fact almost everything except meat and iron".

Stanley did not conceal the arbitrary power of life and death wielded by Mutesa. For the peasants, despotic power was the serpent in paradise, but paradise was a big place where they might hope to avoid the kabaka. For the chiefs, though, insecurity was a fact of everyday life. A young man called Magassa rises through the feudal system (Stanley relates). He is given the title of the pokino and the estates that go with it. He rises higher still, becoming the katikiro. But he is still subject to Mutesa's arbitrary power. He never knows when the "lords of the cord" (the official stranglers) will visit him, and of course in the end they do.

Unsurprisingly, everybody wanted to please Mutesa. His retinue was considerable – about two score of dummers, a score of fifers, half a score of guitar-players, several mountebanks, clowns, dwarfs and albinoes, a multitude of errand boys, pages, messengers, courtiers and claimants, besides bodyguards and two standard-bearers, "either following or preceding him wherever he goes, to declare his state and quality". On a smaller scale the chiefs repeat this display, and so on down to the peasant or cowherd, "who makes an infantile slave trot after him to carry his shield and spears".

As presented by Stanley, the kabaka was a bundle of contradictions. Besides Mutesa's obvious civilised attributes there were "strong evil propensities", as Speke had mentioned already and Mackay was to do later. One of those civilised attributes was a liking for ideas, as when he asked Stanley about angels. Mutesa was no savage chieftain simply gouging goods out of travellers. Every visitor had to give something: arms were especially welcome; goods were acceptable; the fortunate traveller might get away with sharing some of his intellectual property. "Mtesa is the most interesting man in Africa," Stanley wrote, "… through him only can Central Africa be Christianized and civilized."

In neighbouring Bunyoro, which Buganda claimed as a tributary state, no such favourable views about its rulers were held by Sir

Samuel Baker, whose visited the kingdom as an explorer and returned years later when he was governor of Equatoria. His first encounter with the omukama (king) of Bunyoro almost cost him his mistress, Florence; his next encounter almost cost him his life.

On both his visits to Bunyoro, Baker came from the north along the Nile basin unlike Stanley and Speke, who had reached Buganda from the east coast. The two countries were at the fulcrum of the two great routes of exploration.

Baker, the wealthy sportsman and traveller, bought Florence at a slave auction in the Turkish-ruled Balkans. She was still in her teens, and he was twice her age. Together they made some of the toughest and most life-threatening journeys in the European exploration of Africa. In due course they married, although not soon enough for Queen Victoria, who refused to receive Florence because of her previous unsanctified state.

In April 1861 the Bakers (the style is strictly premature because they married later) started up the Nile with the plan of meeting Speke and his companion, James Grant, who were to travel down it from Lake Victoria. Speke and Grant's expedition was intended finally to lay to rest the controversy over the source of the Nile by showing that it originated in the great lake. This was finally proved to be so; hence Speke's famous phrase: "The Nile is settled."

After more than a year the Bakers reached Khartoum, then an isolated Egyptian garrison town and slaving centre. Greater isolation lay ahead because they were heading another 1,100 miles (1,770km) south to Gondokoro, which they reached in February 1863. The settlement, near modern Juba, was a lawless place that existed for just two reasons – slaves and ivory. Here soon afterwards Baker and Florence met Speke and Grant.

The travellers from the south told about the handsome Baganda people. Speke was well placed to know because his stay included romantic dalliances. By a girl called Meri he is supposed to have fathered a child. This was the visit when Speke decided that Mutesa was a blood-thirsty tyrant. The travellers thought little better of Omukama Kamurasi in Bunyoro. His hostility forced them to travel overland rather than along the river whose course they were tracing.

What Speke and Grant reported fired Baker with the prospect of a major discovery for himself. To the north-west of Lake Victoria there was known to be another great lake. Its relation to the Nile, beside which they were now sitting, and to Lake Victoria, where the Nile originated, was not clear. The lake was known locally as Rwita nzige – the killer of locusts (the lake being so big that locusts trying to fly across it would land in the water and die). Baker was to rename it Lake Albert. The connection of the two lakes is as close as their namesakes could have wished: the Nile flows from Lake Victoria into Lake Albert, and out again for its great journey northwards to the Mediterranean.

To reach the Rwita nzige meant entering Kamurasi's kingdom. The distance was about 400 miles (640km), but because of the cataracts of the Nile the boats were sent back to Gondokoro and the small party made the journey overland. With many delays it took the better part of a year.

They found the Banyoro far more developed than the tribes to the north. Baker was struck by their skill at pottery. The men wore gowns of bark cloth and the women, bare-breasted, wore short double petticoats. The stay at Kamurasi's capital was not happy, though. The king was ravenous for the contents of the Bakers' travelling boxes and finally ravenous for Florence. Baker was neither a diplomat nor a coward. When he pulled a gun on the king threatening to shoot him if he repeated the request, Kamurasi retreated. Perhaps to make amends, he provided the party with an escort for most of the way to the lake, which, early in 1864, they were able to gaze upon at last. The journey was most hazardous. Food was often short. Baker and Florence were constantly ill. The risk was all the greater because they had run out of quinine to treat malaria. And now all they had to do was get back again ...

Since coming to Africa the Bakers had had a university course in slavery. The subject must have been particularly sensitive for them because Florence had herself been intended for a Turkish harem. Khartoum was a major slaving centre, while Gondokoro existed for not much else. When the Bakers returned to Kamurasi, they found Bunyoro was under threat from a slaving army from the north. The Bakers' guns helped to see off the attack. It was many months before they could get away. They returned to Gondokoro in March 1865 – almost four years since they started the journey up the Nile.

When the Bakers returned to Bunyoro seven years later, it was at the head of a column of troops. Samuel had become famous, as much for his unusual companion as for his adventures on the Nile. He married Florence, was knighted by Queen Victoria and in 1870 was appointed governor of the Equatoria by the khedive (viceroy) of Egypt. He established a garrison at Gondokoro, which became the province's capital. Then with Lady Baker and the Sudanese troops he set out for Bunyoro. Such a forward policy could hardly be justified when the rest of the province had not been brought under effective administration – but administrative duties were not what Baker was about.

Kamurasi had died, and by 1872 his son, Kabarega, ruled Bunyoro. Florence made a little character sketch of the king, who for more than 25 years kept up the fight against successive rulers of Buganda: "He is a very clean-looking young man of about 18 or 19 years old, he keeps the nails of his feet and hands beautifully clean and wears a very nice bark cloth of a light brown colour, and a necklace of pretty small different coloured beads. His skin is dark brown, his eyes are large, but they always have a frightened look." [Quoted by Richard Hall, see bibliography].

This time, however, Baker was not just passing through Bunyoro. He built a house in Kabarega's capital, Masindi, which was to be the nucleus of a permanent government station. Then he told Kabarega that the country was now a dependency of Egypt, and would share in the bounty of trade. The point was illustrated with an array of cutlery, crockery, watches and cloth as well as spinning tops, tambourines and whistles.

The Bakers also built a house for themselves. Richard Hall, in *Lovers on the Nile*, explains that they decorated this to impress Kabarega – sporting prints, life-sized posters of beautiful women, a framed portrait of Queen Victoria. When the king saw endless images of himself in face-to-face wall mirrors, he thought it was magic. He made all his entourage try the electric shock machine, but did not have a go himself.

It was, however, all bluff by Baker, and the bluff was called. With 100 soldiers, he lacked the strength to impose his rule. The blessings of trade would be unlikely to materialise over the long and difficult route to Gondokoro. He was unlucky, too, in his adversary. Behind Kabarega were merchants like Abou Saood, deeply implicated in slavery, who stood to lose under Baker's rule. Kabarega himself had a particularly strong impulse for independence, which he continually demonstrated in fights with the Baganda and later the British. By stages the Bakers' party found itself under siege in Masindi as Kabarega's regiments camped all around. The Egyptian party was lucky to get out. Before the Maxim gun, 100 men with muzzle-loaders stood little chance by weight of numbers against 5,000 warriors, some of them with firearms. Baker thwarted a couple of attacks, the first by striking up the band and distracting the warriors, the second by torching the grass huts of the capital. The column then made a fighting retreat, under constant harassment, to beyond the Bunyoro border. The grand adventure had ended on a falling note.

Baker in Bunyoro, and first Speke then Stanley in Buganda, had made the outside world aware of these kingdoms beside the lakes. Baker's attempt to take over Bunyoro without the military means was a failure; an attempt by Gordon to extend Egyptian suzerainty to Buganda ended in humiliation when Mutesa captured his soldiers; Stanley's appeal for missionaries for Buganda proved far more potent than either.

5

'My Heart Burns'

*Anonymous gift * Venn's principles of mission * First missionaries at
Rubaga * Death of Shergold Smith and O'Neill * Mackay at the lake *
Rebuilding a boat * Sin of Christian disunity * Rescuing slaves *
Polygamy rebutted * Tribal spirituality * Religion, reading and medicine*

IF the "the people on the shores of the Nyanza" were calling upon
"the pious people of England", in the words of Stanley's 1875
appeal, they were quickly answered from London by the Church
Missionary Society. Two days after the appeal appeared in the Daily
Telegraph, the society's lay secretary received this letter:
"November 17th, 1875
"Dear Mr Hutchinson, – My eyes have often been strained wist-
fully towards the interior of Africa, west of Mombasa, and I have
longed and prayed for the time when the Lord would, by His
Providence, open there a door of entrance to the heralds of the
Gospel.
"The appeal of the energetic explorer Stanley to the Christian
Church from Mtesa's capital, Uganda, taken in connexion with
Colonel Gordon's occupation of the upper territories of the Nile,
seems to me to indicate that the time has come for the soldiers of the
Cross to make an advance into that region.
"If the Committee of the Church Missionary Society are pre-
pared at once and with energy to organize a Mission to the Victoria
Nyanza, I shall account it a high privilege to place £5000 at their
disposal as a nucleus for the expenses of the undertaking.
"I am not so sanguine as to look for the rapidity of success con-
templated by Mr. Stanley; but if the Mission be undertaken in
simple and trustful dependence upon the Lord of the Harvest,
surely no insurmountable difficulty need be anticipated, but His
presence and blessing be confidently expected, as we go forward in
obedience to the indications of His providence and the command of

His Word.
"I only desire to be known in this matter as
AN UNPROFITABLE SERVANT"
[The signature was Luke 17, v10: "We are unprofitable servants:
we have done that which was our duty to do."]
It was an enormous gift. A further £10,000 was soon found, and
within less than half a year a party of eight volunteers were on their
way to Buganda. Among them was Alexander Mackay, the man
whom Stanley was to adjudge "the best missionary since Livingstone".

The Church Missionary Society was (and is, under its revamped
name, the Church Mission Society) a voluntary organisation within
the Anglican Communion. It was founded in 1799 in London by a
small group of Church of England members who felt there was both
room and need for another missionary body alongside the Society
for the Propagation of the Gospel and the Society for Promoting
Christian Knowledge.

The later 18th century had been a bad time for organised religion.
As Britain's empire grew a parallel need was felt to minister to the
overseas settlers and to the indigenous peoples they lived among; yet
the scientific rationalism of the Enlightenment had for many made
God deeply unfashionable, an outdated idea that could be consigned
to history. This was the time when Bishop Butler declined to be
made Archbishop of Canterbury, the spiritual head of the Church of
England, because he saw no future for a "falling church". Then in
reaction came the "Great Awakening". The founders of the CMS
were moved by the same evangelising impulses that moved the
Methodists in England and the Moravians in Germany.
Evangelicals to this day are a major strand in the Church of
England.

Like the Roman Catholic White Fathers – soon to be its rival in
Buganda – the CMS could take pride in a major church figure
within its ranks. With the White Fathers it was their founder,
Cardinal Lavigerie, a leader in the fight to suppress slavery. With
the Church Missionary Society it was Henry Venn, who was the
London-based clerical secretary and effective leader of the society
from 1841 to 1872. Venn kept the Society on its evangelical rails,
echoing his clergyman father's dictum of "the church-principle but

not the high-church principle". He was a pioneer in elaborating the proper relationship of missionaries to the communities they serve. The missionary brings the gospel to those outside the church and the pastor ministers to those within the church. For Venn it was dangerous for missionaries to become tied down in, for example, education and medical work because they then lacked time for evangelising.

Venn became famous as the advocate of the Triple Autonomy principle for indigenous churches – that they should become, as soon as possible, self-supporting, self-governing and self-extending. Jocelyn Murray comments in *Proclaim the Good News* (a history of the CMS, published in 1985): "This teaching is now seen as almost an axiom of the missionary movement, but we do well to remember that this was not always the case, and how much we owe to Venn for his insight. He logically associated it with a high view of the ability of African, Indian and other new Christians to receive a theological education, to take responsibility, and to exercise leadership."

The aim of Triple Autonomy was, in a delightful phrase, the "euthanasia of mission", when local Christians were able to run their own churches. Murray explains how, following Venn's principles, a Christian community steadily grows until there is the basis for forming an Anglican diocese under an indigenous leader – a position, of course, long since reached throughout the Third World. Venn urged the formation of "Christian companies" under an elder. These would become congregations, which in turn would form into conferences, which would support an episcopal structure.

Perhaps most remarkably, in an age when travel to distant places was measured in weeks rather than hours, Venn never saw any of his ideas being worked out on the ground. His ideas were forged in England and he never visited any overseas mission field.

It was to a society alive with Venn's ideas that Alexander Mackay offered himself. He was the son of a presbyterian minister in Aberdeenshire, Scotland. He trained as an engineer at Edinburgh University and at a locomotive works in Germany. He had a wonderfully practical disposition. In Africa he contrived a magic lantern out of some lenses and a biscuit tin. His workshop included a forge, lathe, grindstone and printing press. These practical skills must have commended him to the CMS for Stanley had stressed that "the practical Christian tutor" not "the mere preacher" was needed for Buganda. Mackay also struck the right note when he wrote to the society from his German lodgings, where he had chanced to see an advertisement asking for volunteers.

"My heart burns [wrote Mackay] for the deliverance of Africa, and if you can send me to any of those regions which Livingstone and Stanley have found to be groaning under the curse of the slave-hunter I shall be very glad." It may be hard for us to grasp how so many men and women of goodwill were driven by outrage over slavery continuing in the later 19th century. Similar strength of feelings is called forth in our own day over unpayable Third World debt.

The leader of the CMS party was Lieutenant Shergold Smith, whose Royal Navy career was ended by losing sight in one eye after an attack of fever. Smith had known enough of Africa and its troubles to want to stay there in another role. Like Mackay, he was moved by the spectre of slavery. He also struck the right note, telling the society: "Send me out in any capacity, I am willing to take the lowest place." Aware of his capabilities, the recruiters sensibly decided otherwise.

The march up-country was about 600 miles (970km), from the starting point opposite Zanzibar island to the south side of Lake Victoria, from where the missionaries' own boat, carried in parts, would take them across to Buganda. The CMS party went off in sections. Mackay left on August 27, 1876, in the company of two (unrelated) Smiths – his great friend, Dr John Smith, and the expedition leader. Ahead of them was a trek of about three months. It must have been a bitter disappointment to Mackay that after 73 days he had to turn back. Seriously ill with fever, he returned to the coast helped, and often carried, by faithful bearers.

The party found it necessary to split into several parts. Shergold Smith and an ordained man, C.T. Wilson, had the honour of being the first missionaries in Buganda. Crossing the lake, Smith had met with a personal tragedy. They were stoned by the inhabitants of an island en route. Broken glass from his spectacles went into his one sighted eye, and blinded him. The horror of being so handicapped in such a situation is almost unimaginable. Nevertheless, they continued, reaching Rubaga on June 30, 1877. The the next day, the Sabbath, was passed in retirement. They called on Mutesa on the

Monday. This is Smith's account of the meeting:

"Rubaga, Uganda, July 8th, 1877

"This was our reception. I could not see, so my report is that of ear.

"The king rose as we entered, and advanced to the edge of his carpet, and shook hands. A fine fellow, over six feet [1.83m], broad shoulders, and well made; grace, dignity, and an absence of affectation in his manner. He motioned us to seats. Then five minutes were allowed for drum-beating and looking round. I longed for sight to see.

"Calling one of our guides, I heard his animated report. Then the Sultan of Zanzibar's letter was read, after which the C.M.S.'s.

"It was read in Swahili by a young fellow named Mufta [he was also called Dallington], one of the boys Stanley had brought with him, and left with the king, at his request, to teach him to read the Bible. At the first pause, the king ordered a *feu de joie* to be fired, and a general rejoicing for the letter; but at the end, where it was said that it was the religion of Jesus Christ which was the foundation of England's greatness and happiness, and would be of his kingdom also, he half rose from his seat, called his head musician, Tolé, to him, and ordered a more vigorous rejoicing to be made ...

"The following day we went twice. In the morning it was a full court as before, and from some cause he seemed suspicious of us, and questioned us about Gordon, and rather wanted to bully us into making powder and shot, saying 'Now my heart is not good.' We said we came to do as the letter told him, not to make powder and shot; and if he wished it, we would not stay. He paused for some time, and then said, 'What have you come for – to teach my people to read and write?' We said, 'Yes, and whatever useful arts we and those coming may know.' Then he said, 'Now my heart is good: England is my friend. I have one hand in Uganda, and the other in England.'

"He asked after Queen Victoria, and asked to know which was greatest, she or the Khedive of Egypt. The relative size of their dominions was explained to him, and referring him to our letter, I said how desirous England was that his kingdom should be prosperous ... "

Shergold Smith was soon to die. He and another mission member, T. O'Neill, were massacred with most of their party on

Ukerewe island, on the south side of Lake Victoria, after gallantly refusing to give up an Arab fugitive they were sheltering. Mackay's great friend, Dr John Smith, also died, from fever.

Mackay, after convalescing on the coast, reached the south side of the lake at his second attempt. It was June 13, 1878. The CMS missionaries had established a lakeside base at Kagei. From here he commented in a letter on the lack of technology he found around him: "Among the natives a sail is unknown ... It is a strange fact, and one which I believe is true of every tribe in Central Africa, that the natives are absolutely unacquainted with the art of fastening two pieces of wood together, except by lashing. As a rule, therefore, they prefer the laborious task of hewing everything out of the solid. Oars are unknown. Propulsion is by short paddles like large wooden spoons. Much toil is therefore entailed, but only what one might expect; for no negro knows the use of the lever, or of any other simple mechanical appliance by which to save labour. In all operations, work is done by the application of sheer brute force; hence the people are everywhere worn out at an early age, merely for want of contrivances. It is really astonishing that an old man or old woman is scarcely ever to be found. All are done up, or worked out, in middle life, and then they die."

A knowledge of "contrivances" was to be why he lasted so long in Buganda. Mackay soon had an opportunity to use his remarkable practical skills and ingenuity. Wilson came across the lake in the portable boat, the Daisy, and they set out together for Buganda. In a storm the boat was forced back to the shore, with Wilson, Mackay and the crew being lucky to escape with their lives. The damaged boat needed repairs, but where to find suitable timber? Mackay cut out the boat's middle section to use the wood for the fore and aft sections. The resulting Daisy was stubbier but seaworthy again.

They reached Buganda on November 1, 1878. Mackay, the man who was "burning" for the deliverance of Africa, had already spent more than two years on the continent without even seeing his mission field, but at last the work could begin. With Wilson and Mackay together the work of bringing souls to Christ could be doubled. Soon there was an unseemly competition in salvation. The White Fathers arrived the following year (1879). The two sets of missionaries squared up to each other as well as to heathendom and vice.

Even the physical location of the missions in the capital underlined the competition, the Catholics on Rubaga hill and the Protestants facing them across a valley from another hill, Namirembe. The sin of Christian disunity had already reached Buganda.

The French-speaking White Fathers – the Society of Missionaries of Africa – were founded in Algiers in 1868 by Cardinal Charles Lavigerie. They were so called because they wore an Arab-style white robe and burnous (a hooded cloak), with a rosary around the neck like a Moslem chaplet. Three of the fathers found martyrdom in 1875 on the way to Timbuktu. Their leader in Buganda was Père Lourdel, a man who like Mackay stayed in Africa for many years without a break and left his bones there.

Among the Protestants, great anguish was caused by the Catholic habit of "shadowing" their missions by setting up rivals nearby. This seemed particularly indefensible when so much of Africa was an unsown field. The Catholics, however, felt it their duty to counter the heretics. The Protestants felt a parallel duty to correct the errors of the Church of Rome.

Language was often extreme on both sides, although the comment by the Vatican's *Annals of the Propagation of the Faith* (1828) about Protestant bible societies takes some beating: "Let us hope that the zeal of the children of light becomes as ardent as that of the children of darkness." After such a comment the Annals' observation that the Protestant bibles are "poisoned with the venom of error" seems almost mild!

Both Mackay in letters and a CMS colleague, Robert Ashe, in his book *Two Kings of Uganda*, recorded examples of the Catholic fathers dropping in on Protestant services at the Buganda court, and ostentatiously declining to take part. Mackay vividly describes an incident when the Catholics refused to kneel in prayer. When the Baganda asked why, Lourdel became excited and said: "We do not join in that religion, because it is not true; we do not know that book, because it is a book of lies."

The difficulties were rooted in different understandings of Christianity arising from the Reformation. Partly the dispute was about the relative importance of sacraments and the word of God expressed in scripture. Many Protestants loathed the veneration of the Virgin Mary, which they saw as spilling over into worship, and what they saw as superstitious invocation of the saints: these were felt to diminish the stature of Jesus as our only mediator with God; for many Catholics, the Protestants' denigration of the Blessed Virgin and the saints was part of a trail of heresies that had led them to reject the Pope and spurn the One True Church. Protestants despised the control that Catholic priests wielded over their flocks through the power to grant absolution from sins. There were problems too with the Roman Catholic mass, seen by Protestants as an idolatrous additional sacrifice that denies the uniqueness of Christ's own sacrifice and by the Catholics as a re-enactment and reaffirmation, through the Real Presence, of that sacrifice.

Important, even crucial, as these issues are in the right settings, a new mission field in the African interior is clearly not one of them. Nor were tensions limited to the two Christian communities. When the Mill Hill Fathers, another Catholic group, arrived to make a third missionary presence, there were often tensions between them and the White Fathers. Surrounded by so many forces of darkness, many of the missionaries lost sight of the principle that "the enemy of my enemy is my friend".

Both Protestant and Roman Catholic missionaries were driven by a desire to see the end of enslavement in Africa – warring tribes who made slaves of their neighbours or the organised traffic in human beings for export. In Buganda's wars with surrounding countries no quarter was given to the defeated soldiers. Thus large numbers of women and children became available to be made slaves. The countries of Bunyoro and Busoga were the main source of slaves. The missionaries redeemed as many as they could. There were many small boys at the CMS mission. Some had been given by chiefs and others had been bought. A boy called Lwanga cost a padlock and four yards (3.7m) of calico.

The 1885 Treaty of Berlin, which triggered the scramble for Africa, agreed powers for European nations to suppress slaving, while Cardinal Lavigerie was a prime mover behind the 1890 Brussels conference for the abolition of the slave trade.

Lavigerie's Armed Brethren of the Sahara, founded in 1890, favoured a robust way for winning converts. The publication Truth satirised this approach:

Take this Banner, and if e'er
Arabs will not bow in prayer,
Chant a psalm their shrieks to drown,
Shrive and Bible in your hands
Teach the truth through heathen lands
Preach, convert, baptise, anoint,
Even at the bayonet's point.
Far and wide, without surcease,
Spread the Gospel's news of peace
Far and wide, in Heaven's name,
Spread the news with steel and flame
Brethren! Oh! be not afraid
Heaven your Christian work will aid;
Banish all your doubts and tears,
Rifles cannot fail 'gainst spears.
Take your banner! Onward go!
Christian soldiers, seek your foe,
And the devil to refute,
Do not hesitate to shoot

Roman Catholic mission work, which had tended to lag behind that of Protestantism, was reanimated during the pontificate of Leo XIII covering (1878-1903). Much of the effort went into creating villages to develop a sense of work and community. Many of the inhabitants were children ransomed from slave traders. These Christian converts, boys and girls, were encouraged to marry each other when they grew up, creating the nub of an enduring Christian community.

Protestants too sheltered ex-slave children and orphans – Stanley commented that at Mackay's last mission station, Usambiro, there were boys everywhere – but they also emphasised the growth of commerce as a way to check the slave trade. Another perceived evil was polygamy. The Protestant missionaries often came as married couples. This was partly to offer an example of successful monogamous families in the face of polygamy.

Mackay, who was evidently a skilled debater, recorded this exchange on the subject with Muslims:

"Sunday, October 5th [1879]. – The subject of polygamy was talked on for some time. I told them that I fully recognized the difficulty of the case, but said that we should also go in for many wives were it not that the plain command of God was against it. I said that they could still keep their households of women as servants. The Mussulmans had again much to say. They declared that polygamy had nothing to do with religion. I asked their chief advocate, 'How many wives have you?' 'Four.' 'Why not five?' This they knew to be an injunction of their creed, and could not answer. They then maintained that religion was a thing of pure belief, and had nothing to do with matter of life. I asked, 'Then why did you not join the chiefs and me in the food which the king sent out to us just now?' They were floored again, and Mtesa and the whole court laughed heartily at them.

"The difficulty is this. At present a man's status is reckoned by his establishment, which depends on the number of his wives. These cook the food, and do all the work.

"'How is a man to get on with one wife and several children alone in his house?' asked the king. 'Who will look after the goats, cook the food?' &c. I said that we in Europe had women servants always in the house; but they were not our wives, and need not be necessarily wives here either."

The status of the man with many wives has echoes a century later where for many in Africa a man's status increases with the number of his children. This is a cultural impediment to curbing population growth just as polygamy was a cultural impediment to becoming a Christian.

Both Catholics and Protestants emphasised the ability to read as the way to obtain access to the joys of Christianity. Both have been accused of destroying local cultures but, according to Jean Comby, in *How to Understand the History of Christian Mission*, this was partly accidental: "This emphasis on the written word rather than the oral word, combined with the struggle against pagan literature, meant a certain destructuring of local cultures, though this was not necessarily sought."

The missions were very Western in their style and approach, however. Stephen Neill, in *A History of Christian Missions*, finds that the association of missions with Western governments was "far closer than was wise or right", while "the duty of the convert is clear – to trust in the superior wisdom of the white man". Neither approach would have appeared so outrageous at the time as it does today. Then, commerce and Christianity were seen as elements of the same package so it was considered natural for governments and churches to work together. With the prevailing ethos of social Darwinism, it was to be expected that indigenous people should be evangelised into the whites' mode of Christianity.

Much of the traditional spirituality that the missionaries found was held to be incompatible with Christianity. Propitiating numerous earth spirits cannot be reconciled with worshipping a single God. Present-day efforts to fuse Christianity and animism also express the ethos of a period, our own. No doubt history will decide. Moreover, numerous tribal customs were a problem for the missionaries – for example, slaves buried with their chiefly masters or wives of the dead passed to the husband's brother.

Both Catholics and Protestants stressed sexual continence outside marriage. For the Catholics there appeared to be a further obstacle to the creation of an indigenous African priesthood: the rule of celibacy of the clergy. Neill points out: "Celibacy, entirely unknown in a continent in which early and universal marriage was the rule, seemed to present an insuperable obstacle." That it did not happen that way shows the dangers of stereotyped expectations about behaviour based on race or nation.

Looking at the general picture around the world, Neill found that the Roman Catholics – after a late start – often "with government support, with apparently inexhaustible supplies of recruits, with a very flexible policy in regard to baptism, were able to rival, and in a number of cases to surpass, the Protestants". Opposition between the two sides was the rule. "Protestant and Roman Catholic missionaries could live for years in the same town and never exchange a word. It was taken for granted by the majority of Roman Catholics that the Protestants were the enemy." The Vatican was supposed to have sent a directive calling for "the heretics" to be "followed up and their efforts harassed and destroyed".

The basic institutions of African missions were catechists and schools, with a medical dispensary not far behind. Catechists were local people who had learnt the elements of the religion and were able to pass it on. Mackay realised that all native gods were cure workers, hence "the great influence in favour of Christianity that a medical mission can exert, if prudently conducted".

It was an obvious breakthrough when Africans were able to go into the villages as evangelists. Baganda teachers spread Christianity to Bunyoro, Toro and Koki. Apolo Kivebulaya, an Anglican of simple and profound piety, proclaimed the faith in Mboga, on the far side of the Semliki river in what became part of the Congo. He was a canon of the Church of Uganda and, as a bachelor, an exception to the rule of universal marriage referred to above. Apolo ran a famous mission to the pigmies of the great Congo equatorial forest.

6

An Indispensable Man

*The king's pleasure * Unfavourable view of Mutesa * Rounded picture from Ashe * Trumping the French * Baganda visit London * Mackay a hard-liner * Disputing with Islam * Gospel in Luganda * Cult of Mukasa * 'A mouthful for a cow' * Death of the kabaka*

The early missionaries in Africa survived entirely at the sufferance of the king or chief. Wilson took the earliest opportunity to take Mackay to meet Mutesa – Stanley's "intelligent and distinguished prince", "the light that shall lighten the darkness of this benighted region". Mutesa was courteous as he usually was to visitors, but he did not feel well that day. Mackay gave the kabaka a present of a musical box. He was not certain how the audience had gone, but a reverse present of some cows indicated that it had been successful.

Mackay was delighted by Buganda. The climate he found "like an ever-English summer". In an early letter he wrote: "The people are not savages, nor even barbarians. They are out of sight far in advance of any race I have met with or even heard of in Central Africa."

He was not starry-eyed about the task ahead, however. He wrote on another occasion: "(T)he heathen do not, by nature, wish the gospel, although we know they sorely need it; that in every land people are jealous for their faith, which came down from their ancestors of long-lost memory; that they are greedy of gain, and jealous for their land, which they fancy we have come to possess, or rather spy out with a view to our nation possessing. They understand only material gain at first, and are generally disappointed that we do not aid them more in that way; but it takes time to win their confidence and convince them that we mean to be their true friends. When we have gained that point, but not till then, we can build upon it."

Wilson and Mackay were not on their own at the CMS mission

for long. Three months later (February 1879) a party of three arrived from the north along the Nile route. This was a rival to the East Coast route until it was closed a few years later by the fall of Khartoum to the Mahdi. The party included Robert Felkin, later to be influential in persuading the Imperial British East Africa Company to take on Uganda. In April two more travellers arrived from the south. One of them was Charles Stokes, who later gave up mission and adopted Mammon. He was eventually captured in the Congo Free State by a strategem and summarily executed for gun-running. This quite substantial band in time dispersed, leaving three missionaries including Mackay in Mengo. In April 1881 Philip O'Flaherty, an ordained man, arrived and carried out the first of the CMS baptisms, five in number, the following year. The first communion with African Christians followed in 1883.

As Mackay got to know Mutesa, he was unable to recognise the "enlightened and intelligent king of Uganda" hailed in Europe. In 1880, Mackay wrote to his father: "Some have blamed Mr Stanley for giving far too glowing an account of Mtesa and the kingdom which he rules over ... But I cannot blame Stanley. He and Speke, and every traveller, resided only a few months, at most, at Mtesa's court. They had opportunity of seeing only the outside, and that in many respects is fair enough." He following year (1881) he wrote far more strongly about the kabaka: "Mtesa is a pagan – a heathen – out and out. All the faculties of lying, low cunning, hatred, pride and conceit, jealousy, cruelty and complete ignorance of the value of human life, combined with extreme vanity, a desire for notoriety, greed, and absolute want of control of his animal propensities, – all these seem not only to be combined, but even concentrated in him. All is self, self, self."

Robert Ashe, who arrived in Mengo for his first tour of duty in May 1883, produced a rounded assessment of Mutesa in *Two Kings of Uganda* while insisting how difficult it was to give an accurate judgment. Ashe summed up the king as "easy-going" – not the first quality expected of an African absolute ruler, which may explain why he made a favourable impression of so many travellers.

However, it was with deeply blood-stained hands that Mutesa donned his fine robes. The life of bakopi (peasants) was of little account, and slaughter underlined the monarch's power. An episode earlier in the reign went beyond expected levels of violence. Mutesa had been flirting with Islam, but some the chiefs at court took the new religion further than the kabaka did, undergoing circumcision and refusing to eat meat from the king's butcher because it had not been killed in the halal manner. A furious Mutesa retaliated by slaughtering the chiefs.

No doubt Ashe was aware of the episode when he spoke about Mutesa's cruelty. "To say he was great would hardly be true [wrote Ashe], but to say that he showed some fine qualities, and that he was, in spite of his clogging surroundings, a man who sought after better things, is to give him no more than his due ...

"His generally courteous treatment of all Europeans, and his forbearance, with myself for example, showed a generous spirit. I knew he disliked my intruding religion on him; I did not know the language well enough to put it in a humorous or amusing manner, even if I had possessed the wit to do so; and as Mutesa looked upon religion as an amusement and a recreation, my readings about a great White Throne of Judgment, before which even kings were to stand, must have been most distasteful to the easy-going potentate."

"... (H)is education had been a training in cruelty, brutality, and lust." Ashe complained that men and women might be killed for trivial offences like a breach of court etiquette. "Daily went up the terrible cries of unhappy victims, as they were deliberately hacked to pieces, with strips of reed, sharp enough to be used as knives ..." Brutalities and "such vile obscenities as make daylight ashamed" showed that his "training in these vices had born a plenteous crop of fearful crimes". However, "what was frequent and notorious in his unhappy successor [referring to sodomy by Mwanga], was seldom practised by himself".

Ashe finished with a true Victorian flourish: "But yet, in judging of these things, it is well to remember that there are none to whom the fearfullest crimes are not more than possibilities, for in every human heart are all these things, and out of every human heart they may proceed at any time, as He well knew, who bade His people pray, 'Lead us not into temptation.'"

Ashe was concerned to treat the freed slaves well. He must have been quite put out by the lad called (for a reason not given) James Greenway, or Jimmy. He cost a gun, a white box, a looking glass and some other things. When they got back to the mission, Jimmy promptly said he wanted to return to the slave owner. The rueful Ashe told him that if he still wanted to go back after seven days, he could. When the week was up, Jimmy had changed his mind and stayed.

Both Catholics and Protestants enjoyed access to Mutesa's court, and he did not impede the work of evangelism in and around the court. The early missionaries were largely restricted to the court, but exposing the leaders to the Christian message had the unintended effect of speeding the evangelisation of the Baganda. Mutesa committed himself to neither group, although he was ready enough to debate theology and to order Sunday services. Maybe it was intellectual curiosity and mental sport. But Mutesa also had good reason to balance the factions represented by the two emerging Christian groups as well as the Muslims and the traditionalists.

The CMS missionaries were keen for Mutesa or senior chiefs to visit Queen Victoria. This would cement the relationship with England and Anglicanism. It was also a trump card over the French missionaries. Mackay and his colleagues were in Buganda with the knowledge and informal support of the British government. England was the heartland of the Anglican church. The French had no comparable advantages. French governments had a long history of anti-clericalism. No doubt Cardinal Lavigerie could have arranged a visit to the Pope, but a post-Risorgimento Vatican, its temporal authority reduced to a pocket handkerchief of land, might have compared badly with the world's largest empire.

Mutesa was tempted to visit England but was persuaded by the chiefs that his dignity required visitors to come to him. The chiefs also passed up on the trip. Malamba Kiwanuka suggests in his *History of Buganda* that the reason a trio of ordinary subjects went was the belief that they would not come back. People who went on trips with the Arabs seldom returned.

The three Baganda went to England by the Nile route with the missionaries Wilson and Felkin. The visit was a resounding success. In London they were taken to see the Horse Guards, the Zoo and St Paul's Cathedral – "rather similar to the modern British Council course", Kiwanuka comments. They must have seemed as exotic to the British – when, for example, they sat in on a meeting of the

Royal Geographical Society – as London seemed to them.

They got to meet the queen, presenting her with presents including sandals with leopard skin straps, traditionally reserved for royalty in Buganda, bark cloth and other examples of Kiganda handicraft. In return, Queen Victoria sent Mutesa two bird rifles, ammunition, a sword, jackets and overcoats, fezzes and iron boxes. This was a formidable list. There was no doubt that Victoria was a great queen indeed.

Although Stanley liked to depict Mutesa as lord of all he surveyed, the kabaka of Buganda like any other absolute ruler was absolute only so long as he could contain the centrifugal forces that were ready to tear him apart. Ashe saw the kabaka's work as playing off one chief against another. He did the same with foreigners. Although writing after Mutesa's death, Ashe apparently had him in mind and not his successor when he wrote: "How shrewdly he guesses that it is the devoir [duty] of one party [the Roman Catholics] to counteract the teaching of heresy by the other, and of the latter party [the Protestants] to protest against errors [of the Church of Rome]."

This passage is typical of Ashe's generous approach to the rival faith. Although he was a Protestant clergyman for whom the charge of Christian heresy must have been offensive, he is able equally to balance the "heresy" of one party with the "errors" of the other. His approach, regretfully, was all too rare at the time.

In Buganda, the tiny bands of missionaries could not avoid encountering each other. Ashe recorded that relations with Père Lourdel and his confrère, Père Jeraud, were cordial: "We were always on very good terms with them, and I think by that time we all recognised that there was room for both parties, and that they had learnt the lesson that however much they objected to our doctrine, public denunciation of it was of no earthly use."

When Mackay was ill in 1881 the French fathers sent a note and some wine containing the restoratives of iron and quinine. They also offered to send a cow. Lourdel was repeatedly ill with lumbago, neuralgia and rheumatism, and Mackay visited him.

Mackay, the Scottish Presbyterian, was very much the hard-line Protestant. Ashe wrote of him that he "looked upon the teachings of the Church of Rome with the deepest abhorrence. Their evasions, windings, mysteries, and their hocus-pocus mock-miracle-working formula he could not bear, though he saw clearly that formulas expressing great truths, when properly used, might be of value." Ashe, on the other hand, wrote emolliently after a visit to the Catholics at their Bukumbi mission station south of the lake: "Unable as I am to reverence the system which they support, or many of the doctrines which they believe, I can at least reverence the simple devotion of their lives."

Both Protestant and Catholic missionaries were up against Islam as well as traditional Kiganda beliefs. Mackay recorded in his journal one such encounter in 1883: "Mtesa then began with his usual excuses. 'There are these two religions,' he said. 'When Masudi reads his book, the Koran, you call it lies; when you read your book, Masudi calls it lies: which is true?'

"I left my seat, and going forward to the mat, I knelt on it, and in the most solemn manner, I said, 'Oh, Mtesa, my friend, do not always repeat that excuse! When you and I stand before God at the great day of judgment, will you reply to Almighty God that you did not know what to believe because Masudi told you one thing and Mackay told you another? No, you have the New Testament; read there for yourself. God will judge you by that. There never was anyone yet who looked for the truth there and did not find it.'"

Much of Mackay's work centred on the printing press. He literally did it all, from translating St Matthew's Gospel into Luganda, the local language, to operating the press and even cutting the printing types. He had brought a small stock of lead type with him, but it was not enough and he cut more characters in both wood and lead. On his 30th birthday – October 13, 1879 – he spent all day carving wooden types. It was tedious work: at the end of the day he had made only 10 letters.

Before Mackay could translate St Matthew into the vernacular, he first had to master the language. In an early comment he was far ahead of his time in advocating the Direct Method of language learning:

"February 5th, 1879. – Studied the language. Endeavoured to reduce the seven classes of nouns to four, to find a rationale of concords. I think I see my way pretty clearly. One thing I feel strongly on, viz., the absurdity of multiplying minute differences into distinct classes, thus confusing new learners. Steere's eight classes of nouns in Swahili are a damper to a beginner. The small book with exercises and four classes of nouns is out of sight better for beginners than his handbook. We all learn to speak our mother tongue before we study the grammar of it. This should be the order, as far as possible, in acquiring a new language also. How many years' hard work does it not take to learn Latin by cramming up five declensions? Did Cicero know anything about the declensions? If he did not, and yet knew Latin, how absurd it is to attempt declension before one knows Latin! I learned German first, and afterwards studied German grammar. I never saw any speed by following the inverse order."

Mackay seemed to be equally at home mending a boat, working a printing press, explaining the Christian faith and unravelling the Kiganda theological system. The Baganda acknowledged two principal gods: Katonda, the creator, who however stayed out of human affairs and therefore could safely be ignored; and Lubale, the god of providence, who is actively involved in human affairs and to whom sacrifices were made. The Lubale had an incarnation in a human being called Mukasa, at this time an old woman who lived on an island in Lake Victoria and who was uniquely powerful in Kiganda society.

The Baganda's system of belief was unveiled to the missionaries only bit by bit. H.P. Gale, in *Uganda and the Mill Hill Fathers*, credits Mackay with discerning for the West the mysteries of Katonda and Lubale. In particular, writes Gale, "the Kabaka's divinity was the heart and centre [of Kiganda religion], and in consequence was never clearly revealed to Christian missionaries".

Mutesa's status as a demi-god was based on his descent from Kintu, the first kabaka. Kintu was said to have married a daughter of the Sky Father. Other descendants of Kintu inhabited the Sese Islands, and were therefore also semi-divine. At the time of King Nakibinge, the eighth kabaka – Mutesa being the 30th kabaka, according to the ranking of Sir Apolo Kagwa, a katikiro of Buganda – the Sese Islanders helped the Baganda in a war against the neighbouring state of Bunyoro. In return the grateful king built temples for the worship of these descendants of Kintu.

This was the origin of the cult of Mukasa. The kabaka was an absolute ruler and in practice the Sese cult was under his control. He was semi-divine himself, and so had two ways to control Kiganda religion. Gale comments: "Thus, whichever way we turn, we find the Kingship at the heart of the religion of the Baganda …"

When Mackay remonstrated with Mutesa about the worship of Mukasa, the kabaka replied: "What you say, Mackay, is true, and I know all witchcraft is falsehood." This did not mean that Mutesa was ready to convert to Christianity (which he never did). Gale and also J. Roscoe, in *The Baganda* (1911), say the kabaka was merely acknowledging the truth that he knew better than anyone, that spirits were an emanation of his own kingship, the means whereby the blood of his people brought him life and vigour.

The Baganda, it appeared, had once believed in a single supreme being (Katonda) and immortality of the soul. To the missionaries this implied ancient contacts with Christianity, which was previously more widespread over North Africa. However, Kiganda theology was not exclusively theist. Mackay recorded that each phenomenon of nature had its own divinity: there were gods of food, famine, rain, war, earthquake and plague. Some living creatures, especially snakes and parrots, were worshipped, as were what he called "monstrosities of nature" like misformed trees and rocks. All of this meant a huge amount of propitiation by the hapless human beings. Charms were seen as a potent way of securing a god's goodwill.

Some grass charms, dipped in blood, were brought into court while Mackay was with Mutesa. The missionary realised that credibility forced him to act. Harm was supposed to await anyone who destroyed the charms, but Mackay announced to the court that the grass was just a "mouthful for a cow". The charms were not supposed to burn, but he put a light to the grass to underline the impotence and worthlessness of the idol. Mackay then explained that it was not possible to mix old and new religions just as new cloth cannot be effectively sewn onto old garments.

That settled it for the time being, but the issue has never gone away. The old gods have even tended to travel as many people in the modern West try to integrate the spirits of the earth with Christianity. Nor was the Lubale so easily seen off.

Mutesa died in October 1884. Once more Mackay's practical

skills were called upon. He was asked to make a coffin for the king. Lead for the lining was not available, but he made a suitable alternative by knocking together old copper and brass trays.

7

The Buganda Road

*Mwanga chosen as kabaka * Arab influence * Three boy Christians burned to death * Bishop Hannington captured * Fortified by Scripture * Killed on the king's orders * Year of the Great Terror * Namungongo martyrs * Mwanga's motives * Sir F. Holmwood's telegram * Mackay leaves Buganda*

B ecause the kabaka was an absolute ruler, the death of the kabaka meant a period of potential anarchy. There was no automatic succession – "the king is dead, long live the king" – therefore no continuing fount of authority. It was a hazardous time for the missionaries, surrounded by hostile forces – the Arabs and their Baganda co-religionists, including the mujasi (chief of soldiers), and the traditionalists, who simply resented the foreigners.

The new kabaka was to be chosen by the council of chiefs. Buganda had a highly evolved constitutional system, carefully described by the missionary Robert Ashe in his contemporaneous book, *Two Kings of Uganda*. At the apex was the immensely powerful katikiro, who was both the chief minister and the chief judge. The country was split into five principal divisions or earldoms: the capital district; Budu (whose chief was called the pokino); Bulemezi (headed by the kagawo); Kyagwe (the sekiboobo) and Singo (the mukwenda).

These great offices of state were bestowed by the king, but below these earldoms was an hereditary class of landed gentry, known as bataka. Both the lords and the gentry had the power of life and death in their domains, while anyone could kill his slave at will. A slave was killed for dropping a gourd, for which Mackay remonstrated with the chief and managed to shame him.

Titles attached to offices abounded. For instance, the gabunga was the keeper of the king's war canoes, the kimbugwe was the keeper of the palace and the kasuju was the keeper of the king's children. Three royal persons were recognised constitutionally: the kabaka himself; the namasole, or queen mother; and the nalinya, or king's sister. The occupant of this last office might be a true sister or a cousin. Ashe observed that cousin marriage was forbidden among the Baganda; it was seen as the same as marrying one's sister, and therefore incestuous.

The interregnum passed off without bloodshed, which Mackay ascribed to the moderating influence of Christianity. The council's deliberations were of the highest moment: the kabaka once chosen was not only an absolute ruler but also a demi-god at the head of traditional religion. The choice fell upon Mutesa's son, Mwanga, a boy of 18. He had the strongest facial resemblance to his father, but was shorter and more negroid in appearance.

The Protestant mission was the only one in Buganda at this time, the White Fathers having withdrawn to south of the lake in October 1882. The reason they gave was the corruption of their converts by the court – "giving them presents and practising sodomy on them" – although court intrigues at that time also meant the fathers feared for their lives. Mackay, Ashe and O'Flaherty, the CMS missionaries at Mengo, soon had reason to doubt that the new king would be well disposed towards Christianity. He received them wearing Arab dress, and was under the influence at court of the Muslims and the traditional animists, headed by the katikiro.

In January 1885, when Mwanga had been on the throne less than three months, came a foretaste of tragedies to come for the Christian community. Three young boy Protestants at court were burned to death on the king's instructions. These readers, as those learning Christianity were called, had refused to be sodomised by the kabaka. Sodomy was widespread at the court, but from the missionaries the boys – Kakumba, Seruwanga and Lugulama – learned that it was wrong. Lugulama had a terror of being mutilated before death, and piteously asked (without success) not to have his arms cut off but to be "just thrown onto the fire". The boys went to their deaths singing the moving hymn, Daily, Daily, Sing the Praises.

Mwanga was said to have learned sodomy from the Arabs, but it is hard to know whether this belief was well grounded or an expression of the contemporary European writers' dislike of the Arabs.

In July at Mwanga's request the Roman Catholic mission

returned in the persons of Pères Lourdel and Girault and Frère Amans. This, however, was nothing to do with any particular love for Catholicism. Mwanga feared that the English missionaries were opening the way for a British military invasion, and wanted to offset their influence. For both Christian communities it was a very hazardous time. To attend church, receive instruction or even talk with the missionaries courted death; yet on July 26, for instance, there were 173 at the Protestant service and 35 at holy communion. Mackay and Ashe were both seized, then released. The persecution was spasmodic, however, and the Christian community held its own.

Into this unsettled situation marched Bishop James Hannington. He was a young Anglican clergyman making his second attempt to reach Buganda. He had led a missionary party towards the country three years earlier but had to turn back through illness while still south of the lake. When well enough to return to Africa, he was consecrated as the first bishop of Eastern Equatorial Africa.

There were urgent practical reasons for the Anglican Church to have a bishop on the spot. The CMS had revived East Africa as a mission field. In 1875 a station had been started on the mainland opposite Mombasa. It was named Frere Town after Sir Bartle Frere, a British official who fought the slave trade. Ten years later, there were several inland missions as well as Buganda. Only a bishop was able to make lay missionaries into clergymen, through ordination. Even more importantly, a bishop was needed to administer the rite of confirmation. In this rite, the grace of the Holy Spirit is conveyed in a new or fuller way to those who have already received it in some degree or fashion at baptism (*The Oxford Dictionary of the Christian Church*). Unless confirmed, the African converts could not properly be admitted to holy communion – although this requirement was waived in the special circumstances of East Africa. The position had to be regularised, however.

Hence the need throughout the mission field for Bishop Hannington. He spent several months at Frere Town and at Taita, a new CMS station inland near Mount Kilimanjaro. By mid-1885 he was on his way to Buganda with another clergyman, Ernest Jones, and about 220 porters. He decided to take the northern route around the lake, via Kavirondo. Despite the Masai, whose hostile character Joseph Thomson had exaggerated, it was much shorter than the southern route, via Karagwe.

Mackay warned the bishop not to continue via Busoga because the Baganda had a taboo on strangers entering the country by this route: the conqueror of the country was expected to come this way. Mackay and Ashe told the kabaka that a boat had been arranged so that Hannington could enter by a usual route. Mwanga's fear and anger were understandable when he heard that the bishop had crossed Busoga and was at Lubwa's on the Nile – on the doorstep of Buganda, in fact.

Hannington decided to split the caravan when it was near the lake, taking about 50 men himself and heading for Mengo, leaving the rest to wait with Ernest Jones. Hannington's party was seized by men he took to be robbers. During his captivity the bishop kept a diary, which later came into the hands of the CMS missionaries at Namirembe. Here Hannington describes his feelings at being put on display for the local chief's wives:

"About thirty-three more of the chief's wives came and disported themselves with gazing at the prisoner. I was very poorly and utterly disinclined to pay any attention to them, and said, in English, 'Oh, ladies, if you only knew how ill I feel, you would go.' When my food arrived in the middle of the day I was unable to eat – the first time, I think, since leaving the coast I have refused a meal … Another party of wives coming, I retired into the hut and declined to see them. A third party came later on, and being a little better, I came out and lay upon my bed. It is not pleasant to be examined as a caged lion in the Zoo, and yet that is exactly my state at the present time."

Hannington found that "Mackay's name seems quite a household word. I constantly hear it." A further sentence "But of the others I scarce ever hear a word" was in the diary when it reached Mengo, but did not appear in the biography produced soon afterwards by E.C. Dawson, omitted presumably for diplomatic reasons.

As a captive, the bishop found himself "refreshed" by Matthew vv44/45: "But I say unto you, Love your enemies, bless them that curse you, do good to them that hate you, and pray for them which despitefully use you, and persecute you; That ye may be the children of your Father which is in heaven: for he maketh his sun to rise on the evil and on the good, and sendeth rain on the just and on the unjust." He was "much comforted" by Psalm 28: "Unto thee will I cry, O lord my rock; be not silent to me … The Lord is my strength and my shield … " He was "held up" by Psalm 30: "I will extol thee, O Lord; for thou hast lifted me up, and hast not made my foes to rejoice over me … Thou hast turned for me my mourning into dancing: thou hast put off my sackcloth, and girded me with gladness … "

Hannington's choice of the northern route cost his life and those of most of the party, because Mwanga now ordered them killed. Hannington's end has all the character of a nightmare. His captors kept him apart from the men. Only in the final moments, on October 29, 1885, as he was taken to join them did he realise that they were in a place of execution. His last words were: "Tell the king that I die for Buganda. I have bought this road with my life." Then a horde fell on the men, spearing and hacking them to death.

In the chaos one man escaped and brought the news to Ernest Jones. He could hardly believe it although the proof was inescapable. Eventually, he led the party back to Frere Town with a banner – made up with material from the expedition's trade goods – inscribed ICHABOD, the Old Testament exclamation of regret. The glory has departed. At that moment it seemed never more appropriate than for Bishop James Hannington.

Frederick Jackson (*Early Days in East Africa*) knew Hannington in Zanzibar as the bishop was preparing for his final trek. "Bishop Hannington struck me as inclined to be domineering [wrote Jackson], very impetuous, and intolerant of opposition; but, as subsequent events proved, quite fearless, and a great believer in his own judgment."

Jackson described a lunch party where Hannington frequently made mistakes about the history of the Holy Land, which he had just visited. When corrected by another clergyman at the table, W.E. Taylor, Hannington appealed to his chaplain for support, which was dutifully given. But Taylor "stuck stoutly to his guns, and was certainly the more convincing".

Hannington's death caused dismay in England, although it was not realised at first that Mwanga was behind it. Many African travellers fell victim to robbers or feuding tribes. Mwanga's action was not without reason, however. Even Frederick Lugard, the later conqueror of Buganda, who was no friend of the kabaka, acknowledged it. "Dastardly as this murder was," he wrote in his book, *The Rise of Our East African Empire*, "it must be admitted that Mwanga looked on Hannington's arrival as the precursor of war; and it was most unfortunate that the bishop should have adopted the route *via* Usoga [Busoga]."

Hannington could hardly have picked a worse time to arrive in Busoga. Mwanga, who was only a youth, had not yet consolidated his power in Buganda. Behind the missionaries and their converts lay (earthly) powers that, he assumed, wanted to eat his country. Germany was annexing part of the East African coast. To the north of Buganda, the outlook as he saw it was threatening. The Mahdists were pressing south. Between them and Buganda lay Kabarega's kingdom of Bunyoro, also hostile to him. Bunyoro was claimed as a tributary state but the reality was different: Kabarega had substantial forces and many guns, and a willingness to use both. The bishop's murder cast a long shadow. Lugard believed that Mwanga's association with the pro-French, Roman Catholic political faction, against the British, was because he feared and expected revenge for the killing.

Even in the gunboat era, though, the British government felt no need to avenge the death of a private citizen (a habit that has lasted). The following year, when it was proposed that Stanley would lead an expedition into Equatoria, Sir Percy Anderson of the Foreign Office wrote to the Cabinet: " ... if he [Stanley] lost his life there would be no more obligation on the British Government to avenge him than there is to avenge Bishop Hannington."

Protestants in Buganda remained without a bishop for five more years, until the arrival of Bishop Alfred Tucker in the last days of 1890. This was not through want of trying by the authorities. Soon after Hannington's death, the second bishop of Eastern Equatorial Africa was consecrated: Henry Parker. He arrived near Lake Victoria safely and stayed for a while at Usambiro. This was a CMS "safe haven" south of the lake. But he died of a fever there in 1888. Tucker, however, survived in Uganda for many years and was a major force in developing the Anglican Church.

Hannington's murder left the Protestant missionaries at Mengo in peril. Mwanga demanded to know how Ashe and Mackay knew about the death, as Ashe recorded in *Two Kings of Uganda*:

"We put off our cross-examiners as well as we could; finally we said, 'We have not come here to "ropa" (inform on) people.' Whereupon they waxed angry, and the king called us hypocrites, and added that we were 'bagwagwa' [the most stupid], the most insulting term in the language. Manoga, the king's tailor, now came back to the question of who had told us about the Bishop. The king said, 'They refuse to tell because they think I shall kill the person.' Then he tried a wheedling tone. 'Tell me,' he said, 'and you will be "baganze enyo" (great favourites).' Our continued silence made them very wroth, and then came angry words about killing. 'What if I kill you?' said the king. 'What could Queeni [Queen Victoria] do? Was she able to touch Lukonge or Mirambo [chiefs outside Buganda] when they killed white men? What could she do, or all Bulaya (Europe) together? How would they come – would they fly?' Père Lourdel now kindly attempted to create a diversion in our favour. He said, 'If you killed these white men, then I should not care to stay in your country.' 'If I killed them,' insolently replied the king, 'should I spare you? Are you not a white man like them?' The Père reflected on this in silence during the remainder of the interview.

"Mwanga then said he would not have the east road used. Was he not the king? Who was Queeni?

"We replied, 'We are not messengers of Queeni, but messengers of God'."

Despite the defiant talk, Mwanga feared to kill the missionaries but, encouraged by the Muslims, he showed no inhibitions about persecuting the African converts. The master of the king's pages, a Catholic called Joseph Balikudembe, was killed for remonstrating with the kabaka over Bishop Hannington's murder.

In the great terror of the following year, 1886, about 200 Christians – Roman Catholics and Protestants – were killed for the faith. Anyone attending a Christian meeting or receiving religious instruction risked betrayal and death. Yet still the number of converts grew including some of the senior chiefs surrounding Mwanga. The martyrs' willingness to die for a faith so recently learned made the profoundest impression in both Buganda and Europe. The kabaka could not understand why young men and women went to their deaths praying joyfully instead of voicing the customary mournful wails.

A young boy, Kiwobe, asked to be baptised at the height of the persecution. He became Samweli (Samuel) and a pillar of the Christian community. He was so conscientious to duty that he fled only after delivering a tribute of cowrie shells that he had been entrusted with.

The terror reached a ghastly climax when 32 were burned on a single pyre at the Namugongo execution ground, triggered, according to Ashe, by a royal page, Sabagabo, refusing to be sodomised. The victims included Walukaga, a smith, who had warning but refused to flee. The Christians were accused of disloyalty and sedition. Walukaga wanted to plead his case, but his confidence in the justice system was tragically misplaced. Much uncertainty surrounds who died there, and even the precise number, but by one count the dead included 13 named Catholics and nine named Protestants. Ironically, some non-Christians may have found themselves on the pyre having been caught in the round-up.

For Mwanga the burning of the 32 was a serious mistake. To lash out at what you hate and fear is human enough, but it is not statecraft. A small incident is supposed to have triggered the mass burning. Mwanga had spent an unsuccessful day hippo hunting. On his return he found no pages to attend him. He flew into a rage when he realised they had been having religious instruction. Every Christian he could find he handed over to the executioners. The executions were a calculated act, however. Another week went by while the funeral pyre was made ready. Mwanga, backed by some of the chiefs, had decided to rid himself to the Christians.

Official lists of the Uganda martyrs list the various ways in which they died: dismembered and burned, burned to death, speared, speared and hacked to pieces, speared and beheaded, speared and savaged by dogs, castrated, clubbed and burned, hacked to pieces, dismembered and left to die, beheaded, beheaded and hacked to pieces, beheaded and thrown into swamp.

Yet nothing better dramatises the cause you are trying to suppress, or enlists spectators' emotions on the other side, than a public burning. You hope for a very visible recantation but you are unlikely to get it. The victims are beyond that; they have in a sense already crossed to the other side. Nor can the idea and sight of death en masse be any deterrent for onlookers when killings have become commonplace.

So Mwanga's terror did not destroy Christianity in Buganda but entrenched it. The Roman Catholic Church later canonised 22 of its converts who died in the great persecution, including Charles Lwanga, the Catholic leader. Jocelyn Murray, in her history of the Church Missionary Society, *Proclaim the Good News*, writes: "In no other Anglican mission has there ever been such a testing and such a response." H.P. Gale, in *Uganda and the Mill Hill Fathers* (although this group of Roman Catholic missionaries did not arrive until 1895), remarks that the persecution had the opposite effect to that intended: it forged the two Christian groups into "parties", opposed to the Muslims and traditionalists. The Christian parties were known as the ba-Fransa and the ba-Ingleza from their association with the respective missions.

Lugard, whose *The Rise of Our East African Empire* showed no particular religiosity, spoke of the admiration and sympathy in England for the martyred Christians, recalling as they did the zeal and fortitude of the early Church. "Men asked what kind of people were these [he wrote] who would thus brave death for their belief, and ceased to scoff at the reality of conversions which could stand so terrible a test."

An article in the (London) Times said: "The existence of the Mission, lying altogether in Mwanga's power, yet staying against his declared will, is infinitely more conclusive evidence of the strength of Christianity in Africa than would be its predominance by the tyrant's dethronement. There would have been no shame had the Mission voluntarily broken itself up in the face of the young king's insolent enmity. Its persistency is not merely magnanimous; it is the one way of testing the ability of Christian truth and humanity to hold its ground, without the accessories of gunboats and rifles, against both Heathendom and Islam."

Mwanga's actions were driven by immaturity but he was not the crazed and blood-soaked tyrant sometimes depicted by European writers. He was also illiterate, unlike some of his chiefs, which says nothing about his intelligence but speaks about his temperament. Ashe described how he tried but failed to teach Mwanga to read:

"... wayward and flighty, he seemed unable to concentrate his attention on the same thing for any length of time." In his near-contemporary account (1893) of the event, Lugard acknowledged that from Mwanga's point of view both Christian and Muslim religions were dangerous because they were "disintegrating his country". Mwanga's fears were rational enough, but under the influence of bhang – a commonly smoked narcotic in Buganda – he was capable, according to Mackay, "of the wildest unpremeditated actions".

Ado K. Tiberondwa, in *Missionary Teachers as Agents of Colonialism*, argues that Mwanga was not brutal as such, but was aiming to defend his power and his people by cutting out elements that threatened to destroy them. His persecution of the Christians was fuelled by anger that their first loyalty was to God, not the king.

While no theologian, Mwanga was correct in sensing the same dilemma of church and state that runs through Western history. In England, for instance, Roman Catholics were penalised and excluded from public life for three centuries on the assumption that they owed their ultimate loyalty to the pope not the king. The feeling died hard, perhaps only ended by two world wars that showed Roman Catholics could fight for king and country with as much commitment as the Protestants. The balance between church and state in modern Western nations, imperfect as it still is, derives from a long history of mutual accommodations and a sensitive understanding by Christians of their religious and patriotic obligations.

Mwanga knew – the three boy readers proved it – that, unlike his predecessors, he could not through his deified status as kabaka automatically command the allegiance of the Christians. They listened to their priests and their consciences. In general, a Catholic priest has more authority over his flock than a Protestant minister does over his, but in the fledgling churches of Buganda we can suppose that both groups of missionaries were similarly influential.

For the moment the state, in the person of Mwanga, had the upper hand, and some of the missionaries decided to withdraw. Two of the Catholic priests left in the caravan of Wilhelm Junker, a traveller who arrived from Equatoria in June, and was allowed to continue to the coast. In August Ashe left. Mackay and three of the French fathers remained in Mengo.

Junker brought out with him letters from Emin and his own

apocalyptic assessment of the situation in Equatoria and Buganda. By August he was at Msalala, from where he wrote in emotional terms to a friend, Dr Schweinfurth: "Escaped at last from the clutches of Mwanga at Uganda ... Must we believe that nothing will ever be done for these unhappy Equatorial Provinces? Write, write on, dear friend! Send forth words of thunder that will open the eyes of all the world! ... It is absolutely necessary that Emin Bey should receive help without delay ... It is with this hope alone that I essay to return to Europe." [Quoted by Iain R. Smith, see bibliography]

Junker's information reached Frederic Holmwood, the acting British consul-general in Zanzibar the following month. He immediately cabled London in melodramatic style: "News from Uganda, 12 July. Junker left for Zanzibar. Terrible persecution broken out, all native Christians being put to death. Missionaries in extreme danger; urgently requests our demanding from King their being allowed to withdraw. Emin at Wadelai holds province, but urgently needs ammunition and stores. Objects, if he can avoid it, deserting the 4,000 loyal Egyptian subjects there. No time to be lost if assistance decided on."

In Britain, momentum developed to send help to Emin. The Buganda mission, which Holmwood had made clear was also threatened, attracted less attention, although many hoped that a relief expedition could help both situations. Eugene Stock, in his official *History of the Church Missionary Society* (1899), complained that the British newspapers were not interested in the plight of Mackay, now on his own at Mengo: "For the English missionary they cared nothing; for the Austrian Pasha [Emin] they cared a great deal."

Charles Allen of the Anti-Slavery Society published a letter from Emin; so did Robert Felkin, who had been in Buganda as a missionary in the earliest days. Felkin, who was campaigning for Emin in Scotland, wrote to Allen: "In order to get the Scotch to stir I must have a good humanitarian, utilitarian and several other 'arian' objects in my paper. Can you help me? Do try – think of all poor Emin has tried to do and really has done, of his long weary holding out." [Quoted by Smith, see bibliography]

All this effort had its effect. The British cabinet on December 3, 1886, approved the idea of a relief expedition. The details were uncertain but one thing was clear: there would be no official British government involvement.

In Buganda, persecution and harassment of the Christians continued sporadically. Mackay stayed on for almost a year after Ashe left. He completed his translation of St Matthew's gospel into Luganda. He was careful that the translation was authentic – "every page criticized and revised by the most advanced pupils," as he put it.

Eventually Mwanga demanded that he leave, but he would not do so until a successor had been arranged. The brave person who agreed to take over was E.C. Gordon. There was to be a short gap until he arrived. Relations between the two Christian missions were at best mixed, but Mackay's last action before leaving Mengo in July 1887 was to hand over the key of the mission building to the French fathers.

Mackay had not been home throughout his 10 years in Buganda. Headquarters had often tried to persuade him to take leave. Again he turned down the entreaties. He went no farther than Usambiro, south of the lake, but it was far enough to be beyond Mwanga's reach.

Gordon was joined by Robert Walker. After all the blood-letting and with continued risks, between 150 and 200 attended morning service one Sunday, with nearly as many at two o'clock. This moved Walker to remark: "Really Ashe, Mackay, and the others have done, by the grace of God, a glorious work here."

8

Three Kings

During the persecution of the Christians Mackay and Ashe clandestinely distributed a message to their followers. It read:

"People of Jesus who are in Buganda. Our Friends, – We, your friends and teachers, write to you to send you words of cheer and comfort, which we have taken from the Epistle of Peter the Apostle of Christ. In days of old, Christians were hated, were hunted, were driven out, and were persecuted for Jesus' sake; and thus it is to-day.

"Our beloved brethren, do not deny our Lord Jesus, and He will not deny you on that great day when He shall come with glory. Remember the words of our Saviour, how He told his disciples not to fear men, who are only able to kill the body: but He bid them to fear God, Who is able to destroy the body together with the soul in the fire of Gehenna.

"Do not cease to pray exceedingly, and to pray for our brethren who are in affliction, and for those who do not know God. May God give you His spirit and His blessing! May He deliver you out of all your afflictions! May He give you entrance to eternal life through Jesus Christ our Saviour!

"Farewell. We are the white men: we are your brethren indeed who have written to you."

The passage printed on the back was from 1 Peter ch4, v12 to the end. The passage begins: "Beloved, think it not strange concerning the fiery trial which is to try you, as though some strange things happened unto you: But rejoice, inasmuch as ye are partakers of Christ's sufferings; that, when his glory shall be revealed, ye may be glad also with exceeding joy."

It was both a message of encouragement and a call to martyrdom. The missionaries could have said flee. They could have said stay quiet. Instead, they asked the converts to acknowledge their faith even though renouncing it would save their lives. It was a great responsibility Mackay and Ashe were taking on themselves. It can be explained – and justified – only in terms of profound faith and the fervent conviction that denial of the Lord meant a worse fate than death of the body. Perhaps the missionaries agonised over this message, knowing that they were themselves less at risk. They had been threatened, certainly, but Mwanga already feared revenge for Bishop Hannington's death. He was unlikely to provoke "Queeni" further.

After the mass burning at Namugongo, the persecution of the Christians continued although with less intensity. In London the Church Missionary Society was pleased to receive this letter from Buganda converts:

"Buganda Mission, May 13th, 1887

"Beloved of authority in the Church of Jesus Christ, our English fathers, and all Christians who love us; our brethren. We, your Buganda brethren, write to you to thank you for the letter which you sent us. We rejoice much to hear news which came from where you are to cheer our hearts through our Lord Jesus Christ.

"We thank God that you have heard of our being persecuted. Thank God who brought our brother where you are, whom we love, Mr. Ashe, and made you understand the evil which has befallen us Christians in Buganda, your children whom you have begotten in the Gospel.

"Mr. Ashe has told you how we are hunted, and burned in the fire, and beheaded, and called sorcerers, for the name of Jesus our Lord. And do you thank God who has granted us to suffer here at this time for the Gospel of Christ.

"We hope indeed for this thing which you hoped for us in your letter, namely, that in a short time other teachers will come to teach. And you who have authority continue earnestly to beseech Almighty God, who turned the Emperor of Rome to become a Christian, who formerly persecuted the name of Jesus as to-day this our king in Buganda persecutes us. And do you our fathers hope that we do not in the least degree give up the Word of Christ Jesus. We are willing, indeed, to die for the Word of Jesus; but do you pray for us that the Lord may help us. Finally, our friends, let your ears and eyes and hearts be open to this place where we are at Buganda. Now we are in tribulation at being left alone. Mr. Mackay, the Arabs have driven away out of Buganda. Oh, friends, pity us in our calamity. We, your brethren, who are in Buganda, send you greetings. May God Almighty give you His blessing. May He preserve you in Europe. We remain, your children who love you,

HENRY WRIGHT DUTA.

EDWARD.

ISAYA MAYANJA."

The date of the letter was a puzzle for the CMS because Mackay did not leave until July. The letter may have been started in May, when he was expected to leave, and finished in July after he went.

The following year, 1888, Mwanga completely overreached himself by plotting with traditionalists at court to destroy all the foreigners – that is, both sets of missionaries and the Arabs – and their followers. To unite the Christians and the Muslims was a mistake that his father, with his sensitivities to the balance of forces, could not have made.

After consulting sorcerers, Mwanga laid plans for a general massacre, but the news leaked out. His next attempt was more subtle. The Mukasa, the embodiment of the Lubale, the Kiganda god, lived on an island in the lake. The kabaka announced that the island was to be attacked and Lubale worship extinguished. The real intention was to lure the Christian and the Muslim fighters onto a nearby island under the guise of assembling for the attack; then leave them there to starve. With the loss of most of the men in their prime, the heart would have been torn out of the two communities.

This plan, too, became known. Leaders of the three groups – Honorat Nyonyintono (Catholic), Apolo Kagwa (Protestant) and Lubanga (Muslim) – agreed on united resistance. In September Mwanga ordered the fighters to board the war canoes for the fake attack, but few obeyed him. He fled into his palace and was later allowed to leave Mengo unharmed. He went south of the lake with a retinue of pages and a small following, finding refuge first with Arabs and later at Bukumbi, the Roman Catholic mission station.

Leaving Mwanga alive was a mistake of realpolitik, for which the Muslims would pay heavily. The kabaka, good or bad, *was* Buganda, so a living ex-kabaka was a standing challenge to the legitimacy of the replacement. The crucial need to have a kabaka in place was underlined by the forced installation of Mwanga's eldest brother, Kiwewa. Nyonyintono became the new katikiro, and a Protestant and a Muslim were appointed respectively for the key roles of muk-wenda and kimbugwe.

During Kiwewa's brief reign all the religious groups were able to practise their faith openly. Posts were distributed among the factions – Catholic, Protestant, Muslim and traditionalist. It was too good to last, and it lasted less than two months. The Muslims were by far the weakest of the religious factions. They had an estimated 300 guns against 1,000 apiece for the Catholics and the Protestants. Even so, the next month (October) they succeeded with a coup d'etat, forcing the two Christian groups out of the capital. Nyonyintono and Kagwa led their followers westwards to Ankole, where they were welcomed by King Ntare.

Alexander Mackay, in exile at Usambiro, wrote a vivid account of the exodus: "That sad 12th of October will never be forgotten by our people. Chiefs and commons, rich and poor, free and slave, they fled before their foes, who hotly pursued them. Everything was lost; wives and children, home and country. No man could return to take anything from his house. Clothes, books, their all, gone."

It was not a mass movement. The numbers affected by these manoeuvres at court were relatively small – about 200 Protestants, rather more Catholics. The missionaries decided to stay in the capital. The mission stations were attacked and pillaged. The missionaries were detained and then expelled. Kiwewa, who had refused the Muslim rite of circumcision, fled but was soon captured.

The new kabaka was another of Mwanga's brothers, Kalema. He was much more receptive to Islam. His order for universal circumcision was resisted with much violence and bloodshed.

The missionaries went into exile together: Gordon and Walker of the CMS, and four White Fathers, including Bishop Livinhac and Père Lourdel, with around 30 followers between them. They used the Anglican mission's sailing boat, the Eleanor, which Mackay's sister in Scotland described as "a poor, comfortless thing compared with a Scotch herring-boat, being perfectly open, and having neither cabin nor deck, nor any protection for the crew from the pitiless rains". On the road to the lake Walker was robbed of his hat, coat and even trousers. One of the Frenchmen gave him a pair of corduroy trousers and a blanket.

During the crossing, the Eleanor was attacked by a hippopotamus, causing it to capsize. An island was nearby. Some swam to land, others clung to the boat until rescued by an islander in a canoe; even the Eleanor herself was recovered. The occasion was suffused with sadness, however. Although all the missionaries were safe, five Baganda boys drowned.

Walker, although an archdeacon, set to with an ingenuity that vied with Mackay's when he repaired the Daisy (the Eleanor's predecessor), finding ways to make the damaged boat lakeworthy again.

After more than two weeks crossing the lake, the party reached the Catholic mission station at Bukumbi. After being hospitably entertained by the priests, Gordon and Walker moved on to join Mackay at the CMS station of Usambiro, which was nearby.

We do not have to imagine Père Lourdel's sad feelings about being forced into exile because he expressed them in a letter: "After shipwreck and the many miseries of the crossing, fever, and dysentery, caused by the emotions and fatigue of the voyage, have come in their turn to pay us a visit. I am beginning to recover a little and I have not lost hope of returning again to dear Uganda, which was producing such fine apostolic fruit and promising even more ... The trials and miseries do not discourage one's spirit but they make the flesh feel weak and aged, so that at 35 years I find myself old; my hair and my beard are becoming white."

Mwanga with an entourage arrived at Bukumbi in December 1888, having slipped away from his Arab hosts in exile, whom he found too greedy. The fathers could not condone polygamy so he was lodged with one wife in quarters for married converts and his other wives lived separately. In April 1889 he received envoys speaking for both Baganda Christian communities in Ankole, asking him to join them in their bid to overthrow the Muslims in Buganda. A steady flow of refugees had boosted the exile numbers to the point where Honorat Nyonyintono and Apolo Kagwa believed they could beat Kalema. It is curious that the Christians should want to reinstate as kabaka the man who had persecuted their brethren, but Mwanga listed among his present virtues the fact that he was not Kalema: installing him as king would mean by the fact alone that the Muslims were beaten. No doubt also the Christian chiefs expected to be able to control a restored and chastened kabaka.

The missionaries were in a quandary. A revival of the civil war to overthrow Islam could increase the persecution of the Christians. For the Protestants, a further issue was that Mwanga seemed more closely linked than ever to the Catholics. The movement went ahead anyway. Mackay refused the use of the Eleanor, but the king found the former missionary turned arms trader, Charles Stokes, ready to oblige. They crossed the lake and landed in Budu, where the king was well received. He was joined by the Christian army after a successful encounter with Kalema's forces, during which the Christian leader, Honorat Nyonyintono, had been killed – apparently needlessly as the Christian forces launched a helter-skelter pursuit of the fleeing Muslims.

Nine months of see-saw fortunes for the two sides followed. Mwanga was obliged to leave the mainland for Sese, a large and strategically sited cluster of islands, while his army dispersed towards Ankole. The Sese islanders, like the people of Budu, declared for Mwanga, which gave him control of the lake. Kalema, however, had a big advantage in firepower: some 2,000 guns, twice as many as Mwanga.

Kalema, faced with the invasion threat, responded by killing over 30 of his relatives including his brother, Kiwewa, the former kabaka. These gruesome acts further boosted support for Mwanga (who had an even greater number of ghastly murders to his name).

In June Mwanga moved to the small island of Bulingugwe, less than a mile (1.6km) from the mainland and close to Mengo. Because Kalema did not have the war canoes to attack the island, the Christians were brilliantly sited close to the centre of Muslim power. From Bulingugwe Mwanga invited both sets of missionaries to join him. Père Lourdel and Père Denoit – another of the party that crossed in the Eleanor – came in Stokes's boat; Gordon and Walker from the CMS entrusted themselves to a canoe. Mwanga also wrote appealing for support to Frederick Jackson of the Imperial British East Africa Company, who was at that time believed to be in Kavirondo. This was a letter that a wiser or better advised ruler would not have written. It was like inviting a leopard up for a meat tea – of oneself.

In October 1889 the Christian forces under Apolo Kagwa drove the Muslims out of the capital. Kalema fled and the Christians returned to Mengo a year almost to the day after they had been driven out. Kagwa became katikiro, a post he was to hold for many years. Mackay, from Usambiro, wrote: "The greatest, and, till recently, the most tyrannical power in all East Africa is now in the hands of men who rejoice in the name of CHRISTIAN. But is the power in the hand of *Christianity?* Shall a nation be born in a day? It is born, but being only just born it is at this moment in the most helpless and critical condition conceivable."

The October victory proved to be transient for next month Kalema's forces, reinforced by King Kabarega of Bunyoro, retook the capital. Mwanga went back to the fastness of Bulingugwe, where Père Lourdel lamented conditions on the overcrowded island: "In our island, disease and famine, following the flow of war, rage more violently each day! How many poor folk have not even a rag with which to cover themselves! And how many sick people die of cold and misery! The bark-cloth with which the Baganda clothe themselves is nearly all used up, and no-one is able to make more because of the disturbed conditions…"

Instead of the Protestant Apolo Kagwa, the Christian forces now agreed to serve under a young Roman Catholic, Gabriel Kintu. By February 1890 he had 3,370 guns under his command and was able to drive the Muslims out of Mengo, this time for good. True to a pact they had made before the decisive battles with the Muslims, the Catholics and the Protestants shared out the official posts and the shambas (landed estates) that went with them. Chiefdoms were allocated between the two groups, each office-holder having a member of the opposite faith under him, and so on down the line. The distribution was admirably fair in theory, but became the source of many problems in practice. Given the hostility between the two Christian groups, which had been put aside for the fight with the Muslims but not ended, members of the opposing faiths found it hard to work together. Then there was the matter of what happened to the post – and the shambas – when someone wanted to change faiths. This was particularly a problem for the Protestants. With the kabaka supporting the Catholics, loyal Baganda were tugged that way.

At this point in Buganda's affairs, Walker of the CMS identified three separate interests among the Europeans. The CMS missionaries wanted to see a British occupation "to ensure peace, and to put an end to the ceaseless war and carnage". The White Fathers, who through Lourdel had exclusive influence over the king, believed that Buganda should be left alone and Africans able to buy arms for their defence. The third interest was the arms trader and former missionary, Charles Stokes, who wanted to be able to offer terms to any Europeans who came to Buganda. It is a measure of Stokes's extraordinary position that Walker picked him out for mention alongside the two religious groups.

John S. Galbraith, in *Mackinnon and East Africa 1878-1895*, makes clear that the "French" and "English" labels, while deriving from the presence of the two missions, referred essentially to politics, not religion: "In the convulsions in Buganda after the death of Mutesa, the 'Arab' party derived much of its strength from the fear of the extension of European influence and European values, and Mwanga when he had initially accepted Muslim support had been similarly motivated. Bunyoro's backing of the Muslims after Mwanga had shifted to the Christian party had nothing to do with doctrine, much with the ambitions of its ruler, Kabarega, to restore his kingdom to its earlier greatness by capitalizing on the internal weaknesses of rival Buganda. The Fransa and Ingleza chiefs, on the other hand, saw the future of Buganda as within the sphere of European influence but were divided as to which of the European powers should be their protector."

The defeated Kalema retreated northwards towards the Bunyoro border. He soon died of smallpox and the Muslim succession went back a generation, to Mbogo, a brother of Mutesa. As Elizabeth Mary Matheson points out in *An Enterprise So Perilous* (a history of the White Fathers), Mbogo was "one of the few [royal] survivors of the 1889 massacre". He was "much less aggressive a character than his predecessor, though his followers carried on raiding in Singo and Kyagwe county for some time". Indeed, while the two Christian groups aimed to settle their differences after their joint victory, the

Muslims remained an unintegrated part of the Buganda body politic. Walker's contemporaneous comment was: "The Mohammedans were for the moment overpowered, but neither was their strength nor their spirit broken."

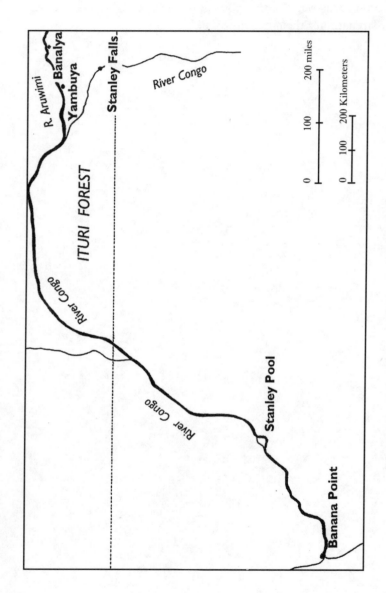

Fig 3 The Emin Pasha Expedition – outbound to Yambuya

9

Equatoria Alert

*Egypt looks south * Threat of the Mahdi * Death of Gordon * Emin isolated in Equatoria * Eating their boots * Relief expedition * Stanley's astonishing route * Recruiting the men * Tippu Tip brought in * By sea and river * A colourful procession * Yambuya taken by force*

To Buganda's north (beyond Bunyoro), along the Nile after it emerges from Lake Albert lay the Equatorial Province, the final remnant of the Egyptian empire in the Sudan. At this time, in the late Eighties, Equatoria was under great pressure from the Islamist followers of the Mahdi pushing ever southwards after the fall of Khartoum. Comes the moment comes the man ... Henry Morton Stanley re-enters the story with his mission to bring relief to the beleaguered governor of Equatoria, Emin Pasha.

Stanley had spent several years working for King Leopold of Belgium after he finished the expedition upon which he met Kabaka Mutesa. Travelling west, he traced a then-unidentified river, which turned out to be the infant Congo. He followed it to its mouth, completing an historic east-west crossing of Africa. For Leopold he knocked heads together and split rocks apart to make the roads that created the Congo state, earning himself his African name, the Breaker of Rocks. The Conference of Berlin in 1885 – the defining event in modern African history because in European terms it legitimated the scramble for Africa – recognised the Congo Free State as the king's private property.

That same year Khartoum fell to the besieging Mahdists, and General Charles Gordon died a hero with a relieving column only two days away. He was the most spectacular victim of the vanished power of the Egyptian state. The country had found itself ruined in the best possible cause – modernisation. Over much of the 19th century Khedive Muhammad Ali and his successors set about modernising Egypt in everything from education to cotton growing.

Nominally part of the crumbling Turkish empire, the country had achieved considerable autonomy and wanted to find its place in the modern world. Meanwhile, costs mounted. Debt, particularly to British and French capital, eventually became unsustainable. In 1875 Khedive Ismael, to raise money, sold his 44 per cent holding in the Suez Canal to Britain, giving that country control of its vital link with India. In 1876 he was obliged to accept an international commission to manage the Egyptian debt. In 1879 the British and French seized the arteries of Egyptian self-rule, taking over the treasury, customs, telegraphs and railways. In 1880, according to Lawrence James in *The Rise and Fall of the British Empire*, Egypt's debts were more than £100 million – or about eight times the average annual value of her exports, £13 million.

Anglo-French control of Egypt was challenged the following year (1881) when a high-ranking soldier, Urabi Pasha, staged a coup d'etat. Foreign control was only one of the issues, which made the revolt even more threatening to the Western powers. Urabi and his associates had grievances over pay and conditions; behind them stood the Egypt for the Egyptians movement of constitutional reformers. "What united them was a determination to break the power of the Turkish oligarchy," writes Thomas Pakenham in *The Scramble for Africa*. "They were not, at least at first, anti-Western. Indeed, they admired Western institutions and planned to set up a Western-style democracy with an elected Parliament and with the Khedive playing the role of constitutional monarch."

Doubtless Urabi's admiration of things Western did not extend to the ironclads that in July 1882 bombarded Alexandria. When this did not do any good, a substantial British expeditionary force of about 30,000 was landed at Ismaelia. It engaged Urabi's army in September at Tel-el-Kebir, 60 miles (97km) from Cairo. The commander, Sir Garnet Wolseley, decided on a daring night attack. It took the enemy by surprise. The battle was over in just 35 minutes.

"Down the slopes, through the camps, over the railway and across the Canal, the white-clad fugitives were flying south and west in dots, in dozens in hundreds." The words were written by a battle participant, Colonel William Butler. He praised the fighting spirit of Urabi's forces: "Not a moment was given them to awake, form up, prepare, or move into position. The assault fell upon them like a thunderbolt might fall upon a man asleep ... they fought stoutly wherever ten or twenty or fifty of them could get together in the works ... the heaps of dead lying with and across their rifles facing the upcoming sun bore eloquent testimony to that final resolve of those poor fellows." [Quoted by James, see bibliography]

Urabi gave himself up, Wolseley returned to Cairo in style and British control over Egypt was consolidated, in the cause of saving the country from anarchy or protecting its creditors' investments, depending on your viewpoint. The khedive, by now Ismael's son, Tewfik, nominally stayed in control, but the real power was with his British officials. Already, though, that power was threatened from another direction – the south.

Egypt's provinces stretched deep into Africa, even gnawing from time to time at the Great Lakes kingdoms of Bunyoro and Buganda. For the most part it was not settled administration, but rather garrisons of troops more or less holding down recalcitrant tribes. This tenuous control disintegrated over most of the Sudan with the uprising of Muhammad Ahmad. The son of a boat builder called himself the Mahdi, meaning the Expected One or the Redeemer. The state formed by his fundamentalist movement was to last for most of two decades, until destroyed by Major-General Kitchener at the Battle of Omdurman in 1898.

The Mahdi soon had much of the Sudan in his grip. An Egyptian army of 10,000 was sent against him under Colonel William Hicks (Hicks Pasha). On November 5, 1883, this large force was ambushed, overcome and massacred at El Obeid in the southern Sudanese province of Kordofan. Much of the story of 19th century Africa is about small European-led forces, better armed and better disciplined, overcoming essentially medieval hordes. The Battle of El Obeid is one of the few occasions where weight of numbers prevailed. The zeal of the Dervishes, as the Mahdi's troops were known to the Europeans, was shown again 14 months later at the Battle of Abu Klea, where they nearly managed another massacre by prising open the British defensive square.

Rudyard Kipling produced a famous poem about the battle. His brilliant metre and rhyming has worn better than the sentiments of this Cockney soldier's tribute to his opponents. It is only too easy to see why Kipling is in deep disfavour in post-imperial times. The final lines are:

So 'ere's *to* you, Fuzzy-Wuzzy, at your 'ome in the Soudan;
You're a poor benighted 'eathen but a first-class fightin' man;
An 'ere's *to* you, Fuzzy-Wuzzy, with your 'ayrick 'ead of 'air –
You big black boundin' beggar – for you broke a British square!

After El Obeid the British Cabinet decided to disengage Egypt from the Sudan. Gordon, who had been governor of the southernmost Equatorial Province, 1874-1876, reached Khartoum in February 1884 to supervise the withdrawal of the Egyptian garrisons. He allowed himself and the garrison to become trapped by the Mahdists. Eventually, a relief expedition under Wolseley was sent. Wolseley was advancing slowly – too slowly, the critics charged afterwards – through Abu Klea, where the battle was fought, and Al Matamma. His forces arrived just too late to save Gordon. Ironically, it was the news of the relieving force that drove the Mahdi to risk storming the city on January 26, 1885.

Gordon's death echoed across Europe. In the Equatorial Province, or Equatoria, his lieutenant, the German-born Emin, remained cut off and under threat. Slatin Bey and Lupton Bey, other European satraps ruling provinces of the Sudan for the khedive, had surrendered to the Mahdists. Only Emin remained. A correspondent wrote the the the Times: "Having betrayed the master [Gordon], we might well exert ourselves a little to deliver his man."

As his admirers saw it, the governor of Equatoria was keeping alight the flame of civilisation in the heart of Africa. Local tribes, as Iain Smith shows in *The Emin Pasha Relief Expedition, 1886-1890*, saw instead a string of garrison stations, administering little more than themselves but still exacting supplies, concubines and taxes from the surrounding countryside. However that may be, Emin was stranded in the remote reaches of the upper Nile, and Stanley's mission was to reach him.

Emin as not trapped personally; no doubt he could have marched out, abandoning "Emin's people" – the soldiers, administrators and clerks who had come up from Cairo, Alexandria and Khartoum – but Equatoria's position was untenable both short-term and long-term. Emin lacked the military strength to stop the Mahdists. He had abandoned Lado (near the present-day Sudanese city of Juba) as his headquarters, and moved ever southwards along the Nile: to Muggi, Labore and finally Wadelai (the last in modern Uganda). Emin also lacked reliable supply routes. The Nile route was closed indefinitely while astride the other feasible routes were the powerful kingdoms of Bunyoro and Buganda. He had no assured ways of bringing in equipment, spare parts or the ammunition on which his rule ultimately depended.

The route that brought Emin to Wadelai was long in miles and even longer in terms of a life's journey. He was born Eduard Schnitzer in Germany in 1840, and qualified as a doctor. However, he failed to complete the formal requirements to practise medicine in his own country so that employment in his profession was impossible. In a wandering life he found himself employed in the medical service of the Ottoman Empire, calling himself by a Muslim name. Later, he assumed a different Muslim name – Emin. By an oddity of history, Emin and Stanley greeted each other by names that were not their own, Stanley having been born John Rowland.

Emin from his time in Turkey became enthused by Islamic culture so it was natural to drift on to North Africa. He arrived in Equatoria when Gordon was the governor, and their association for the better part of a decade cemented him in the public mind as "Gordon's man". Emin by every account was a most likeable character, unselfish and ascetic. Even as governor he treated medical patients. It is no surprise that he won the loyalty of his ragbag of soldiers and followers. As a keen naturalist, Emin was greatly pained that in the eventual evacuation of Wadelai he had to leave his collections behind. He was not, however, heroic in appearance. He was extremely short-sighted. He is said to have several times passed by the famous Ruwenzori Mountains (the Mountains of the Moon) and never known they were there. He was also quite short, around 5ft 7in (1.7m). Stanley brought a pair of trousers for Emin. They had been made in Cairo to measurements based on a traveller's account of the Pasha, and six inches (15cm) had to be cut off the legs for them to fit.

Equatoria had been founded as a province of Egypt by Sir Samuel Baker between 1870 and 1873. Emin reached Equatoria in 1876 near the end of Gordon's own time there as governor. He was appointed as medical officer, but soon he was sent on a mission to Mutesa in

Buganda. The following year Emin declined to join Gordon in Khartoum as major-domo and was back in Equatoria as chief physician. He visited Omukama Kabarega in Bunyoro and met Mutesa again. In 1878 Emin was appointed governor of Equatoria.

Emin was beset from the beginning. Before the Mahdist threat was felt from the north, he had to guard his southern stations from harassment by Kabarega. In 1878, too, his communications with Khartoum were cut: the sudd, an impenetrable mass of floating vegetation, blocked the Nile, which continued closed for 2 1/2 years. Nevertheless, Emin, helped by his ascetic temperament, had a considerable degree of self-sufficiency and the work of opening stations went forward. In 1884 the Equatorial Province reached its fullest extent before the combination of the Mahdi and Stanley, the one by design, the other by accident, brought about its contraction and eventual collapse.

The province consisted, according to Major C.H. Stigand, a British officer who served in the area years later, of the following districts and stations: 1. Rol. Capital Ayak plus five stations; 2. Lado. Capital Lado plus five stations; 3. Makaraka. Capital Wandi plus 11 stations; 4. Mangbettu. Capital Mbaga plus five stations; 5. Kiri. Capital Labore plus three stations; 6. Dufile. Capital Dufile plus two stations including Wadelai; 7. Fowera. Capital Foda plus one station; 8. Fadibek. Capital Fajuli plus five stations; 9. Latuka. Capital Tarangole plus three stations; 10. Bor. Capital Bor, no other stations.

The forces in the province were two regular battalions, about 1,300 men, and 3,000 irregular troops. The expatriate population also included Egyptian and Sudanese administrators and clerks, many of them with criminal records because Equatoria was seen as a virtual penal colony, and their dependants. Emin had with him two faithful associates, who stayed with him to the end: an Italian soldier, Captain Gaetano Casati, and a Tunisian medical dispenser, Vita Hassan. Emin's Abyssinian wife died before the final evacuation, leaving him with a young daughter.

This structure plan suggests a degree of control over the province that Emin never had. For the tribes of the area life went on more or less irrespective of the local station. In that sense Equatoria was more of a construct in the European mind than a reality on the ground. Emin never enjoyed the resource base, the infrastructure and the involvement of the local population to move beyond garrisoning to complete administration. However, the regime did make successful efforts to reduce the slave trade in its area. One of the historical might-have-beens is how the southern Sudan would have evolved if an assured route to the coast – one of the possible outcomes of Stanley's expedition – for supply and trade had been secured.

Certainly the province was rich in ivory, or would have been if it could have been got out. Paradoxically, the humane government of Equatoria was involved in heavy stockpiling of ivory, which was obtained at terrible human cost. In pursuit of slaves and ivory, Arab traders fought their way into Africa's deepest recesses. Stanley wrote in *In Darkest Africa* (not specifically about Equatoria): "Every tusk, piece and scrap in the possession of an Arab trader has been steeped and dyed in blood. Every pound weight [0.45kg] has cost the life of a man, woman or child, for every five pounds [2.3kg] a hut has been burned, for every two tusks a whole village has been destroyed, every twenty tusks have been obtained at the price of a district with all its people, villages and plantations. It is simply incredible that, because ivory is required for ornaments or billiard games, the rich heart of Africa should be laid waste at this late year of the nineteenth century..."

Emin wrote a letter from Wadelai on the last day of 1885 which, when it was published in The (London) Times months later, caused a sensation and started the movement to bring him "relief", in the classic term of the period. The letter was to Charles Allen of the Anti-Slavery Society. "Forgotten, and abandoned by the [Egyptian] Government, we have been compelled to make a virtue of necessity," Emin wrote. "Since the occupation of the Bahr-Ghazal we have been vigorously attacked, and I do not know how to describe to you the admirable devotion of my black troops throughout a long war, which for them at least, has no advantage. Deprived of the most necessary things for a long time without any pay, my men fought valiantly, and when at last hunger weakened them, when, after nineteen days of incredible privation and sufferings, their strength was exhausted, and when the last torn leather of the last boot had been eaten, then they cut away through the midst of their enemies and succeeded in saving themselves."

This was the letter that caused such a stir in Britain, described in the earlier chapter, THE BUGANDA ROAD. In the same month Emin sent a "local letter" to Mackay in Buganda, which ominously foreshadowed the events to come. One of Mackay's many roles was to act as Emin's postmaster, establishing regular contact between Equatoria and Buganda and from there to the world beyond via the route to the coast. Emin told Mackay: "All my people, but especially the negro troops, entertain a strong objection against a march to the south and thence to Egypt, and mean to remain here until they can be taken north."

That route, using the Nile, was closed by the Mahdists' occupation of Khartoum and most of the Sudan. This sentiment was not realised in London when the Emin Pasha Relief Expedition was created, however. The task was taken up by William Mackinnon, whose Imperial British East Africa Company had an avowed philanthropic as well as trading purpose. The IBEA Company included among its sponsors one of Britain's most influential African specialists, Sir John Kirk. He had travelled with Livingstone and in the 1870s was the British consul-general in Zanzibar. Like the Doctor, he believed that commerce was the way to bring civilisation to Africa.

When Kirk was in post in Zanzibar, Frederick Jackson (*Early Days in East Africa*) found Kirk's knowledge of what was going on, both important and trivial, "little less than downright uncanny". It was founded on a great network of eyes and ears. At Jackson's first meeting with Kirk, the consul led him on about his trip and then threw in "Oh yes, that's where you gave the headman far too much baksheesh [gratuity]", or "I know, you shot a topi there", or "And then the gun-bearers you dismissed came along and frightened them away", and so on.

Mackinnon and his colleagues were inspired by the East India Company's success as a trading company that also exercised the powers of government, but the IBEA Company lacked some of the crucial advantages of the earlier company. The east African coastal hinterland was not favoured with great natural resources and was not very promising for cultivation; nor were the tribes advanced in social development. The company was in its earliest days when

Stanley was appointed leader of the Emin expedition, but it soon became obvious that if the company was to have a future, that future lay in Buganda and the surrounding states. Here the soil was fertile and the population advanced.

On the British side the Emin Pasha Relief Expedition was entirely privately funded. The Egyptian government met almost half of the expedition's costs. Stanley was not the only possible leader, especially because he was still in the service of King Leopold of Belgium building the Congo State, but he was by far the most eminent and experienced explorer available. He was the natural choice, although another well known explorer, Joseph Thomson, was disappointed not to have been chosen.

Stanley's instructions, which were later the subject of bitter controversy, appear to have been to (a) invite Emin with his men to accept repatriation to Egypt, all to receive arrears of pay and allowances from the Egyptian government, or (b) to stay under another flag, in which case the Egyptian government accepted no further financial responsibility. Emin himself wanted nothing more than resupply of goods and ammunition, which begged the question of what would happen when they in turn ran out. In any case, there were bigger stakes in play.

Controversy soon broke out over the route to reach Emin at his base near Lake Albert. The more established course ran from Bagamoyo on the coast of present-day Tanzania north-westwards and around the southern tip of Lake Victoria. Thomson suggested leaving from Mombasa in what is now Kenya and passing the opposite (northern) end of Lake Victoria. This was the shorter route, although Stanley pointed out that it was far more dangerous. It ran through Masai country and also Busoga, the "back door" to Buganda. The Baganda were very sensitive about this strategic area, so there was a risk that an expedition taking this route would destabilise the situation for the Christians in Buganda still further. The same could and was said to a smaller extent against the route from Bagamoyo.

Stanley now proposed the seemingly extraordinary idea of starting from the other (west) side of the continent, using the Congo River and its tributaries to reach the deep interior. This route meant circumnavigating half the continent to reach the starting point and was more than double the distance across land. It also meant crossing the unexplored vastness of the Ituri Rainforest.

Stanley put the weight of his reputation behind the route. He stressed that desertion would be easier if the expedition started from the east coast, and the desertion of porters with valuable supplies had wrecked other expeditions. He made the Congo route sound easy: the river would take the expedition to barely more than 300 miles (480km) as the crow flies from Lake Albert, its destination. He conjured up dangers of the other routes, like the Wanyankori with the unimaginable number of 200,000 spears.

Even so, Stanley could not prevail over the organising committee until providentially – too providentially, some historians have felt – a letter was received from King Leopold's aide, the Comte de Borchgrave. The king, Stanley learned, "considers that he would be failing in his duty towards the [Congo] State were he to deprive it of your services" over the 18 months the expedition was expected to take via the east coast. Stanley's estimated time for the Congo route was the same – 18 months – but by passing through untraversed parts of Leopold's domains he would be combining exploring with the relief of Emin.

A letter from Mackinnon to Stanley showed that Leopold's intention had been understood: "I had a pleasant short letter from the King [wrote Mackinnon] showing how anxious he is the Congo route should be taken, and how unwilling to allow a break in the continuity of your connection with the Congo State, as he considers you a pillar of the State." So, the Congo route it was.

It is hard to believe that Stanley, the servant of King Leopold, did not have a double agenda in suggesting the Congo route. It was not dishonourable to allow for Emin bringing Equatoria under the the king's flag. This was one of the possible outcomes of the expedition. It depended on adequate communication across the Nile-Congo watershed, and the traverse of the unexplored Ituri Forest might establish that.

Mackinnon and King Leopold were in fact closely associated in business activities and as friends. Mackinnon had been an early supporter of the International Association, Leopold's means of establishing himself in the Congo. Mackinnon, like Stanley, believed in the Congo as an important area for British investment. But the pair failed in a bid to build a Congo railway, which Leopold wanted built by Belgians. Iain Smith sees this as a crucial event: "September 1886 [when the railway contract was lost] marks an important watershed in the careers of both Mackinnon and Stanley. After this date, they both turn away from the Congo and their real interest is in East Africa." Leopold, Mackinnon, Stanley, the Germans on the coastal strip of what is now mainland Tanzania would all have been aware that at the heart of Africa there was the political vacuum of two established but unstable adjacent states, Equatoria and Buganda. It was becoming a question of which power would fill that vacuum. Equatoria was unstable because of the Mahdist threat and lack of supplies; Buganda because of chronic unrest under Mwanga. Stanley was in what now would be called a conflict of interest, although he may have seen it as simply advancing civilisation in whatever way was to hand. He was working for one employer and seconded from another, both of whom wanted to possess Equatoria. In Zanzibar before the expedition set out, Stanley underlined his dual allegiance with what he called "a little commission" to the ailing Sultan Barghash. He persuaded the sultan to grant Britain a concession over what is now the coast of Kenya. This was the springboard from which Frederick Lugard half a decade later penetrated the interior on behalf of Mackinnon's company.

An Anglo-German agreement in 1886 settled arrangements along the East African coast. Kirk described it enthusiastically to Mackinnon as covering deep into the interior: "Thus we have Mombasa under the Sultan [of Zanzibar] and a free run inland to the Lake [Victoria] etc. but not Kilimanjaro. We have the best of any line for a rail if ever one is made. We also have the Equatorial Province now held by the brave Emin Bey, well-governed and quiet to this day. Germany will rent Dar Salaam from the Sultan, which arrangement we may make at Mombasa. This is the outline of the scheme and you will see we have an opening as good as any." [Quoted by Smith, see bibliography]

The Emin Pasha Relief Expedition was organised on military lines, despite its leader's only army experience being as a ranker in the American Civil War. Stanley answered operationally to Mackinnon and the relief committee in London, but the expedition flew the Egyptian flag and was partly funded by the Egyptian government. From this perhaps Stanley could infer legitimacy for the harsh discipline he imposed on his men, including execution, and his readiness to fight tribespeople in his path – actions that otherwise would be common assault and murder. Three army officers were among the seven expedition officers chosen in England. Two more expedition officers were added en route.

The soldiers were Major E.M. Barttelot, Capt R.H. Nelson and Lt W.G. Stairs. A Congo veteran, John Rose Troup, and William Bonny, who was to be the medical assistant, were selected. The two other civilians were James S. Jameson, a naturalist, and A.J. Mounteney-Jephson, whose merits included their willingness to pay the then enormous sum of £1,000 each for a place on the expedition. A medical doctor, Thomas H. Parke, joined the party in Cairo. The final officer to join, when the expedition was already on the march, was Herbert Ward, a veteran of service with Stanley in his Congo state-building days.

In Cairo, the khedive gave Stanley 61 Sudanese soldiers and he later recruited about a dozen Somalis. In Zanzibar 620 men and boys were recruited, mainly as porters, most of them slaves.

Stanley now made the fateful decision to bring about the appointment of Tippu Tip as governor of Stanley Falls (near present-day Kisangani) on the Congo River, a few days' march from the expedition's staging point of Yambuya. Tippu Tip was a Arab trader of strongly negroid appearance, a slaver or reputedly ex-slaver, whom Stanley knew from years before. The Arabs had reached all over the eastern side of Africa, many of them seeking slaves and ivory. They were spreading ever westwards and had become a force in the Congo. When Stanley crossed the Ituri Forest on this expedition, it was unexplored by Europeans but already well known by Arabs, who had opened up trails across it and built villages. Tippu Tip was "an uncrowned king of the region between Stanley Falls and Tanganika Lake" who had the power to disrupt the expedition, and worse. The loads of ammunition being carried for Emin might be expected to attract attack; between Tippu Tip and Mwanga of Buganda Stanley felt "there was only the choice of the frying-pan and the fire". Once landed in the Congo, the expedition would need more carriers. Who better to supply them from the local tribes than Tippu Tip?

The trader was found to be "fully prepared for any eventuality – to fight me, or be employed by me". Stanley chose the second, and Tippu Tip was duly appointed as a salaried official under King Leopold. He was to defend the station against all Arabs and natives; defeat and capture slave raiders; and abstain from slave-raiding himself. He had also to accept a European officer as Resident to see that the duties were carried out. Otherwise he was free to carry on his trading activities. Tippu Tip's main value to Stanley was as the provider of carriers: he was to supply 600 carriers to take ammunition to Emin Pasha and to return with ivory. Each man was to carry 70lb (32kg) of ivory. The matter-of-fact way in which Stanley described this arrangement in *In Darkest Africa* does not play well alongside his impassioned plea against the ivory trade, quoted above. Tippu Tip was named as governor of the Falls over the strong opposition of many of Stanley's Belgian colleagues, who doubted the depth of the trader's conversion to king and country. As the events of the Emin Pasha Relief Expedition unfolded, the 600 carriers were indeed to decide the outcome of the whole venture.

In February 1887, the SS Madura left Zanzibar on its improbable route to relieve Emin: down the east coast of Africa, around the Cape of Good Hope, then up the west coast to the mouth of the Congo at Banana Point. Included in the cargo was a Maxim automatic gun, which Lieutenant Stairs later demonstrated at 330 shots per minute to general admiration.

Stanley left Zanzibar with 706 men plus Tippu Tip and his party, making about 100 more. The casualty rate was to be extraordinarily high, for only 246 returned to Zanzibar in December 1889 after the winding down of the expedition. Almost all the rest had either died or deserted, with little to choose between the two outcomes. No doubt some of the deserters did survive among alien tribes and impossibly far from home, but most were condemning themselves to death the fast way – which may have been the plan.

From the Congo mouth the expedition's route lay up the river to Stanley Pool, where the young settlement of Leopoldville (now Kinshasa) was located, then continuing up-river to Bangala and, after the main river forked away to Stanley Falls, along the Aruwimi to Yambuya. The navigation was interrupted in several places by cataracts, requiring long and tedious treks.

Herbert Ward, the last officer to join, engagingly tells how he ran after the expedition when it was in the lower Congo – stretched out in line of march with almost medieval magnificence and colour – and persuaded Stanley to sign him up. Ward's writing is very typical of the period, the language for us both clear and curious: "(I)n the distance coming over the brow of a hill I saw a tall Soudanese soldier bearing Gordon Bennett's yacht flag. [Bennett was the proprietor of the New York Herald, who sent Stanley on the expedition to find Livingstone.] Behind him and astride of a fine henna-stained mule, whose silver-plated strappings shone in the morning sun, was Mr. Henry M. Stanley, attired in his famous African costume. Following immediately in his rear were his personal servants, Somalis with their curious braised waist-coats and white robes. Then came Zanzibaris with their blankets, water-bottles, ammunition belts and guns. Stalwart Soudanese soldiers with dark-hooded coats, their rifles on their backs, and innumerable straps and leather belts around their bodies; and Zanzibari porters bearing iron-bound boxes of ammunition, to which were fastened axes and shovels as well as their little bundles of clothing which were rolled up in coarse sandy-coloured blankets.

"... Passing along I became further acquainted with the constitution of Stanley's great cavalcade. At one point a steel whale-boat was being carried in sections, suspended from poles which were each borne by four men; donkeys heavily laden with sacks of rice were next met with, and a little further on the women of Tippoo Tib's harem, their faces partly concealed, and their bodies draped in gaudily-covered cloths; then at intervals along the line of march an English officer with whom, of course, I exchanged friendly salutations; then several large-horned East African goats, driven by saucy little Zanzibari boys. A short distance further on, an abrupt turn of the narrow footpath brought into view the dignified form of the renowned Tippoo Tib, as he strode along majestically in his flowing Arab robes of dazzling whiteness, and carrying over his left shoulder a richly-decorated sabre, which was an emblem of office conferred on him by H.H. the Sultan of Zanzibar. Behind him at a respectful distance followed several Arab sheiks, whose bearing was quiet and dignified. In response to my salutation they bowed most gracefully.

"'Haijambo,' said I.

"'Sijambo,' they replied.

"'Khabari gani?' (what news?), I inquired.

"'Khabai njema' (good news), was the reply, and in that way I passed along the line of 700 men, in whose ranks were represented various types from all parts of eastern equatorial Africa, each wearing the distinguishing garb of his own country. All the costumes and accoutrements looked bright and gay, for the Expedition had disembarked but a few days previously. As the procession filed along the narrow, rugged path, it produced an effect no less brilliant than striking. Its unbroken line extended over a distance of probably four miles."

Stanley reached Leo on April 1887 and two months later (June 15), with two steamers, had reached Yambuya. The inhabitants being unwilling to share their village with the arrivals, it was occupied by force and the villagers driven off. Yambuya was the starting point for the crossing of the Ituri Forest and the Congo/Nile watershed. It was also the point where things started to go wrong.

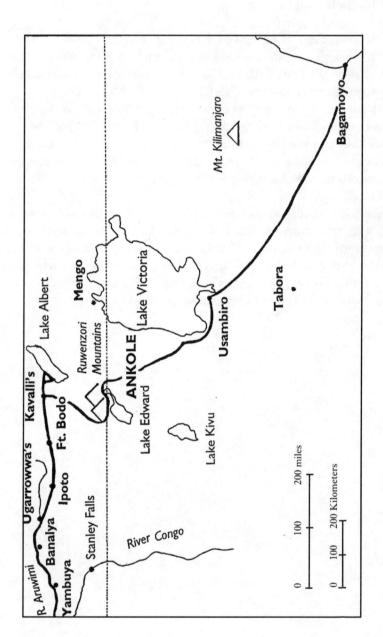

Fig 4 The Emin Pasha Expedition – to the lake and coast

10

The Ituri Forest

*Crossing the 'region of horrors' * Clashes with pigmies * Music of the molimo * Breaking out * Terrible toll of the forest * Search for Emin * The Pasha encountered * Into the forest again * Tragedy at Banalya * Barttelot's orders in dispute * Wasting away * Third time to the forest*

B etween Stanley and Emin Pasha now lay many miles of fearsome jungle, uncrossed by Europeans. The Ituri Forest was to cause numerous deaths, cost the expedition its chance of success and enmesh the great explorer in controversies that have continued to the present day.

Stanley's column to find Emin left Yambuya on June 28, 1887. He had with him 388 men including four European officers. The rear column under Barttelot, which was to follow, had more than a third of the men and most of the supplies for Emin. Stanley expected he would take two months to reach Lake Albert. In the event, he took 5 1/2 months – a difference that proved crucial in several ways. When the rear column failed to come up as arranged, Stanley made two more traverses of what he called "this region of horrors", to find the missing column and then to rejoin the main party.

The difficulties and delays of crossing the great Congo forest, which Stanley described as measuring 321,057 square miles (831,538 sq km), were caused by the terrain and the pigmy inhabitants. The atmosphere of the trek is well caught by Frank Hird in an authorised biography of Stanley: "For over five months he and his men had marched through a continuous, unbroken primeval forest under conditions which equalled some of the horrors in Dante's Inferno. At high noon only a dim green light filtered through the foliage from forty to a hundred feet [12-31m] thick above them. When they started the day's march at six o'clock in the morning, the forest would be buried in a cheerless twilight, the morning mist making every tree shadowy and indistinct. A path had to be hacked with bill-hooks, cutlasses, and axes through thick and entangled undergrowth, along which the Column crept slowly, the carriers often sinking to their necks in quagmires of stagnant water and decaying vegetation. Moisture dripped from the archway of impenetrable green above them; they were stung by wasps and hornets, and during many nights sat shivering under ceaseless torrents of rain. Underfoot the ground was soft black mud; oozy creeks had to be forded or bridged, causing hours of delay."

Stanley himself wrote of the long months "without ever having seen a bit of greensward of the size of a cottage chamber floor. Nothing but miles and miles, endless miles of forest ..." Colin Turnbull, an anthropologist who two generations later befriended the ba-Mbuti pigmies who so beset Stanley, acknowledges (in *The Forest People*) how overpowering the forest can be – "the heaviness of everything; the damp air, the gigantic, water-laden trees that are constantly dripping, never quite drying out between the violent storms that come with monotonous regularity ... the seeming silence and the age-old remoteness and loneliness of it all". He might have added the threatening feeling of disorientation, when one can wander 10 yards (metres) off the trail and amid the dense vegetation not find it again.

For most of the route the advance column followed the river (the Aruwimi changes its name to the Ituri), so except where there were rapids a river party and a land party were formed. The expedition had a portable steel boat, the Advance, which Jephson soon assembled, and some canoes were acquired along the way. The Advance was in 44 sections, representing 44 loads, and could carry 50 loads and at least 10 sick. That meant relief for almost 100 porters.

The expedition ate what it could find in the rainforest. A staple was patties of vegetables, herbs and leaves of the manioc. Some tribes were happy to trade: sugar cane, Indian corn (maize) and tobacco were bartered for empty sardine boxes, jam and milk cans and cartridge cases. Dr Parke bagged weaver birds with his gun. On October 15 Stanley's faithful donkey from Zanzibar, which had been ill, became part of the food chain. The meat was fairly shared, but a free-for-all occurred over the skin. Bones and hoofs were used; "a pack of hyaenas could not have made a more thorough disposal of it".

In a very Victorian comment, Stanley said: "That constituent of the human being which marks him as superior to all others of the animal creation was so deadened by hunger that our men had become merely carnivorous bipeds, inclined to be as ferocious as any beast of prey."

With the constant preoccupation of obtaining food, it was perhaps inevitable that someone of Stanley's temperament would clash with the forest inhabitants. The ba-Mbuti, at least as perceived by Stanley, were vicious dwarves and cunning thieves. All this from a people described as ranging from* 3ft to 4ft 6ins in height. (Turnbull in the 1950s found them averaging 4ft 6ins, although he does not distinguish male and female heights.) An average male might weigh 90lbs (6st 6lbs). One man was measured very comprehensively by William Bonny, the expedition medical assistant, whose findings include: height 4ft 0ins, length of leg 22ins, length of foot 6 1/4ins, length of arm to tip of finger 19 3/4ins.

Stanley felt sorry for the settled tribes around the forest. They "have much to bear from these fierce little people who glue themselves to their clearings, flatter them when well fed, but oppress them in their extortions and robberies". The expedition was often attacked by the pigmies, armed with poison-tipped arrows. Stanley supposed one of the poisons was made from a species of arum. Another seemed to be made from dried red ants, which with even deadlier insects gave the pigmies a limitless supply of poison. The main antidote was a heavy solution of carbonate of ammonium injected into the wound, after it had been sucked out and syringed. There were deaths, however, which Stanley ascribed to the poison not having been fully removed.

For all Stanley's hatred of the pigmies as a people, he had with the expedition for a year and more two individuals, a young man and a girl, both of whom he described affectionately. The "damsel" was

---

* The metric equivalents are: 0.9m to 1.4m in height. (Turnbull in the 1950s found them averaging 1.4m, although he does not distinguish male and female heights.) An average male might weigh 41kg. One man was measured very comprehensively by William Bonny, the expedition medical assistant, whose findings include: height 1.2m, length of leg 56cm, length of foot 15.9cm, length of arm to tip of finger 50.2cm.

the servant of Dr Parke, carrying his satchel, collecting fuel for his fire and preparing the surgeon's "cheering cup of tea". She became ill and was eventually left with a chief far beyond her forest home, on the way to the coast. The young man, who worked for one of the other officers, was frequently robbed of his stock of fuelwood. He "would show his distress by his looks, but presently gathering courage he would abandon it and collect another pile, as though time was too precious to waste in useless argument over the inevitable". Stanley commented: "And thus the Pigmies showed by their conduct that they were related to all that was best and noble in human nature."

When Colin Turnbull lived with the pigmies two full generations later, he found that Stanley's expedition was only too well remembered. A chief of one of the settled tribes had a father who was a boy when the expedition came through. Old Effundi Somali "used to tell stories of the dreadful wars that were fought in those days, and of the trail of destruction that Stanley had left behind him". Yet Turnbull found the pigmy world essentially non-violent. The ba-Mbuti are hunter-gatherers who roam about the forest in hunting groups. They have no chiefs and no hierarchy. Punishment means ostracism rather than chastisement. Pigmy wars, which are about territory, consist of mutual threats until, after a respectable interval, the group that invaded runs away.

Stanley commiserated with the villagers for the way the pigmies "glued themselves" to the clearings and stole the villagers' goods. Turnbull, however, discovered that this was the expression of an extraordinary symbiotic relationship. The two sides dislike each other but need each other. The villagers supply the pigmies with vegetables, plantains and metal arrowheads; the pigmies provide meat from the forest, where the villagers rarely care, or dare, to go. The pigmies steal from the villagers and have no sense of guilt about it. The villagers scarcely react. It is sanctioned thievery, as one might indulge a child.

The tribes of the villages claim to "own" the pigmies. Individuals have "their" pigmies, but the supposed rights are often unenforceable. For much of the time the pigmies are in the forest and out of reach; but when they are in the villages the pigmies go along with the system because it suits them. This even extends to the nkumbi initiation ceremony for boys, with its painful circumcision rites. The pigmies go through the nkumbi because it would be inconvenient for their young men not to be accepted as adults in the villages, but every mu-Mbuti knows that the only real initiation is in the forest hunt. They join in the nkumbi not because they lack culture of their own but because it makes sense to do so.

Turnbull lived with the boys at the nkumbi camp, a privilege normally allowed only to the "fathers" of the boys (brothers sometimes also fill the role), and saw what the ceremony really meant to the pigmies. One played punchball with the sacred banana; another mockingly imitated the action of the bull-roarer, which the candidates were supposed to think was the voice of a forest demon. The boys washed themselves in a rain shower, although they ought to have kept the white clay on as a sign of their death as children. All of this was not mere play: "The villagers hoped that the nkumbi would place the pigmies directly under the supernatural authority of the village tribal ancestors, the pigmies naturally took good care that nothing of the sort happened, proving it to themselves by this conscious flaunting of custom."

This must have been as an insurance policy because pigmies, Turnbull found, do not believe in the power of the dead. The villagers live in constant fear of spirits and those who summon them. Freeing human beings from crippling, superstitious terror was a driving force for the first missionaries. The pigmies' God is the forest, but they revere it rather than worship it. Stanley's "region of horrors" is to them a cool, friendly and familiar place. Since the forest is God, why should one be afraid of it? Turnbull in his three years with the ba-Mbuti felt at home there too, but even towards the end of his time he acknowledged the forest's capacity to frighten. He wanted to make a final visit to a favourite spot but he had to force himself to go alone. "(T)here is something about the forest, not exactly threatening, but challenging, that dares you to travel alone … I knew what that challenge was: for to be alone was as though you were daring to look on the face of the great God of the Forest himself, so overpowering was the goodness and beauty of the world all around."

The pigmies' own great ceremony is the molimo, which Turnbull witnessed daily for a month. The music was made by two "trum-

pets" (hollow tubes) found in the forest. Turnbull had been expect-
ing elaborate and beautiful ritual objects. Instead, the pigmies
picked up a couple of metal pipes left behind by construction gangs.
"What does it matter what the molimo is made of?" he was asked.
"This one makes a great sound and besides, it does not rot like
wood. It is much trouble to make a wooden one, and then it rots
away and you have to make another." The dancing, with dramatic
spurts out of the forest and rampages through the camp, was strictly
by the men. The women were bundled into the huts before it
started. They were supposed to think the molimo was an animal of
the forest and to see it meant death. Needless to say, they didn't
think that, and later Turnbull was surprised to find the women
singing the sacred songs, led by an old woman under a head-dress of
vine and feathers and backed by the camp belle, with the men in
supporting roles.

Finally, old Moke explained the meaning of the molimo. He said:
"Normally everything goes well in our world. But at night when we
are sleeping sometimes things go wrong, because we are not awake
to stop them from going wrong. Army ants invade the camp, leop-
ards may come in and steal a hunting dog or even a child. If we were
awake these things would not happen. So when something big goes
wrong, like illness or bad hunting or death, it must be because the
forest is sleeping and not looking after its children. So what do we
do? We wake it up. We wake it up by singing to it, and we do this
because we want it to awaken happy. Then everything will be well
and good again. And when our world is going well then we also sing
to the forest because we want it to share our happiness."

Turnbull found that the pigmies have a strange perception of
death. Life and death are not either/or states. The daughter of a
man called Cephu was announced to be dead, but the child was
actually still alive although critically ill with dysentery. Degrees of
illness are expressed as hot, with fever, ill, completely or absolutely
dead and finally, dead for ever. Unhappily, the next day the girl was
dead for ever. After Stanley's forays in the Ituri Forest so were
many others.

For all the ordeals of the crossings, Stanley maintained his metic-
ulous observations. Among the trees and bushes he noted were cot-
tonwood, teak, camwood, mahogany, greenheart, lignum vitae,

ironwood, yellowwood, skinkwood, ebony, copalwood, wild mango, wild orange, wild fig, butter tree, acacia and mpafu.

Even in the gloomy rainforest, there were better times, although Stanley's way of describing them is curiously buttoned-up. The master of the vivid journalistic phrase was not at his best describing the lyricism of nature: "But during the march, Providence was gracious; the sun shone, and streamed in a million beams of soft light through the woods, which brightened our feelings, and caused the aisles and corridors of the woods to be of Divine beauty, converted the graceful thin tree-shafts into marbly-grey pillars, and the dew and rain-drops into sparkling brilliants; cheered the invisible birds to pour out, with spirit, their varied repertory of songs; inspired parrot flocks to vent gleeful screams and whistlings; roused hosts of monkeys to exert their wildest antics; while now and then some deep, bass roar in far-away recesses indicated a family of soko or chimpanzees enjoying some savage sport."

Breaking out of the forest at last was dramatic and the entire column was overjoyed: " ... then, to our undisguised joy, [we] emerged upon a rolling plain, green as an English lawn, into broadest, sweetest daylight, and warm and glorious sunshine, to inhale the pure air with an uncontrollable rapture. Judging of the feelings of others by my own, we felt as if we had thrown all age and a score of years away, as we stepped with invigorated limbs upon the soft sward of young grass. We strode forward at a pace most unusual, and finally, unable to suppress our emotions, the whole caravan broke into a run ... Leagues upon leagues of bright green pasture land undulated in gentle waves ... far away to the east rose some frowning ranges of mountains beyond which we were certain slept in its deep gulf the blue Albert."

That was on December 5, 1887. A few days later (December 13) they had completed the easy route to the shores of Lake Albert. Crossing the forest had taken a terrible toll. Of the 389 including Stanley who started from Yambuya, only 169 now stood beside him. The rest had died, deserted (which far from home came to the same thing) or had been left sick at several points along the route.

At the cost of fragmenting his expedition, Stanley had made finding Emin his overriding priority. It had all been for nothing, though. Beside Lake Albert, Stanley was astonished to find that the local people not only had no message from Emin but did not even know who he was. It was to be four more months before the two met. Meanwhile, there was nothing for it but to create a stockaded camp, which Stanley did inland from the lake at a site he called Fort Bodo.

The pressing need was to reunite the scattered expedition. Lieutenant Stairs led a party back into the forest making for Ipoto, a settlement founded by Arab slave traders. A section of the advance column under Captain Nelson were stranded there (having been left even further back on the trip out, a decision for which Stanley was greatly criticised later). Also there was another of the expedition's officers, the surgeon, Thomas Parke, the Maxim gun and the portable steel boat. Stairs brought them all back to Fort Bodo and before long – in February 1888 – he had dived into the forest again. This time he was sent even further, to a settlement called Ugarrowwa's, where more sick had been left on the march out. Stairs's mission was to find news of the rear column, which was overdue. Stanley had hoped that by a detailed system of marking trees and blocking forks in the trail the rear column would have made good time through the forest.

In April, Stanley led a party on a return to the lake, making camp close by at Kavalli's. This time there was a letter from Emin. It was dated from Tunguru, a station on the lake northwards. Jephson was sent in search of the elusive pasha, and before the end of the month (April 29) a steamer brought Emin to meet Stanley on the lakeshore. It was evening and dark. We can imagine that Stanley was conscious of his poor record in historic greetings, stating the obvious to Livingstone and getting the wrong man with Mutesa of Buganda. This time he played it straight.

As he told it: "At eight o'clock, amid great rejoicing, and after repeated salutes from rifles, Emin Pasha himself walked into camp, accompanied by Captain Casati and Mr. Jephson, and one of the Pasha's officers. I shook hands with all, and asked which was Emin Pasha? Then one rather small, slight figure, wearing glasses, arrested my attention by saying in excellent English, 'I owe you a thousand thanks, Mr. Stanley; I really do not know how to express my thanks to you'.

"'Ah, you are Emin Pasha. Do not mention thanks, but come in and sit down. It is so dark out here we cannot see one another'."

The object of the Emin Pasha Relief Expedition appeared in clean suit of snowy cotton drill, "well-ironed and of perfect fit", as Stanley noted. He wore a well kept fez. As for his face, there was "not a trace on it of ill-health or anxiety; it rather indicated good condition of body and peace of mind". It was the rescuers who from their appearance were more in need of relief. Stanley and Emin spent almost a month together at Kavalli's. But there were few supplies to hand over: before the "relief" of Emin could be completed, Stanley had to rescue his own rear column, about which there was still no news.

It was agreed that Emin, accompanied by Jephson, would tour the stations of the Equatorial province to explain arrangements to the garrisons and to sound out their opinions, while Stanley would make a return journey through the Ituri Forest to find the missing column. On June 16 he started the return march accompanied by his personal servant (if he was going to starve, he would do so in style), 113 Zanzibaris and 95 carriers supplied by Emin. It was an astonishingly determined crossing of the forest: the party was back at Banalya, only 90 miles (145km) from the original starting point of Yambuya, in 62 days (the outbound march had taken 2 1/2 times as long). At Banalya Stanley saw from the river a camp flying the Egyptian flag. Asked who they were, they answered, "We are Stanley's men." This was the rear column, or what was left of it.

It was a terrible tragedy. Of the officers, only Bonny, the medical assistant, remained at the camp. An incredulous Stanley heard that the commander, Major Barttelot, had been assassinated by one of the carriers over a trivial dispute, Troup had been invalided home, Ward had been sent 1,500 miles (2,400km) down the Congo to send a telegram to the expedition committee in London, and Jameson had also gone downriver in yet another hunt for carriers. On the very day that Stanley reached Banalya, Jameson died of fever at Bangala nursed by Ward.

Stanley caused Bonny to make a return of all personnel at Banalya on August 17, 1888. It showed 75 Zanzibaris present out of 223 accounted for when Stanley handed over command of the rear column to Barttelot. Ten more were with Jameson at Bangala, but there had been 78 deaths – more than one third of the total – and many desertions. Of 53 Sudanese, Somalis and Syrians, 22 were present and 23 were dead. The futility of these deaths was particularly shocking because for whatever reason – and that became a bitter national, indeed international, controversy – the rear column had not moved for almost a year and when it did, it got just a fraction of the way. Stanley's role was naturally at the centre of the storm that followed.

Stanley had left Barttelot with detailed written instructions that at least in theory covered every possibility. But Barttelot was in an unfavourable position from the start. The rear column was already split with Troup, Ward, Bonny and their parties downriver bringing up more loads. Nor had Tippu Tip, upon whom so much depended for the supply of carriers, arrived in Stanley Falls yet. The question arises why Stanley rushed on when the situation at Yambuya was unresolved. The memory of Gordon's death at Khartoum just 2 1/2 years earlier, when a British relieving force arrived hours too late, must have been fresh and haunting. Now the Mahdists were threatening Emin, one of Gordon's loyal lieutenants, and Stanley would not want to repeat that tragic delay. With his odd dual loyalty to King Leopold and to the British, he would know that the Germans might get to the interior territories first and annex them. Stanley's temperament did not lend itself to waiting and watching. We also have to beware of judging his actions from the perspective of a hundred more years' experience of the dangers of splitting expeditions in hostile terrain.

And so Stanley marched away into the jungle. In his detailed instructions, he told Barttelot: "The goods that will be brought up are the currency needed for transit through the regions beyond the Lakes; there will be a vast store of ammunition and provisions, which are of equal importance to us. The loss of these men and goods would be certain ruin to us, and the Advance Force itself would need to solicit relief in its turn."

If Tippu Tip did not supply enough carriers "you must consider, after rope, sacking, tools, such as shovels (never discard an axe or bill-hook), how many sacks of provisions you can distribute among your men to enable you to march ... If you still cannot march, then it would be better to make two marches of six miles [10km] twice over, if you prefer marching to staying for our arrival, than throw too many things away".

Barttelot never attempted this plan of short double marches, which would have allowed the expedition to move with half the complement of carriers and all the loads. Instead, he awaited for many months the full strength of carriers, seemingly always about to turn up. The waiting proved as lethal as the forest. Food was inadequate: for much of the time the men lived on nothing but the manioc root, while the Europeans managed with boiled rice and fried plantains. Arab slave traders and ivory hunters camped nearby competed with the expedition for supplies from the surrounding countryside. One by one, day by day, men died of fever or malnutrition.

The question at the crux of the tragedy was whether Barttelot had been instructed to move in some form or another. Stanley afterwards expressed amazement that Barttelot did not carry out the double marches, but it seems clear, even from a dispassionate reading of *In Darkest Africa*, that Stanley left Barttelot the option of moving or staying. That was how the rear column commander understood matters. It appears Stanley expected to return rather than necessarily wait for the rear column to find him. He planned to be back in five months. As it was, it took almost 14 months. Whatever the instructions, the ultimate cause of the tragedy was Stanley's under-estimate of the terrain.

The wasting away of the rear column was graphically chronicled by Herbert Ward, who had joined the expedition when it was already in the Congo in the hope of adventure and found himself, like the rest at Yambuya, hungry, fever-ridden and bored. He spent much of the time sketching and writing his diary.

"Rheumatism, fever, and biliousness was the order of the day amongst the white men [Ward wrote], while the poor fellows under us were growing weaker and weaker, and dropping off day by day. By December 5 there were thirty-one deaths amongst the blacks. Each morning a miserable sight met our eyes as, crowding round Bonny's hut, their number growing each day, a mass of suffering Zanzibaris and Soudanese sought relief and medicine, from the scanty store he had at his disposal. The wet weather, the wretched food, and the weary, miserable existence we were forced to lead was telling on us all, but with most deadly effect on the poor creatures, whose uncared-for flesh broke into festering sores of the most painful character."

On February 18, 1888 – with the rear column still at Yambuya almost eight months after Stanley left – Ward commented in his diary: "Death is written in plain letters on many faces in this camp. Almost as many lives will be lost over this philanthropic mission as there are lives to save of Emin's people."

The Manyemas, a tribe much used by the Arabs, had a reputation for cannibalism. Ward records: "Had a chat with Selim bin Mohammed this morning about cannibals. He told me he had frequently seen the natives he used to have with him in these parts ... kill a slave, cut it up, and eat the flesh in front of him." A few days later, matter-of-factly: "To-day was very hot, the sun registering 135° outside; no news of the captured Arabs; they have undoubtedly been eaten. Drew two Manyema warriors this morning, and sketched a number of heads &c."

If small episodes can tell all, Ward's description, from his diary entry of January 10, of how he and his fellow officers spent their time is revealing: "Jameson and I are generally sketching; Major B. walking up and down; Troup and Bonny smoking, chatting, reading, &c." By far the least productive of these activities was "walking up and down". For the commander to extricate the expedition, more was needed.

The jungle trail from Yambuya on the Aruwimi to Tippu Tip's base at Stanley Falls on the Congo was relatively short, around five days' marches. Barttelot and his fellow officers made the journey several times: Jameson and Ward in August 1887, Barttelot and Troup in October, Barttelot and Jameson in February 1888, and Barttelot again in April and May. They were kindly received by Tippu Tip or, in his absence, by other leaders, but the necessary carriers did not appear. The reason has always been disputed. That Tippu Tip was hoping to bring about the final wreck of the rear column so he could plunder its guns and other stores is the most unfavourable construction. Another possibility is that as governor of Stanley Falls he felt he had been promised money and assistance by Stanley that had not been given. He may have been unwilling to help Stanley until the debt had been paid. He may simply have been unable to produce such a large number of carriers (600) at any one time. Whatever the reason, the Europeans would never have been told No and would have thought just a little bit longer ... With no word about Stanley for almost a year, and with a growing feeling that the advance column must have met with disaster, the rear column officers would have felt even less inclined to venture into the Ituri Forest. They had fewer men than Stanley – and he had the Maxim gun.

Finally, Barttelot managed to collect 430 Manyema carriers (still only two-thirds of the number specified by Stanley) and on June 11, 1888, the rear column left Yambuya, almost a year after the advance column. On the other side of the great Congo forest, Stanley had met Emin Pasha and was about to trek back in search of the missing rear column.

Barttelot was a well qualified army officer and an able commander of his Sudanese soldiers, but he now showed he was no Stanley in the control of a mob of irregulars. Amid much chaos and very slowly, the column reached Banalya, 90 miles (145km) upriver. While it was halted there, Barttelot was shot dead in the most trivial circumstances. He complained to a woman about the noise of her singing during a Manyema festival and her husband, taking offence, killed him. This was on July 19, one month before Stanley's return.

Stanley found only 60 men "likely to survive" and scarcely one-third of the loads. The fear he had expressed to Barttelot the year before, that the loss of the men and the goods "would be certain ruin to us", had nearly come about. The lack of supplies that Stanley was able to offer Emin had a direct bearing on what the pasha did next, which in turn affected the course of events in Equatoria and Buganda. Stanley now led the bedraggled expedition through the Ituri Forest – some, like him, traversing the forest for the third time. Passing through Fort Bodo, he was back at Lake Albert in January 1889. There he found astonishing news. There had been a rebellion in Equatoria. Emin and Stanley's lieutenant, Jephson, were prisoners. The beloved pasha upholding civilisation in the wilderness became a captive of his own men.

11

Emin's Adieu

*Emin's choices * Garrisons spurn message * The Pasha arrested * Pressed by the Mahdists * A Roman sense of honour * Free again * Casati's close shaves * Character of Kabarega * Blood sacrifice * The expedition reunited * March for the coast * Emin humiliated*

After Stanley left to find the missing rear party, Emin made a tour of his stations to discover the views of the garrisons. He was accompanied by Jephson and just three soldiers from the relief expedition. This was a misjudgment by Stanley: Emin's troops could not believe that their master, the mighty khedive of Egypt, would send word to them with such a meagre force. Thus even before the message was delivered, the messengers had failed to convince. While it was their governor, not Jephson, who explained the khedive's options, the suspicion grew that Emin had "turned" and was about to betray them.

In their month together by the lake, Stanley and Emin had reviewed the choices offered by the khedive's message. The proposition was for Emin and his people to come out, and receive their arrears of pay and allowances, or to stay on without further Egyptian responsibility. Only after Emin had said he wished to stay did Stanley feel able to mention the offers from his two employers: King Leopold wanted Emin to attach Equatoria to the Congo state and to continue as governor; Mackinnon wanted Emin to work with his Imperial British East Africa Company, which involved relocating his people to Kavirondo (at the north-east end of Lake Victoria). Both Stanley and Emin seemed inclined towards the Kavirondo scheme, but to sell it to the garrisons might be another matter.

Most of the main stations of Equatoria could be reached by steamer, being on Lake Albert or along the Nile. In the south–north direction taken by Emin and Jephson, they were : Mswa and Tunguru on the west side of the lake (in present-day Congo);

Wadelai, Bora and Dufile (now in Uganda); Labore, Muggi, Kirri, Bedan, Rejaf and Gondokoro (still in Sudan). These stations were strung out over more than 200 miles (320km). Lado, the former capital of Equatoria, further north still and near modern Juba, had been abandoned the year before because of fire. Its garrison was distributed between the stations at Rejaf and Makaraka.

Emin and Jephson began their tour of the stations in June 1888. The first stop was Tunguru. In his address to the troops and other station residents, the governor did not mention the Kavirondo scheme but presented the khedive's choice of evacuating the province or staying on under another master. The message was not well received. The idea of going to Cairo was deeply unattractive to many Sudanese, who saw destitution staring at them in an alien city. Since everyone knew that the seat of the khedive lay down river, the plan to evacuate by marching in another direction was profoundly suspicious. The soldiers refused to believe that Khartoum had fallen, although it was now more than three years since that event. Jephson and his insignificant entourage were clearly imposters. Emin must be planning to march them away and sell them into slavery.

It was the same reaction at other stations. At Wadelai, Emin's capital, Jephson nevertheless was impressed by the neatness and order with which the governor had arranged the station. Emin's own comfortable quarters, filled with his well arranged natural history collections, described the man. After passing through Dufile, Emin and Jephson reached Labore where, on August 13, the unthinkable happened: one of the once loyal troops made a rush at the governor. The incident was contained, but it was a portent.

Stanley's expedition had brought next to no relief – just 34 cases of ammunition and two bales of calico – because most of the loads were with the rear party. His presence, however, had combined with the Mahdist threat to bring about the unravelling of Equatoria. The same effect was felt in Bunyoro, where Captain Casati was Emin's emissary to Kabarega. When the king heard about the expedition, he had Casati arrested.

Above Labore, Emin learnt that the 1st Battalion in Rejaf had mutinied and he was advised not to proceed any further north. The party returned to Dufile, but it was too late. The disaffection had spread to the 2nd Battalion and Emin, with Jephson, was put under house arrest. On August 31 evacuees from Rejaf, which was under threat from the Mahdists, reached Dufile. The garrisons finally began to accept the truth of Khartoum's fall.

On September 3 Jephson left Dufile on Emin's steamer Khedive. The rebel leaders had allowed him to go so he could tell the southern stations how things stood. He visited Wadelai, Tunguru and Mswa, then, showing a truly Roman sense of honour, returned to Dufile by the end of the month. Emin was formally deposed on September 27. The state of Equatoria, what remained of it, was in the hands of two of the officers, Fadl al-Mula and Hamad Agha. Selim Bey, the governor of Labore station, who was to play a continuing part in the Buganda story, was consistently loyal to Emin.

Late in October came the news that the Mahdists had captured Rejaf. Emin and Jephson were freed. On November 17 they left for Wadelai, but even that southerly station began to look insecure as the Mahdists swept on. On December 4 Emin heard that the Mahdists had taken more northern stations including Labore, and had attacked, but failed to take, Dufile, the scene of his recent captivity. It was later taken by one of the local tribes, the Danagla, who no doubt relished the chance to pay back on the oppression of the soldiers. Two days after he heard about the Mahdists' capture of the northern stations, Emin began to evacuate Wadelai.

In Bunyoro Gaetono Casati had some close shaves. Stanhope White, in *Lost Empire on the Nile*, records how from a favourable start Casati ended up hiding for his life. He had met Kabarega in June 1886 as Emin's unofficial envoy. He wanted to persuade the king to allow a flow of letters from Equatoria through Bunyoro to the missionary Alexander Mackay in Buganda, and so on to the coast. He also wanted to arrange passage for Emin's troops if they had to retreat from the Mahdists.

Casati and Emin, who had also visited the king, give us two of the most complete pictures we have of Kabarega. The fiery ruler, whatever his other failings, kept the field constantly and repeatedly against those he feared would eat the country until he was finally deposed by the British after the creation of the Uganda protectorate. In person Emin found Kabarega talkative, cheerful and ready to laugh. He wrote: "The next day I was called again to the king whom

I found surrounded by ten or twelve persons. Anyone who has seen the strict etiquette in Buganda could not fail to be greatly surprised at the nonchalance and informality of the Wanyoro who lie about the floor chewing coffee in a completely unceremonious manner." The king was a young man, much attached to his cattle of which, according to Casati, he had more than 150,000. He seemed to be more interested in the cattle than administering the kingdom. He was notably fair-skinned because of his Bahuma (Nilotic rather than Bantu) blood.

At the time of Casati's stay (1886-88) Bunyoro had had very little contact with Christian missionaries, although these had been established in neighbouring Buganda since 1877. Kabarega followed custom in sacrificing human beings. No doubt it never occurred to him not to: for the most extreme crises, this was the way to appease the spirits of ancestors, who would otherwise destroy you. Casati offers a vivid account of one such occasion, when the king thought he was about to be caught in the pincers of an alliance between Emin and Mwanga of Buganda.

The ceremony of the mpango (axe) was carried out. A great bass drum boomed out over Kabarega's capital. After three days, numerous villagers were seized at random and their throats cut in order to regain the protection of the king's dead father. "But the great sacrifice was not to be completed until the morning of the next day [Casati wrote] … The King made a sign with his hand; the nobles rose and bowing in sign of reverence approached him; he touched the shoulder of one of them with the point of his spear; the chief advanced and extended his neck; the axe descended and the blood was caught in the cup. The King then sprinkled some of the blood on his own forehead and cheeks, then on those of the nobles; then the remainder was poured over the drum and the chair … At a sign from the King, the sorrowing parents took away the body of Kisa, late chief of the District of Muenghe. The drums called to a feast; oxen were killed and jars of beer brought and the drunken people danced upon the ground bathed with the blood of the late victim." [Quoted by White, see bibliography]

Kabarega had gathered a force of some 3,000 rifles known as the Banassura. In the best tradition of palace guards, the soldiers were mostly not Banyoro. They included youths from other countries, runaway slaves, even some deserters from Emin's Equatoria. The king was right to fear an invasion by Buganda: early in 1887 (when Stanley's expedition was on its way to the Congo to relieve Emin Pasha) it invaded, with around 6,000 troops. In Buganda eyes, Bunyoro was a tributary state, although Kabarega had other ideas. However, his Banassura and regiments of spear-men were no match for the Baganda, so he retreated. Casati was caught up in the invasion, but was unharmed. He was even offered safe passage back to Buganda, which he refused. This decision nearly cost him his life.

Casati had not pleased the king by negotating with Zanzibari merchants, as well as with Kabarega himself, over the transport of mail to Mackay in Buganda. His position was now weakened further when Emin's troops occupied Kibiro on the Bunyoro (east) side of Lake Albert. The decision to stay on must have seemed the right one, but at the start of 1888 Casati, along with a Zanzibari named Mohammed Biri, an Egyptian soldier and Casati's personal servant, found himself under arrest.

At a signal from the royal vizier the "unbridled crowd pounced upon us; we were seized and barbarously tied to the large trees close to the great magician [a reference to the high priest]. I was stripped of my tarboosh and my pockets were rifled; my neck, arms, wrists, knees and ankles were bound to a tree with such atrocious force that I was unable to make the least movement. The rope round my neck was so tight that my respiration was hindered and one of my arms was twisted and tied in a painful position." [Quoted by White, see bibliography]

Later, the vizier addressed the crowd about the captives: "'This man,' he said pointing me out, 'together with that other, Biri, brought the Waganda to our country; he was the cause of your children and wives being ravished, your goods stolen and your crops destroyed. For these crimes the King has struck them with his justice and entrusted his vengeance to my arm'"

From this situation the party, improbably, cheated death. Casati, his servant and the Egyptian soldier (Biri was left behind, and later died) were taken to a killing ground but managed to escape through a wood. Fleeing their pursuers, they eventually reached a hilltop overlooking Kibiro. We can imagine their anguish when, so close to safety, they were seized by Banassura. Kabarega liked to deal in large numbers; on this occasion, according to Casati, there were about 1,000, partly Banassura and partly spear-men. Once again it seemed inevitable that they would be killed. The chance appearance on the lake of one of Emin's steamers threw their captors into a panic. They fled. Casati and his group were free.

The Italian was thus back in Equatoria in time for the evacuation of the province. To Emin's great regret he had to leave behind at Wadelai his books, instruments and natural history collections. On February 17, 1889, he reached Stanley's camp at Kavalli's with just 65 followers. These included the loyalist Selim Bey. At this point the governor (or former governor, because he refused to take up his old title) looked more like a refugee than a ruler with a choice of action. Stanley, it seems, now dropped the plan for Emin to settle in Kavirondo – a springboard for Buganda – and simply prepared to bring his charge out.

The day after Emin reached Kavalli's, Capt Nelson, Lt Stairs and Dr Parke returned to the camp, bringing with them more loads. Mostly these were too late to do any good: with the collapse of Emin's administration, the ammunition was superfluous and much of it was buried and left. Since Jephson and Bonny were already with Stanley, the expedition officers were reunited for the first time in two years – reunited at least if one disregards two dead (Barttelot and Jameson) and two repatriated (Troup and Ward).

An example of the protracted time scale that was typical of those days and which we find so hard to relate to followed. It was almost two more months before the march to the coast began. Partly this delay was caused by Emin's temporising. He must have known that Equatoria held nothing for him any more, but he may also have felt the shame of making the journey, figuratively, in Stanley's baggage train. Or perhaps it was less rational than that; perhaps he just could not make up his mind. Meanwhile, Selim Bey returned to Wadelai with the invitation to the troops and their followers to join the evacuation.

Eventually, it all became too long even by the more relaxed pace of the times, and Stanley set a deadline for departure. He had become obsessed with the idea that some of the Sudanese were planning to seize the expedition's ammunition and stores. After an attempt was made to steal guns from the Zanzibaris, Stanley announced that he was assuming control of the entire party – a move that humiliated Emin. Stanley refused Selim's pleas for more time to gather the troops, or to wait en route, although he did promise to go slowly so the late-comers could catch them up.

The expedition set off from Kavalli's on April 10, a ragbag crowd of about 1,500. It was a far cry from the splendid force that Herbert Ward so vividly described after it first landed in the Congo. To Stanley's depleted original force he had added 130 Manyema carriers recruited from the Arabs, and more than 500 carriers press-ganged into service locally. Emin's people numbered 570 men, women and children, but the men were administrators and clerks, not troops. In other words, the Emin Pasha Relief Expedition was relieving Emin himself, but it was leaving behind far more of Equatoria's expatriate population than it was bringing out.

Nor did the soldiers join the expedition later, even though the expedition soon halted for a month because Stanley had fever. Remnants of the Egyptian battalions remained at Wadelai and Kavilli's. Selim Bey was driven out of Wadelai by Fadl al-Mula, and established himself at Kavalli's – helped by finding the buried ammunition – with about 90 soldiers plus women and children. Later, he was to play an important part in the Buganda story.

Relations on the march between Emin and Stanley quickly became strained. Even without the gun incident, that was was always likely between men of such different temperaments: the all-action and brutal Breaker of Rocks and the scholarly, caring, indecisive German. But Emin was a former ruling plenipotentiary and a commander of men on a scale that Stanley had never known; Stanley had redeemed himself from an upbringing in the poor house to become the gentleman, the commander of soldiers and the arbiter of life and death, but by background was not a gentleman, a soldier or a judge. In Emin's reduced circumstances they did not march as equals, and it was clear to all whose expedition it was.

Stanley was drawn by Captain Casati in a vivid and balanced pen-picture: "Stanley is a man remarkable for strength of character, resolution, promptness of thought and iron will. Jealous of his own authority, he does not tolerate exterior influences, nor ask advice. Difficulties do not deter him, disasters do not dismay him. With an extraordinary readiness of mind he improvises means, and draws himself out of a difficulty; absolute and severe in the execution of his duty, he is not always prudent, or free from hasty and erroneous judgments. Irresolution and hesitation irritate him, disturbing his accustomed gravity; his countenance is usually serious. Reserved, laconic and not very sociable, he does not awaken sympathy; but on closer acquaintance he is found very agreeable, from the frankness of his manner, his brilliant conversation and his gentlemanly courtesy." [Quoted by White, see bibliography]

Emin now found himself doing what he had always insisted he did not want to do – leave. His wish to hand over his province to Britain had come to nothing. His withdrawal left behind not a political vacuum but something worse, a dangerous half-vacuum containing remnant military groups, as well as Stanley's buried arms.

The expedition had hardly even fulfilled its first duty, to survive. Two of the European officers were dead, and the overall loss rate by death or desertion was awful. It was to be almost two-thirds at the end of the journey. Consul Holmwood's hope that the expedition could also help with the troubled situation in Buganda had long been off the agenda. The subject was about to return, however. This was the time when the Baganda Christians were in exile in Ankole, looking for ways to go home.

12

Encounter at Usambiro

*Appeal by the Baganda * Mackay's welcome * 'Best missionary since Livingstone' * Books galore * The journey resumed * Death of Mackay * His last stirring appeal * Bagamoyo at last * Peters's coup * Anglo-German treaty * Death of Lourdel * Controversy boils over*

Stanley's expedition came out by the southern route, passing through Ankole. Here he went through a blood-brotherhood ceremony with one of King Ntare's sons. At this time the Baganda Christian refugees were in the country. Two emissaries – one of them was Samweli, the boy who insisted on delivering the king's cowrie shells before fleeing from the king's persecution – to ask for his help to overthrow the Muslims in Buganda. The expedition was soon to meet both sets of missionaries, now established south of the lake. Stanley's officers were fed by the Protestants (British) and re-clothed by the Catholics (French), although, doctrinal considerations apart, they might have done even better by reversing the sequence.

Stanley refused the Christian refugees' request to intervene in Buganda. With his motley party, far more followers than fighters, he was hardly in a position to. However, he had a Maxim gun, that single-handed conqueror of thousands, and for those who see an imperialistic master-plan behind the expedition the decision is hard to read. By now it was not a question of whether a European power would take over Buganda, but which and when. In 1889 tensions between Germany and Britain over the interior were at their peak, with the governments in both countries, Bismarck and Salisbury respectively, deeply involved with chartered companies that ostensibly ruled over East Africa. In Britain's case this was the Imperial British East Africa Company, headed by William Mackinnon, the chief sponsor of the Emin Pasha expedition. Stanley had been in the African interior for more than two years, and may not have fully realised how far the scramble had moved into its end-game.

From Ankole, Stanley's expedition continued through Karagwe, where according to the leader the numbers were down to 800, or scarcely more than half the total starting from Kavalli's. Losses came from deaths and illness, desertions or simply being unable to keep up. It was a fearsome loss rate, however, over relatively known and straightforward terrain.

On August 28 the expedition reached Usambiro and Stanley came face to face for the first time with Alexander Mackay, the man who more than any other was the embodiment of Stanley's famous appeal years ago for missionaries to serve in Buganda. Emin. too, was able to meet the man with whom he had corresponded for so long. Mackay had come out with the first Church Missionary Society party in 1877 and, amazingly, had never been home since. Sometimes alone, sometimes with one or two colleagues, Mackay survived against the odds in Buganda until at last he was compelled to continue his work and witness south of the lake in what is now Tanzania.

Stanley called Mackay "the best missionary since Livingstone", and readers of *In Darkest Africa* were left in no doubt about his fortitude: "A clever writer lately wrote a book about a man who spent much time in Africa, which from beginning to end is a long-drawn wail. It would have cured both writer and hero of all moping to have seen the manner of Mackay's life. He has no time to fret and groan and weep, and God knows if ever man had reason to think of 'graves and worms and oblivion,' and to be doleful and lonely and sad, Mackay had, when, after murdering his Bishop [James Hannington was killed on Mwanga's orders when approaching Buganda], and burning his pupils, and strangling his converts, and clubbing to death his dark friends, Mwanga turned his eye of death on him. And yet the little man met it with calm blue eyes that never winked. To see one man of this kind, working day and night for twelve years bravely, and without a syllable of complaint or a moan amid the 'wildernesses,' and to hear him lead his little flock to show forth God's loving kindness in the morning, and His faithfulness every night, is worth going a long journey, for the moral courage and contentment that one derives from it."

Mackay himself, dressed in white linen and grey Tyrolese hat, came out to greet the visitors. The mission station was in a rather barren location but was within sight of an inlet of Lake Victoria. Stanley found the station full of activity, with an extensive workshop, the boiler from a launch being prepared, a canoe under repair, sawpits, a cattle fold, a goat pen and scores of fowls pecking around. Boys of all ages looked "uncommonly sleek and happy" and quiet labourers wished the visitors a polite good morning.

Stanley was shown into a room with substantial, two-foot (0.6m) thick clay walls, which were evenly plastered and covered with missionary pictures and placards. The room was filled with books. The headman confided: "Mackay has thousands of books, in the dining-room, bedroom, the church, everywhere."

The expedition stayed at Usambiro for three weeks, enjoying the company of Mackay and another missionary, David Deekes. Everyone was able to catch up on good food and rest. Stanley enjoyed real coffee and home-made bread and butter for the first time in 30 months. On the party's final night, September 16, Mackay and Deekes produced a sumptuous dinner of roast beef, roast fowls, stews, rice and curry, plum pudding and wine. The last item was described by Stanley as "a bottle of medical wine", no doubt to avoid the suggestion of a mission awash with alcohol. The healths of Emin and Stanley were drunk.

Stanley's high opinion of Mackay was reciprocated. Mackay's comment after meeting the explorer adds to the paradox of Stanley because its portrayal of the kind uncle differs from the more familiar view: "He is a man of an iron will and sound judgment, and besides is most patient with the natives. He never allows any one of his followers to oppress or even insult a native. If he has had occasionally to use force in order to effect a passage, I am certain that he only resorted to arms when all other means failed."

On another occasion Mackay wrote: "Wherever I find myself in Stanley's track, in Uganda, Ugogo or even Ukerewe itself, I find his treatment of the natives has invariably been such as to win from them the highest respect for the face of a white man."

The expedition left Usambiro and continued better equipped towards the coast. Fourteen pack donkeys were distributed to Emin's followers, and three riding asses – for the Pasha, Stanley and Captain Casati – were bought from the Roman Catholic missionaries at their nearby Bukumbi station. From the French Stanley's officers were able to buy much-needed items of clothing.

Stanley received a letter from Mackay dated January 5, 1890, in which he noted "what a strange loneliness hung about this place – physically and mentally – after you left". He was active as always: the steam engine, including the "serious job" of the boiler, had been fitted up; the canoe that Stanley saw was about to be transformed into a steam launch. This work was behind because of other jobs, including printing for Buganda. Mackay was both a printer and a translator of Christian texts. All this work, however, had ended because a month later, on February 8, 1890, Mackay died of fever, still only on the edge of middle age.

Mackay always took the broadest view of the Church's mission, raising his eyes beyond the day-to-day work of evangelising. In an earlier letter to Ashe he wrote: "To relieve men from the wrongs under which they perish, to secure freedom for the oppressed, yet not by Blut und Eisen [blood and iron], is a crux indeed for statesmanship. We want not so much an 'arm of flesh,' but heads of wisdom, human hearts, and helping hands. There is no need for gunpowder. That remedy is even worse than the disease.

"The rotten, mortifying state of this continent cannot be healed by more lacerations and wounds. A transfusion of fresh blood, and new life into it, not in miserable driblets as hitherto, but in a full stream, will alone save it from utter corruption.

"This African problem must be solved, and in God's name it shall be solved, for God means it to be solved. It is not for the sake of the few scattered and despised missionaries that we are determined that this end shall be attained, but for the sake of Africa itself."

Soon after he arrived at Usambiro, he showed himself ever the realist, writing: "Hereabouts we are so far from the reaping stage, that we can scarcely to be said even to be sowing. We are merely clearing the ground, and cutting down the natural growth of suspicion and jealousy, and clearing out the hard stones of ignorance and superstition. Only after the ground is thus in some measure prepared and broken up, can we cast in the seed with hope of a harvest in God's good time."

Mackay's last public appeal was written just a month before his death, and received by the CMS afterwards. It was a call for more missionaries, which had strong echoes of Stanley's letter that had won him for Africa: "You sons of England, here is a field for your energies. Bring with you your highest education and your greatest talents, you will find scope for the exercise of them all. You men of God who have resolved to devote your lives to the cure of the souls of men, here is the proper field for you. It is not to win numbers to a Church, but to win men to the Saviour, and who otherwise will be lost, that I entreat you to leave your work at home to the many that are ready to undertake it and to come forth yourselves to reap this field now white to the harvest. Rome is rushing in with her salvation by sacraments, and a religion of carnal ordinances. We want men who will preach Jesus and the Resurrection."

With this article, which was published in the CM Gleaner, was a personal message to the Society's headquarters: "But what is this you write – 'Come home'? Surely now, in our terrible dearth of workers, it is not the time for any one to desert his post. Send us only our first twenty men, and I may be tempted to come to help you to find the second twenty."

Deekes, himself ill, was the only other missionary at Usambiro when Mackay died. He arranged the burial, at which the small band of Baganda Christians at the mission sang the stirring hymn, All Hail the Power of Jesus' Name. Later on, Mackay was moved to Kampala to lie alongside Bishop Hannington.

From Usambiro, it took Stanley 79 days to reach the coast at Bagamoyo, where the expedition arrived on December 4, 1889. The German commandant gave a celebratory banquet, during which there was a near-tragedy. Emin fell from a first-floor window and sustained head injuries. Being extremely short-sighted, he apparently mistook the window for a balcony. He was unconscious for several days.

Stanley had brought the expedition in at fearful human cost. The people whom he had come to rescue – Emin's people – had been few enough to begin with. A total of 570 men, women and children had started for the coast, and only 290 arrived. Stanley had left Zanzibar in February 1887 with 706 men and boys. This had become almost exactly half, 350, at the start for the coast in April 1889 and a hundred or so more were to be lost before the expedition was wound down with 246 survivors. To this must be added untold numbers from the tribes who died in fights in the Ituri Forest and elsewhere. Nine European officers were enrolled with the expedition, but only five finished it with Stanley. Of the others, Major Barttelot and James Jameson were dead, John Rose Troup had been invalided home and Herbert Ward had been dropped from the expedition by Barttelot and made his own way to England.

While Stanley was on his march back to the coast through most of 1889, the German Carl Peters was marching the other way, and his moves created near-panic among the British government. Peters, a resourceful free-wheeler not to mention loose cannon, headed another Emin Pasha relief expedition, in the German interest, which he himself called "no pleasure trip, but a large-scale, colonial-political undertaking". Forbidden to proceed by the German colonial authorities, who were co-operating with the British, Peters made a secret landing on the African east coast in June 1889. With very few men, he managed to traverse Masai country and was quickly in the region of Lake Victoria. He heard that Emin was coming out with Stanley, but he made a discovery that offered better prospects. It was to raise the Buganda stakes dramatically. Peters did not act the gentlemen, however; he opened and read letters sent by Mwanga and Lourdel to Frederick Jackson of the IBEA Company. Mwanga in his extremity against the Muslims asked for help in regaining his throne. In return, the kabaka offered to accept the flag of his rescuer, a trade monopoly and other inducements. Peters saw his opportunity. He rushed to Buganda, where he found Mwanga newly restored to his capital and in February 1890 he signed a treaty with the king.

Jackson had been sent out with orders to make for Wadelai. It greatly vexed Stanley when he learnt about it that the company had seen fit to send a second expedition in search of Emin. Jackson, who had a force of 500 men, also had specific orders not to enter Buganda. This was the reason for his lukewarm response to Mwanga's letter sent in June 1889. Jackson offered a flag – which horrified the kabaka – and not much else. The letters that Peters read included one from Lourdel on behalf of the king, dated December 1 and repeating Mwanga's appeal for help.

When Jackson returned to Kavirondo in March 1890 from an ivory hunt near Mount Elgon, he heard about Peters's seizure of the letters, and knew he must put aside his orginal orders and follow the German to Mengo, which he reached in April after Peters had left. By now Mwanga had little use for Jackson. He had no need of military help, and in any case he had the treaty with Peters. Frederick Lugard said the appearance of Jackson's men was felt to compare badly with the scarlet and gold lace of Peter's escort. The kabaka was strongly under the influence of Lourdel, who was acting as his private secretary. British political control was the last thing the French missionaries wanted. They associated it, quite reasonably, with Protestant supremacy. Nor did they want French rule (although this was never a practical possibility): France in the 19th century had a long history of anti-clericalism. The fathers' choice was for the status quo ante described by Walker in which the Baganda would continue to rule themselves, buying goods and arms (for self-defence) where they would. Apart from Britain, the only European country in a position to take over Buganda was Germany. Of the two powers, the fathers preferred Germany.

With Mwanga and Lourdel both uninterested in his treaty, Jackson was getting nowhere. It looked as if Buganda, the "Pearl of Africa", was slipping away from the IBEA Company and Great Britain. Jackson's presence further destabilised the fragile political situation. It was decided to send two envoys, one Catholic and one Protestant, to the coast to find out which country had the stronger claim on Buganda. It was unclear because the Anglo–German boundary agreement of 1886 had left the hinterland undefined.

It is hard to say which is more surprising: European countries coolly appropriating other people's lands without even the physical presence of the conqueror, or the Baganda's apparent fatalistic acceptance at this point that their country was to be taken over by someone, and it just remained to find out who.

Empty-handed, Jackson left on May 14 for the coast, leaving behind his colleague, Ernest Gedge, with about 35 men and some 180 rifles. The day before Jackson left, Lourdel died of fever. It was just three months after Mackay's death. Lourdel, too, was a young man even though he felt himself prematurely old. Like Mackay, he had never been home: they spent 14 years and 11 years in Africa respectively.

Meanwhile, at Bagamoyo Emin Pasha had recovered from his fall. In March 1890 he surprised the world, and angered a chunk of it, by entering German government service with a brief to open stations south of Lake Victoria in the German sphere. The man whom Britain had rescued at enormous financial and human cost was to return close to Equatoria and even closer to Buganda, which was still the unpicked plum. The ultimate destination, it is clear, was Buganda itself. It was too much for the Times correspondent, who wrote from Zanzibar: "The news of Emin's decision is received very unfavourably here. His rescue, effected at so great an expenditure of time and money is absolutely resultless regarding himself. Within four months of reaching the coast he returns, as a paid subordinate of the German Company, to the very latitude where he so recently lived as heroic governor of immense provinces amid world-wide admiration."

World-wide admiration was at first Stanley's lot, too. Soon, however, he was caught up in a vicious controversy as the relatives of the dead officers, and the surviving officers of the expedition, had their say.

Major Barttelot's brother issued a rejoinder to Stanley. Jameson's widow published her late husband's letters and diaries. The nation and beyond were caught up in a heated debate about Stanley's decision to split the expedition at Yambuya. Stanley himself was forced into a series of public pronouncements in his own defence. He had already produced an eloquent account of the expedition with *In Darkest Africa* (1890). His raw energy – in a man approaching 50 – is shown as clearly in this production as it was in marching three times through the Ituri Forest.

For speed of writing, it is one of the most astonishing feats of authorship of all time. Stanley immured himself in a Cairo hotel and generated the text of about 400,000 words in 50 days. This is an astonishing 8,000 words on average, or around 20 printed pages per day, where many modern writers consider they have done a day's work in producing 1,000 words. The book was candid about what the author saw as Barttelot's inexplicable failures at Yambuya, although if he had been able to foresee the controversy to come it would no doubt have been even stronger.

Stanley was answered with equal eloquence, but with brevity in place of length, by H.R. Fox Bourne in *The Other Side of the Emin Pasha Relief Expedition* (1891). This is high-quality journalistic commentary, which still reads well today. Without making a claim to any first-hand knowledge of the events, Fox Bourne put the "case for the prosecution". Stanley, he argued, promised Emin ample ammunition and stores to be delivered to Wadelai. In fact, he came late and never got to Wadelai; by sending Jephson there with Emin, but accompanied by just three soldiers, he "quickened and strengthened the disaffection" among the pasha's people.

Fox Bourne was among many to claim that Emin was brought out of Equatoria as a captive. He pointed out that barely more than half of the pasha's followers who left with the expedition survived to reach the coast. Interestingly for the period, he complained about the colonialism behind the expedition: it was a pretence for an "empire-making errand" for Mackinnon's company.

Fox Bourne quoted from *In Darkest Africa* and ended his book with a venomous comment: "'How to adhere to a promise seems to me to be the most difficult of all tasks to 999,999 men out of every million whom I meet.'

"For Mr Stanley himself the task was too difficult. He has shown that he, at any rate, is not the one man among a million who can be trusted to keep a promise."

While Fox Bourne was concerned about Stanley's failure to relieve Emin in the way originally announced, the dead officers' supporters wanted to drive home the point that the decision to split the expedition at Yambuya effectively condemned Barttelot and Jameson to their deaths. In the detailed written instructions that Stanley left behind before marching off into the Ituri Forest, every probable situation was foreseen and Barttelot given suggested means of moving forward. On the other hand, Stanley must have known that he was blessed with an unusually high level of drive and determination, and that this could not be assumed in others. Splitting an expedition in difficult terrain is always potentially hazardous. This expedition was not so much split as scattered, with Troup, Ward and Bonny still at various points downriver when Stanley left Yambuya. Barttelot was an accomplished officer, but he was unproved in Africa. Much depended on Tippu Tip, but Barttelot was also unversed in dealing with Arabs. Yet again, it remains hard to explain why Barttelot and the other rear party officers were seized with inaction while the force wasted away over many weeks.

Stanley, amid all the controversy, had been portrayed in newspapers and elsewhere as "a nineteenth-century conquistador resolutely cutting his way across Africa at the head of a slave army and leaving a wake of destruction behind him", says Iain R. Smith (*The Emin Pasha Relief Expedition 1886-1890*). In typical British fashion, the questions over his conduct did not prevent Stanley going on to continued successes. Until now a lifelong bachelor, he married. He became an MP and a knight of the realm. He was able to build a fine house in Surrey. But he remained the former work-house boy and not everyone was won over. His fellow explorer, Colonel James Grant, had been unable to get Stanley into membership of the Athenaeum Club in London before the Emin Pasha expedition; afterwards (Smith records) he quite despaired of doing so.

It is easy is to see how the controversy over the expedition divided the nation. There is enough to be said on each side to explain why the controversy has never completely gone away.

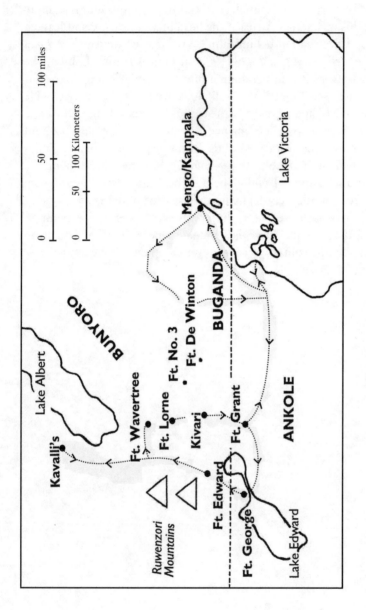

Fig 5 Lugard's marches

13

Lugard's Year

*'Dividends in philanthropy' * The Maxim gun * Encamped at Kampala
* First treaty obtained * Enter Captain Williams * Ba-Fransa and Ba-
Ingleza * Fight with the Muslims * March to the west * Selim Bey *
Sudanese brought back * Chain of forts * Lugard's year of achievement*

The year after Stanley completed the Emin Pasha relief expedition, declining on his trek to the coast to intervene in Buganda, Captain Frederick Lugard left Mombasa bound for the kingdom. He was in his early thirties, and possessed those ideal accompaniments of the Victorian expeditioner: a war wound and a broken heart. He had followed his lady from India to England, to suffer the traumatic shock of finding her in a hopelessly compromising position with a lover. In the circumstances the isolation and danger promised in Buganda can have been no hardships for Lugard, who was the first choice of the Imperial British East Africa Company for the job.

The Company needed Buganda as much as it considered Buganda needed the Company. Since Stanley half a decade earlier had won it land cessions from the sultan of Zanzibar its rule had been lethargic. Little development had taken place. The interior remained largely untouched, with few stations established. Part of the problem was that much of East Africa lacked exportable natural resources. The IBEA Company's chief, William Mackinnon, had declared that its shareholders would "take their dividends in philanthropy", but so far there was little economic or humanitarian activity to pay dividends on. Buganda was the Company's inevitable destination. Here were massive supplies of ivory and an established system of agriculture. On the back of commercial success, the war against Arab-led slave-raiding would be successfully prosecuted.

Stanley's advice to Mackinnon caused a delay with Lugard's expedition. The advice was that a major force would be needed to assure control of Buganda. In the Mackinnon Papers, John S. Galbraith (in *Mackinnon and East Africa 1878-1895*) found that Stanley advised 500 white men, 2,000 porters and an expenditure of at least £100,000. He also suggested that the undertaking was not worthwhile until a railway was built.

An expedition on that scale was far beyond the resources of the Company. It was obvious that successful trade with Buganda depended on a rail link to the coast, but to delay until the line was built – it was actually completed in 1901 – would be to hand the country to other powers. Buganda was a political vacuum, which Mackinnon realised. Stanley's advice was so wayward that again we must wonder at the motive behind it.

Lugard proved Stanley completely wrong about the size of the force needed. He was eventually cleared to proceed to Buganda with three other Europeans, a Somali interpreter called Dualla and about 300 porters. The fighting force, such as it was, consisted of 50 Sudanese and Somali soldiers, but backed by a Maxim gun – the weapon that wrote the history of Africa in the closing years of the century:

> Whatever happens we have got
> The Maxim gun, and they have not.

As Hilaire Belloc put it.

The expedition left Mombasa on August 6, 1890. With the porters carrying standard loads of 65-70lb (30-32kg) each, it covered up to 20 miles (32km) a day but usually much less. On September 20 the Company post of Machakos (later to be the seat of Britain's Kenya administration before yielding place to Nairobi with the coming of the railway) was reached. Lugard passed uneventfully through Masailand and Busoga, the "back door to Buganda" where Bishop Hannington had been killed, to cross the Nile on December 13 and enter Buganda proper. Five days later he was flying his flag on Kampala hill near the kabaka's palace on Mengo hill (Mwanga had moved the palace here from the nearby Rubaga hill site used by Mutesa). Lugard coolly helped himself to the campsite as a show of strength, as his book *The Rise of Our East African Empire* makes clear.

Lugard was fortified by the knowledge that earlier in the year Germany, as Britain's main European rival for Buganda, had given up its claim. The Peters treaty with Mwanga was washed away by the Anglo-German agreement of May 1890. Germany accepted Britain's protectorate authority over Buganda and Equatoria, as well as Zanzibar. Britain ceded Heligoland to Germany. This barren rock in the North Sea was of vital strategic importance to Germany because it was the key to the Kiel Canal and the country's main naval base. But Britain also had to give up a five-mile (8km) wide strip of land in central Africa, which marked the end of the Cape-to-Cairo dream of a railway taking the "red route" – running in British territory throughout. It also spelled the end of any north–south railway; the line was never built.

If Lugard was afraid that his tiny armed band could simply be swept away by Mwanga's thousands of warriors, there is no suggestion of it in this passage:

"As a result of international negotiation, Uganda and the countries round about had been ceded to the influence of Great Britain. I, myself an officer of the army, had been deputed, as the representative of a great chartered Company, to make a treaty with a semi-savage king noted for his cruelty and incapacity. I sought no unfair advantage, no acquisition of territory, no monopoly of trade, no annexation of revenues. My task was to save the country from itself; and for such a treaty as I proposed to make, I saw no need to stoop to bargaining by presents (of arms, a Maxim gun, &c., as had at first been suggested), and no cause for obeisance or deference. It was for this reason, as well as to hasten my arrival before any crisis between the factions took place, or the expected munitions reached Uganda, that I crossed the Nile without waiting for permission, and, marching rapidly on the capital, selected my own camping-ground. Mackay and Ashe relate how they knelt before the king, when praying for permission to leave the country. Such an attitude seemed to me to lower the prestige of Europeans, and I determined to make my own methods the more marked by contrast."

Robert Ashe in his *Two Kings of Uganda*, published in 1889, told how he and Mackay always followed local custom by kneeling or sitting in the presence of the ruler, never standing. The missionaries evidently lacked both Lugard's sense of status and his 50 armed men.

Lugard rubbed the point in by declining Mwanga's invitation to call at the palace on the day he arrived, saying he was tired and had much work to do. The first meeting took place the next day (December 19). He took a dozen Sudanese whose bugle flourishes vied with the fervour of the king's drummers. The durbar hut was packed with a mass of humanity. Lugard, who had been warned on the point, was careful not to tread on the king's carpet. He then shook hands with Mwanga "cordially and frankly". (He discovered only later that it was Mwanga who ordered the death of Bishop Hannington.) The kabaka's face, he felt, "betokens irresolution, a weak character, and a good deal of sensuality".

Lugard explained that he had come in the hope of bringing peace to the country and he had full powers to make treaties. For the present he was there to pay salaams; he would talk of other matters "by-and-by". The court was very relieved that there had been no mention of a flag, "understanding that it means that they give away their country". Carl Peters, Frederick Jackson and other visitors had "talked of nothing but a flag", Lugard found, but he was much more delicate in the matter: "If I can get a treaty, the flag will come of its own accord, and at their own request later on."

Lugard must have felt he had taken the initiative firmly into his hands as he left the first meeting. Meanwhile, on Kampala hill the tiny force was making sure of its security. A neat, stockaded camp was created. The fort was close to the Protestant (Church Missionary Society) settlement at Namirembe. The major buildings and compounds of the capital were scattered among banana groves and dense high grass on several hills. Across the valley from the CMS mission, on Rubaga hill about one mile (1.6km) away, was the Roman Catholic mission of the White Fathers. The royal palace was at the apex of a triangle with Namirembe-Rubaga as the base and was about two miles (3.2km) from each. The layout of the place afforded plenty of space for politicking while the location of the church missions, facing each other across a valley, symbolised the bad feelings between these supposed brothers and sisters in Christ.

Lugard wanted to regularise his position and pressed for a quick treaty. On December 24 a preliminary meeting was interrupted by armed rowdies, and he narrowly escaped being shot. On Christmas Day he missed the magnificent dinner, with champagne, that had been put up by the tiny European community in Mengo in order to confer with the kimbugwe, the senior chief of the Roman Catholics. On December 26, the chiefs of the Catholic and Protestant factions came to the Company's camp to sign the treaty, then they all went to the king and obtained his signature. The scene gives us a glimpse of literacy in Buganda at that time: Mwanga made a mark and a ba-Fransa chief who could write put the king's name against his cross. Several of the other head chiefs were able to sign although "they took very long struggling with the letters of their names".

From a first impression of Mwanga's irresolution and sensuality, Lugard came to see the king as a monster of depravity. With the persecution of the Christians men had been "slowly hacked to pieces, each member being thrown into the fire, and lastly their mutilated but living limbless trunks", while the court was mired in immorality: "Mwanga's court was the public scene of all the vices of Sodom and Gomorrah – vices not indigenous, I believe, amongst African tribes, and the result of contact with coast people ... His dominant motive was a thirst for arbitrary despotic power, and his antagonism to European influence arose, not from high patriotism, but from a fear lest this exercise of despotism should be curtailed." Lugard adds that Mwanga was particularly afraid of the British because he expected vengeance for the murder of Bishop Hannington.

This character sketch of the king may or may not be accurate, but it is no more than an artist's impression; it cannot claim the first-hand authority of much of Lugard's reportage. The killing of the Christians occurred before he arrived. He makes no claim that he witnessed the vices of Sodom and Gomorrah being played out at court, nor could anyone else say with certainty what the king's motives were for resisting European influence.

Lugard's success (and the style of the book matches the confidence he showed on the ground) was founded on an unshakeable belief in the rightness of his mission – and strong genes. The empire builder who created a British territory before Queen Victoria's diamond jubilee lived to see the last stages of Hitler's war. When Margery Perham was publishing her biography of Lugard in the 1950s, a brother and a sister were still alive.

Although he was not a large man, his robustness apparently allowed Lugard to withstand the ailments big, small or fatal that were everyday occurrences for Europeans in Buganda. (Years later it was said that the anti-malarial drug Paludrine created a new, less friendly society among whites in the tropics because now everybody expected to see tomorrow.) In his book Lugard compared his good health with the problems of his associates with a simplicity that can easily be read as hubristic:

"Williams came back [from a mission south of the lake] full of health, but broke down the day after his arrival, and was in a serious state of collapse. The others were ill from time to time. As for myself, I remained, as usual, impervious to all sickness, but neuralgia, toothache, and dizziness, &c., warned me that the strain was almost too great even for me." Later he remarks: "Grant and Wilson were both so unwell at this time that I advised their making a trip for a few days to our little island on the lake, which they did in the company of Mr Smith (Church Missionary Society). I was myself considerably pulled down, for I had hardly been outside my office for four months. The breaking out of the wound in my arm, accompanied by toothache and neuralgia, were the signs which always warned me that the pressure was a little too high."

The Rise of Our East African Empire is an important account of Lugard's activities in Buganda (and of a previous assignment around what is now Lake Malawi), written in his own defence when he was being challenged over some of his actions. The style suggests the high self-confidence of a man convinced about the morality of his position. He had come to Buganda to take possession of it as the property of the company he represented. It had been awarded to Britain by the forces of international diplomacy, and the IBEA Company was the chartered representative of the British people. That the king or people of Buganda had not asked to be taken over, or even consulted about it, would have seemed to Lugard as beside the point: in their state of under-development, although Buganda was advanced compared with its neighbours, there was no occasion to. The debt was the other way: the advanced nations were bringing the blessings of commerce and Christianity.

Lugard did not see himself as a conqueror but as a treaty-maker and administrator. He was always careful to follow the forms, as when he made blood-brotherhood with the son of the king of Ankole: "I made a very formal ceremony, drawing up all the

Sudanese [troops] in a hollow square, which I had cleared of grass and bushes. I greatly pleased them by consenting to go through the full ceremony according to their own rites, and I founded upon our mutual pledges the treaty which I submitted to England. I had this treaty read and most carefully translated to them. Its main provisions were, that the British were to be free to pass through Ankoli, or to build and settle in it, and that the king would do all in his power to suppress the import of arms and powder, by the Waziba traders in German territory to Kabarega and the Mohammedan Waganda, and would seize and confiscate all he could.

"In return, I gave him a flag and a copy of the treaty, and promised him the protection and the alliance of the Company. We exchanged presents, and the ceremony was complete, and this large country of Ankoli was added to the Company's territory."

It is tempting to see in the last sentence a wry comment on the unequalness of the bargain (particularly since the Company lacked the means to guarantee protection), but perhaps that would be to use the hindsight of a hundred years later.

Whatever the missionaries might say, Lugard had no illusions about the equality of the races in Buganda, and the job of the whites was to hang together. Complaining about two of the leading Church Missionary Society members, he writes: "... it became patent to me that both Mr Ashe and Mr Pilkington allowed the Waganda to imagine that they could turn to them with complaints against myself. 'The pity of it!' I exclaim in my diary, 'that natives should find that they can set off one Englishman against another. This means death to British prestige with black men; and once let our prestige go – by which alone we hold our own in Africa – and *we* must follow fast. Langheld, a German officer, was more loyal than my own countrymen. He told Williams that when they came to him "he very quickly let them understand that they could not play off one European against another," and that we all stand by each other'."

Lugard was no Colonel Blimp but he was certainly a paternalist as we understand the word today. Throughout his book he makes clear his respect for the Baganda, both in comparison with surrounding tribes and for their innate capacities. Even so, they were at a lower level of social evolution than Europeans, whose service to

Africa lay in the models they represented of superior technology and development. This needed to be underpinned by social distance; appearance and form were vital. Even the katikiro, the king's chief minister, had to request an audience to see Lugard, and no followers were allowed to hang around the meeting place as was customary in Africa.

"Trivial as these things may appear [Lugard wrote], I think that in dealing with natives they are of the utmost importance ... the European should assert his superiority – not merely in intellect, in appliances, and in knowledge, but in his dwellings, his manners, his every surrounding; and the superiority, which he thus unostentatiously asserts, will be instinctively accorded to him. Above all this is important in Uganda, where a scale of deference is insisted upon, varying in its degree from the king down to the very pettiest chieflet, and every slightest detail of etiquette is punctiliously followed and understood by the smallest pageboy or most ignorant peasant."

With the treaty obtained, Lugard was soon joined by two other key players in the Buganda drama. Just after Christmas 1890 Bishop Tucker reached Mengo. He was the third CMS missionary bishop to be sent to the kingdom and the first to reach it. He was to stay in post and build up the Anglican Church for almost two decades. The country he found on arrival he described as "like a volcano on the verge of an eruption". Early in the new year of 1891 a second Maxim gun arrived, brought by Captain W.H. Williams with 75 Sudanese soldiers and 100 porters. There was a potentially ticklish problem of Williams being slightly senior to Lugard in length of army service although assigned to serve under him in Buganda, but the two men hit it off. *The Rise of Our East African Empire* is full of cordial references to Lugard's deputy.

If the first task had been to ensure the survival of the tiny Company force amid rival factions awash with guns, the second was to pacify the capital. With Kampala Fort made safe from attack, Lugard set about securing the dispersed settlement beyond the stockade. He gave some of the porters basic military training, creating a useful auxiliary force which he called the Zanzibari Levy. He used these men to mount police patrols around Mengo.

At least twice, Lugard's soldiers prevented war between the factions and he was able to bring about a shaky accord between the

Catholics (ba-Fransa) and the Protestants (ba-Ingleza). The situation was made doubly unstable because the kabaka was with the ba-Fransa. This was the obvious political choice for Mwanga. The ba-Fransa were the larger faction, and with the IBEA Company poised to eat the country they were his best bet to thwart the British. Lugard, officially neutral, inevitably found himself in bed with the ba-Ingleza. Aside from any feelings he had for the Protestant religion, this was the faction that supported Britain's side in Buganda.

The interchangeability of the terms ba-Fransa/Catholic and ba-Ingleza/Protestant was a contemporary recognition of how politics and religion had become mixed up. The factions were not essentially about religion, but religious belief affected the political equation because the triumph of one or other European power would entrench one or other religion. Many of the missionaries, both French and British, engaged in plainly political activities, which in religious terms made practical, possibly moral sense since the country that emerged victorious would determine the religion. This duly happened under British rule, when the Protestants grew in support and political influence at the expense of the Roman Catholics.

Conversely, it was sensible for the Muganda supporter of French or British political hegemony to attach himself to the appropriate religious faction. However, not everyone was motivated by such cynical calculation. Buganda had purchased its admission to the Christian world with the blood of martyrs. Many of the leaders were sincere Christian converts; others just adopted religion as a useful label for a political cause. Meanwhile, followers for the most part accepted the religious denomination of their feudal lord.

"The two factions called Wa Ingleza (English) and Wa Fransa (French) were led by chiefs of the Protestant and Roman Catholic creeds respectively [Lugard explained]. These chiefs were the rulers of the country, and the lesser chiefs and peasantry, who followed them in war as their retainers or serfs, declared themselves, of course, of the same faction as their lords. The two parties were thus composed largely of men of no religion, nor were they religious in their designation. But religious differences had embittered the leaders and a large portion of the rank and file against each other, and their animosity was taken up and intensified by their respective followers."

The Catholics and the Protestants were in temporary alliance, but the third main faction, the Arab party (the Muslims), remained to be dealt with. They had fled towards and into Bunyoro, where they were helped by the ruler, Kabarega. Whatever his feelings towards Islam, the Muslims were a good weapon for the king against the traditional enemy, Buganda, now that Mwanga had gone over to the Christians.

A large army set out from Mengo in April led by the katikiro, Apolo Kagwa. Lugard and Williams followed a week later with about 600 men. Half of these were former porters, now proud members of the Zanzibari Levy. Lugard estimated the Baganda fighters at about 25,000. Spears outnumbered rifles by five to one, and there was a vast following to carry the guns, bedding and other equipment. He was mystified over where the food was found for such a host.

Just inside the Bunyoro border, on May 7, the Christian army – so called because its opponents were mainly Baganda too, but with a sizeable stiffening of Kabarega's rifles – overcame the Muslims despite the disadvantages of attacking uphill and having no significant edge in firepower. Lugard's force was scarcely involved, and the Maxim guns could not be used because of the dense grass. The victory was achieved by turning the enemy so they fled rather than wearing them down with heavy casualties: deaths on the Christian side were about 30 while the Muslims lost 300–400 killed, many of them butchered after capture.

Lugard could not persuade the Baganda to march with him on Kabarega's capital so the army broke up with the warriors dispersing to their home areas. Williams returned to Kampala, taking one of the Maxim guns and fewer than a dozen soldiers. Including the troops already there, the fort would find itself with barely more than 200 soldiers while Lugard went marching away to the west with 110 of his own troops, some Baganda (whose numbers he does not give) and the more effective Maxim gun. He also had with him 138 of the Zanzibari Levy and 185 porters, as well as two of his European associates – Grant and Dr Macpherson. At home later, he was to be criticised for leaving the capital exposed, but his luck held in that regard.

The Muslims and the forces of Bunyoro that lay behind them had been checked but not mated. Lugard had secured neither a total military victory over them nor a political settlement with them. His object now, however, was to make contact with the remants of Emin Pasha's Equatoria garrisons known to be established at Kavalli's under Selim Bey.

The expedition marched into Ankole, where a treaty was signed with King Ntare, and on to Lake Edward, where Lugard built a stockaded camp to control the salt supplies at the adjacent Salt Lake. This camp – Fort George, which he immediately garrisoned – was sited on a neck of land only 40 yards (37m) wide separating Lake Edward from the Salt Lake.

On August 6, the expedition had the second of three encounters with Kabarega's troops. It was a dramatic illustration of the power, actual and psychological, of the repeating gun. Lugard, with only about 40 soldiers, had got ahead of the main party and at that moment ran into a large force of Banyoro by the Mokia river. The enemy delayed too long for their own good allowing some 60 more soldiers to join Lugard's small band. With night approaching, he ordered an advance and at the same time sprayed Maxim fire on a knoll 950 yards (870m) off. This caused panic. Disciplined charges on the two flanks by Somali and Baganda completed the rout. Later they heard that the score or so of rounds from the Maxim had killed 20-30 Banyoro.

Three weeks later (August 26) the expedition, now numbering about 300, offered a remarkable example of the effect of disciplined movement by overturning an army of many thousands without firing a shot. The enemy was thought to contain a large portion of Kabarega's main army, with considerable firepower. Lugard described what happened next: "We steadily came on, while the enemy kept up a tremendous firing. The bullets, however, came nowhere near us. We advanced without replying, and the Wanyoro fell back as we came on. The result was that, scared by the reports of our terrible shooting at incredible ranges, and at our stolid and orderly advance, they did not dare to await us at close quarters, and we actually defeated this great army without firing one single cartridge , and without the loss of one single life!"

Heading generally north-east on a line between Lake Edward and Lake Albert, the expedition made a march through a country near to paradise in the spectacular variety of its scenery. Constantly climbing, they crossed endless streams bringing snow-waters from the Ruwenzori Mountains. The terrain alternated between bush and elephant grass and great areas of cultivation. Vegetation was luxuriant. At 5,300ft (1,615m) they found a trio of pretty lakes. They dropped down into the Kiaya valley and down again onto the great plain of the Semliki river. Far away Lugard could see the edge of the Kavalli plateau – their destination.

The Semliki was at least 100 yards (90m) wide. Some of the Zanzibaris, braving the crocodiles, swam across to obtain canoes on the other side, and in this way the party was able to get over. They were still shadowed by Kabarega's troops. They ran into heavy firing along the Semliki, although again without casualties. They entered swamp, sometimes up to the waist, troubled by grass with a fret-saw edge that caused deep gashes and with stalks shedding white thorns that produced intense irritation. A forest composed mainly of scarlet and yellow flowering trees, criss-crossed by paths of elephant and hippo, was followed by a park-like country studded with acacia bushes.

Hidden away in another stretch of forest the expedition came upon villagers of the Banyabuga people, whom Lugard described as "the most affable savages I had ever met, and ... the first friendly people we had seen since we left Fort George". The chief explained that they washed the saline hills and sold the salt; they dared not cultivate because they knew Kabarega's men would seize the produce. In fact, the Banyoro had recently visited them, carrying off everything. The chief also gave the welcome news that the Sudanese settlements were nearby.

Guides led the expedition into the hills. At 3,000ft (914m) they saw Lake Albert spread before them. Some of the Sudanese were veterans of the Emin Pasha Relief Expedition, including the leader, Shukri Aga. They could point out to Lugard the harbour from where the goods of Emin's people were humped up the edge of the plateau to Stanley's camp 10 miles (16km) inland. Lugard wondered why the camp had not been made nearer, "that the tired men might be saved a part at least of their toil".

The expedition camped on the top of the plateau and were visited by several Sudanese officers from Kavalli's. Lugard, quoting from his diary, described the scene, although as he acknowledged himself without the "practised pen" of a Stanley: "There was great joy and kissing of my hand (which they touch with their foreheads), and hand-shaking with Shukri and my Sudanese. Every one talked at the same time, and congratulated each other, and every one temporarily became a fool, and smiled extremely, and talked incessantly, as is right and proper on such an occasion." It was another of those climactic encounters with which the history of Africa abounds.

Selim Bey, the commander of Kavalli's, was the master of substantial settlements with a population of around 8,000. Only about a tenth of these were soldiers; the rest were wives, children, slaves and the households of soldiers who had died in Equatoria. Buried among the tribal villages and completely cut off from the world, the Sudanese made do with cotton clothes of their own weaving if they were fortunate, with ox-hides if they were not. The women wore a thick fringe of black strings suspended from the waist, "which served fairly adequately the purposes of modesty and decency". Yet coinage circulated and clerks wrote out Selim's orders to his officers and the out-stations. "In short [Lugard wrote], among all the outward savagery of soldiers dressed in hides, of naked women and grass huts, there was a noticeable, – almost pathetic, – attempt to maintain the status they claimed as soldiers of a civilised Government."

Despite Stanley's distrust of Selim Bey, Lugard found the commander to be "a man of very considerable character". He was a giant of a man and a devout Muslim who did not smoke or drink, even though many of his co-religionists at the settlements had wandered so far off the path as to distil their own liquor.

Lugard learnt what had happened to Selim since he had been unable to link up with Stanley's expedition to the coast two years before. Driven out of Wadelai by Fadl al-Mula supported by most of the troops, Selim had set up at Kavalli's with just 90 men. Finding the ammunition left behind by Stanley was a great bonus. He soon lost 50 of his men in an attack by tribespeople in retaliation for an attack by Stanley. Meanwhile, the Mahdists were as far south as Rejaf. Fadl al-Mula began to treat with them against the wishes of most of his soldiers. Eight hundred of these, with an astonishing 10,000 dependants and camp followers, deserted Fadl and joined Selim at Kavalli's.

Earlier in the present year (1891) Emin Pasha turned up at Kavalli's on what was to be his last expedition. He was murdered in the interior soon afterwards. The subject of Stanley's relief expedition was himself mistaken for the reliever of the station, but he explained he was in German service and he failed to persuade Selim to abandon his loyalty to the khedive of Egypt.

Lugard faced the same problem of negotiation. However, he was able to say that Britain and the khedive were close allies. In this he was backed by Shukri Aga, who had even been to Cairo with Stanley. A complex agreement was struck whereby Selim and his men would serve under the British pending word from the khedive. If the khedive approved the association it would continue; if he did not and summoned them back to Egypt, Lugard would facilitate their journey to the coast in return for their service.

Both Lugard and Selim wanted to go to Wadelai but both recognised that this was not the time. Instead, the course was set for the Semliki plain and the Company's territory. On October 5, 1891, the evacuation of the 8,000 population of the Sudanese settlements began. Much of the time this host had to march single file along the narrow trails. The half of the expedition that Lugard was leading (i.e. 4,000 people) made a column seven miles (11km) long – "Thus the head of the caravan would be nearly arriving in camp, by the time that the last of the people were leaving the old one..."

Most of the Sudanese were settled in a chain of forts running north to south from western Bunyoro to the borders of Ankole, including Fort Wavertree, Fort Lorne and Fort Grant. Some of Lugard's own troops were sent with Grant to link with the garrison at Fort George and secure the Salt Lake, which was being attacked by Manyema tribesman. When Lugard left for Kampala in early December the nearly 9,000 souls making up the expedition at its largest had become 1,200, among them Selim Bey and his retinue. There were "100 good fighting men" in the total of 600 Sudanese, also 350 widows and children to be repatriated to Egypt via the coast and 250 of Lugard's original soldiers.

December 13, 1891, was the anniversary of Lugard's crossing the Nile to enter Buganda proper. He could look back on a year of substantial soldierly achievement, which he set out unembarrassedly in *The Rise of Our East African Empire* – a book written in self-defence (see next chapter, THE BATTLE OF MENGO). Thus far, he could point to the preliminary settlement of Buganda, successful restraining battles with the Muslims, treaty relations with all the country west of Buganda to the the Congo State borders, the routes for the trade of arms and ammunition more or less closed, seven forts built, the Salt Lake annexed, the Sudanese relocated under their officers, the king of Toro (Kasagama) restored with a European to assist (another of Lugard's expedition associates, De Winton) and a feasible transport route opened between Lake Victoria and Lake Albert. But when the expedition returned to Kampala on New Year's Eve he well knew that the capital was bristling with arms and that tensions remained high between the ba-Fransa and the ba-Ingleza.

14

The Battle of Mengo

*An unwelcome mail * Dishonour spared * Row over a gun * Lugard arms ba-Ingleza * Ba-Fransa routed * Pursuit to Bulingugwe * Atrocities denied * New treaty signed * Muslims accept terms * Mbogo's drum * Sad fate of Selim Bey * Campaigning in London*

Among the mail waiting for Lugard at Kampala was a totally unexpected and wholly unwelcome instruction from the Imperial British East Africa Company, his employers: he was to evacuate Buganda immediately. The directors had decided that the occupation simply could not be afforded. There were some fig leaves. The Company might be back later. In the meantime, it was suggested, a British Resident might be found to work there without military support, which Lugard commented was like asking someone to volunteer to be hanged. He was flabbergasted at the directors' decision.

He shared the knowledge only with Williams. Both men were concerned about the breach of faith involved in withdrawal. Treaties had been made in which kings and chiefs had been induced to accept British suzerainty in exchange for military protection from their enemies. They had been told that Britain had come to stay. Now the order was to scuttle out almost before the ink on the treaties was dry.

Lugard and Williams believed that the move would deal a fatal blow to British prestige. They also feared that Buganda would collapse into anarchy as the ba-Fransa took their revenge on the ba-Ingleza, who were the main supporters of the British administration. The Muslims, backed by Kabarega of Bunyoro, would then move in and massacre the Catholics. The position of the Protestant missionaries was inevitably threatened.

Feelings were running high with both men. Lugard did not even understand the instruction. From his point of view, the administration was virtually self-sustaining, particularly with the expected revenues from the Salt Lake. Williams declared that he could not hold up his head in society if he were party to such a betrayal of promises to the local people. He offered £4,000 (then a substantial sum) from his own funds to keep the administration going, and said he would use up all his resources if necessary. Lugard, who did not have much money, was deeply moved by the gesture. They were spared the need to disobey the Company by the arrival of new instructions, which partly countermanded the first ones: the evacuation was to be postponed for 12 months, until the end of the 1892. Later, there was to be another extension, to the end of March 1893.

The British prime minister, Lord Salisbury, accepted Mackinnon's plan for the Company to evacuate the country, but was essentially uninterested in the government saddling itself with the responsibility and the costs of a Uganda protectorate. The extensions were the result of intense lobbying in Britain, where the martyrdom of the Baganda converts was well remembered. So too were the lonely deaths of Bishop Hannington and Alexander Mackay, the one murdered and the other a fever victim after 14 uninterrupted years in Africa. The Church Missionary Society – whose work in Buganda was at risk of being undone – raised funds by public donations to help the IBEA Company carry on. Lugard realised that he had to get to Britain to argue the case, but before he could leave he was caught up in another battle nearer to hand – in Mengo itself.

The showdown between the ba-Fransa and the ba-Ingleza was triggered when an Ingleza was killed by a sub-chief of the French faction in an argument over a gun. Mwanga acquitted the killer on the basis that the other man had entered his compound. To Lugard, this was not justice because the Ingleza was the owner of the gun, which had been seized by the Fransa. As Lugard's trusted Somali aide Dualla put it, if a leopard seized a goat would you not pursue it into its cave?

Since the kabaka belonged to the French faction, the political crisis that developed was a trial of strength between Mwanga and Lugard. According to the latter's acccount, he appealed in vain for the French bishop, Monsignor Hirth, and his priests to defuse the crisis. Their refusal, and their decision to stay put on Rubaga hill, was, he argued, evidence that they expected to win the coming battle.

The ba-Fransa were much more numerous in the capital, and on

January 22 Lugard issued arms to the ba-Ingleza: 40 muzzle-loading guns and a 5lb (2.3kg) keg of powder. Lugard was later to be criticised for fuelling the crisis in this way. He denied that "my own overwhelming force freed me from all apprehension of danger to ourselves". It was "very far from being the case". He knew that if the ba-Ingleza went down, the threat to his expedition – which was sustained not by overwhelming force but by disciplined movement and the Maxim gun – would be immediate.

The Catholic Union of Great Britain saw matters in a totally opposite light when it issued its polemical *Notes on Uganda* the following year (1893). According to this analysis, the Protestants, otherwise outnumbered, had provoked the showdown at their time of maximum strength – when Lugard had returned to the capital with a reinforcement of crack Sudanese troops. The Company's force was not in any way vulnerable (the writer gave the example of two hundred Spaniards being enough to conquer Peru), and Lugard's issue of arms to the ba-Ingleza was with aggressive intent. The Catholics, the argument continued, would not have stayed quiet while the Company was at its weakest in Kampala and then pick a fight just when reinforcements had arrived.

But unless one believes that Lugard fomented the battle in order to smash the ba-Fransa, his own account hangs together. For a time it seemed that the crisis would be contained without a fight, but on the morning on January 24, 1892, the ba-Fransa began to beat the war drums. Lugard issued more arms to the ba-Ingleza: 300 muzzle-loaders and 150 Sniders. The Catholic and Protestant forces were facing each other on opposing hills. The Catholic line extended from the king's compound to the White Fathers' Rubaga mission; the Protestant line was from Kampala fort to the CMS mission at Namirembe. Curiously, both sets of missionaries refused to move, risking being caught up in the battle – which for the French is what happened. Although the forces were facing each other, their main strengths were not. The ba-Fransa's biggest strength was on Mengo hill facing Kampala, whereas the ba-Ingleza's biggest strength was at Namirembe opposite Rubaga, which was defended more lightly.

The Fransa planned to draw the Ingleza on and then create a wedge between them and the Company's troops at Kampala, allowing each to be dealt with separately and consecutively – a plan

Lugard described as "extremely well devised". As a consequence of the unequal battle formation, the Protestants succeded in rushing Rubaga and soon the great Roman Catholic church was in flames. Meanwhile, the Fransa charge from Mengo hill had been broken up by Lugard's Maxim, the second Maxim operated by Williams having failed with a smashed rivet-pin almost at the first shot. Terrified Baganda took shelter in a banana grove. Lugard claimed that the effect was mainly psychological, with only about half a dozen killed. He wrote in *The Rise of Our East African Empire*, with anxious italics: "On the West Coast, in the 'Jebu' war, undertaken by Government, I have been told that 'several thousands' were mowed down by the Maxim. *There was absolutely nothing of the kind in Uganda or previously in Unyoro* [original emphasis]."

Williams now led the Company's Sudanese and Zanzibaris into the battle, taking the king's compound to light opposition. With the defeated ba-Fransa streaming away to the lake, Williams turned his troops towards Rubaga to see what had happened to the fathers.

"As soon as the enemy turned [wrote Lugard], the spearmen and peasantry of the victorious side had rushed in (as is the custom of the Waganda) to complete the victory, and to loot and fire the houses. Flames rose in every direction, in spite of my indignant orders, for the Katikiro and chiefs were powerless to stay the excited rabble, who were scouring the country in every direction – mad to burn the houses of their detested rivals."

Mwanga and the ba-Fransa took refuge on Bulingugwe island in Lake Victoria. It was close to the shore and about seven miles (11km) from Mengo. The bishop and his 10 priests accepted shelter at Kampala fort, where Lugard complained that their swarm of followers "swaggered about as though the place belonged to them". Williams gave the bishop his room and bed in the Europeans' house. Lugard, as he was doubtless happy to tell his readers, was living in a tent. Soon Bishop Hirth and all but two of the priests had left to join the ba-Fransa at Bulingugwe.

They were there on January 30 – almost a week after the Battle of Mengo – when Williams, on Lugard's orders, attacked the island in support of the ba-Ingleza. Lugard acknowledged that he took offence at what he saw as an insulting message from the ba-Fransa, including the offer to return to the capital (which Lugard wanted for the general settlement of the country) if the ba-Ingleza – the winning faction – paid a fine for the fighting. There was also the trigger of the Catholics attacking Protestant estates on the mainland. Again, *Notes on Uganda* offered an opposite interpretation, ridiculing the Protestants' claims to the estates and suggesting that the war was renewed at Bulingugwe because Lugard wanted to avenge the ba-Fransa's insulting message.

The island was only 400-500 yards (370-460m) offshore, and most of the damage was done by the Maxim firing from the mainland. The ba-Ingleza, according to Lugard's account, were ineffective in their canoes, hardly daring to land on the island even under covering fire. The ba-Fransa were driven back to the far end of the island. Mwanga and the bishop fled. The priests were brought to Williams and then returned to Kampala, where they stayed under a genteel form of house arrest. After the battle, Bulingugwe became "like a fair", with guns firing for fun and men dancing and fooling.

Williams's official report about the fighting put the killed and wounded on the island at 25 with 60 more killed in the Fransa canoes: he said he could have killed "several hundreds" if he had wanted to. More died in a panic to get away, but they were not under fire or under pursuit. *Notes on Uganda* blames the Company – that is, Lugard – for the original issue of arms: "The armed natives, accustomed to a savage system of warfare, carrried their ferocity into the fight; and if the agents of the Company deplored the brutality which ensued and endeavoured to mitigate it, – as we may be quite certain they did, – yet, having armed and unloosened forces they could not control, the evil was done, and the responsibility for all that happened, can only fall on them."

Most damagingly back home, *Notes on Uganda* accused Williams of firing on defenceless canoes during the Catholic retreat to Bulingugwe Island. Lugard rushed out *The Rise of Our East African Empire* to defend Captain Williams and himself. Malumba Kiwanuka, in *A History of Buganda* (1971), accepts the claim of canoes filled with refugees being sunk by Maxim fire. He sees the war as provoked by Lugard and the Protestant chiefs at a time when they expected to win it, soon after Lugard had returned to the capital with a reinforcement of crack Sudanese troops. The White Fathers' refusal to leave Rubaga on the eve of the Battle of Mengo is for Lugard a sign of their confidence in victory; for Kiwanuka they stayed because Lugard did not offer them the same facilities for safe evacuation as he had for the Protestant missionaries. Lugard's distribution of rifles to the ba-Inglesa before the Battle of Mengo is for Kiwanuka not a defensive but an offensive move. The Protestant whose death had started the chain of events was in this reading not the victim but the aggressor, and Mwanga was right under Kiganda law to give judgement for the Catholic sub-chief.

It is crucial to Kiwanuka's position that Lugard's actions have not been searchingly examined, largely because of the influence of his principal biographer, Margery Perham. She, it is argued, was too ready to rely on Lugard's own explanations. Certainly Perham, in *Lugard: The Years of Adventure 1858-1898*, does not hide her closeness to her subject. They were on "Fred" and "Margery" terms. This volume of a two-volume work was published in 1956 – 11 years after Lugard's death – with the active encouragement and help of his surviving brother and sister. Kiwanuka might have added that later writers were swayed also by the case so elegantly put by Lugard himself in his book.

In this book Lugard described the claims that Williams deliberately fired on fugitives including women as "hardly worthy of serious refutation". He added: "Under any circumstances it is too monstrous to suppose that a British officer would have purposefully fired on women." In defence of his own role, he said simply that he took no part in any alleged atrocities; he wasn't there.

After the events at Bulingugwe the Catholics, although the larger faction, were roundly beaten with the kabaka a fugitive in German East Africa, where he remained under the influence of (their enemies said as the captive of) Bishop Hirth. The Catholics, however, had a high card: Mwanga. It was vital to get him back to Mengo. A kabaka must always be on the throne of Buganda. *Notes on Uganda* saw Lugard's moves to get Mwanga back as a bid to give the Protestants legitimacy; Lugard presents them as the way to the settlement of the country. Any kabaka was better than no kabaka. If he could not get Mwanga back, he would even contemplate installing Mbogo, the head of the Baganda Muslims and Mwanga's uncle. Installing Mbogo, Lugard recognised reluctantly, would mean Buganda was no longer a Christian country.

However, after extensive negotiations Mwanga and senior ba-Fransa chiefs returned to Mengo after a couple of months (March 30). A treaty soon followed in which the large and fertile – also formerly Protestant – province of Budu was assigned to the French faction. Here Roman Catholics could keep their arms; they were free to live elsewhere provided they were unarmed. Lugard, who constantly tried to separate religious differences (Catholic:Protestant) from political differences (ba-Fransa:ba-Ingleza), stressed that the Roman Catholic religion could be practised anywhere. Both the Fransa and the Ingleza assailed the settlement as unfair, leading Lugard to remark that this was proof of its fairness! The ba-Ingleza were not given a special province, but as the victors in the war, or at least the faction that had sided with the victorious Company, they had most of the country by default.

Notes on Uganda sought to rebut a key part of Lugard's account – the alleged disloyalty of Mgr Hirth. Quoting several times the bishop's comment, "a very little more, and it [Uganda] would have become a Catholic kingdom", it asked what would anyone expect a Catholic bishop to do but propagate his faith. The disloyalty of Mgr Hirth and his companions has "distinctly not been proved". The writer continued, with the elaborate syntax favoured at the time: "Nay more, it is inconceivable to suppose that these Catholic missionaries could have been disloyal; for even were they French Nationalists before they were Catholics, the French were altogether outside of Uganda, and the interests of the White Fathers made them earnestly desire, that some civilized power should assume the direction of affairs in the Equatorial Provinces, to protect them from the Mohammedans, and to establish justice, liberty, and an enlightened government."

With his supporters coming to terms with Lugard, Mwanga's power base had vanished. From now on, his power would be what the British gave him. This was set out in the general treaty of April 11, 1892. The kabaka recognised the Company's suzerainty and would fly its flag. Final authority no longer rested with the king or the chiefs, but with the British Resident. The consent of the Resident was needed "in all grave and serious affairs and matters of the state", like raising taxes and appointments of the higher chiefs.

Lugard in later years was to be known as the architect of "indirect rule", particularly in Nigeria. Here was an early demonstration of it. For a soldier who had turned up in the country, uninvited, with just 50 fighting men, the treaty was the culmination of an astonishing process of persistence, self-belief and legal correctness – all underpinned by the Maxim gun.

He was able, in time-honoured fashion, to turn to his advantage the divisions in the society. Doubtless, too, the Baganda, although famed for their warrior spirit, were growing tired of the fighting, which had lasted on and off for more than three years. Lugard was fortunate also in his deputy. Captain Williams had very much the back-up role, which must have been galling given his army seniority to his commanding officer. Williams played his part very loyally. He showed great commitment in offering money from his own pocket to keep the administration going, he literally held the fort at Kampala while Lugard was enjoying the more glamorous part of exploring the west and he continued the government in the spirit in which Lugard had left it for a few months until relieved.

Lugard's treaty, however, would be just paper unless the matter of the Baganda Muslims was settled. They possessed formidable military power – an estimated 10,000 soldiers – and occupied Singo province to the north of Mengo, towards Bunyoro. Lugard was clear that as long as the Muslims were unabsorbed, faction fighting could always break out again in Buganda. He wanted the Muslims to leave Singo and take over three small provinces in the centre of the country – Kitunzi, Butambala and Busujju. These were near Mengo and between lands occupied by the two Christian factions. Mbogo was to stand down as king and he would live in Mengo. He would not be allowed to reside in any of those provinces, where he might become a focus for disaffection.

Margery Perham in her definitive *Lugard: The Years of Adventure 1858-1898* cannot hide her puzzlement over why the Muslims, with a large undefeated army, accepted these severe terms without getting anything much in return. Certainly, the settlement and the earlier one between the Christian factions were hailed on all sides as "taking war out of the country", according to Lugard. In the short time they were together, Mbogo and Lugard certainly seem to have hit it off. Thousands marched with the two men to Kampala, where on May 28 they were greeted by thousands more. After a rest, they went over to Mwanga's compound on Mengo hill. With great courage, Mbogo entered to compound unarmed and had caused his chiefs to do the same. He was trusting for his safety entirely to Lugard and his troops. In the event, help was not needed.

Lugard vividly described the meeting between the rival kings, uncle and nephew: "Mwanga stood at his gate surrounded by his chiefs. He received Mbogo as though overpowered with delight. They held each other's hands, and gave vent to a long-drawn guttural Oh!-oh! then Ah!-ah! in a higher note, then long low whistles as they gazed into each other's faces. This went on for a long time, and became extremely ludicrous to a European conception; for at times, while thus indicating intense delight and surprise, their eyes would be roaming round in a very inconsequent manner. Then they fell on each other's necks and embraced, and then again began the former ceremony. Then Bambeja (princesses) who had followed Mbogo fell on Mwanga's neck, and those of Mwanga's suite fell on Mbogo's neck, and meanwhile the same performances were going on between chiefs and chieflets and common people on every side, till the crush became so great that it was hard to preserve one's balance among the gesticulating crowd."

The tale of the royal drum casts a pleasant light on the characters of both Mbogo and Lugard. The sultan had in his possession one of two large drums that were emblems of Buganda kingship. (Mwanga had the other one.) Since he was no longer a king, Mbogo gave the drum to Lugard. It stayed for many years at Lugard's house in Abinger, Surrey. In the 1930s, Lugard heard from Uganda that its return would be appreciated. He sent it back at once, and a copy was made for him.

At last, Lugard was able to leave for England, where he knew he was urgently needed to fight for retention of the British presence in Buganda. He had been north of the lake for 18 months almost to the day, and within this neat period he saw his activities falling into three broadly equal phases: first half-year, preliminary settlement of Buganda, including containing the Muslims; second half-year, outside in tributary states (in the "march to the west" he brought the Sudanese remnant force out of Equatoria and resettled it, and also established treaty relations with the kings of Ankole and Toro); third-half year, the "closing of the story", with the Catholic,

Protestant and Muslim factions united in acceptance of the British flag. It was a feat of will and energy, but the story was not quite as closed as Lugard liked to suggest. On Buganda's northern border, Kabarega of Bunyoro remained untamed and as well disposed to the British as a hungry leopard is to an antelope.

At Kampala, Williams took charge. In haste, and to avoid depleting his successor's stock of arms, Lugard decided not to form his own caravan and joined the one being taken down to the coast by Captain James Macdonald, who had been conducting a railway survey. The party left on June 16. Lugard soon found himself in the same difficult position as Emin marching with Stanley: both were used to command but had to submit to someone else's decisions. Between Lugard and Macdonald there was much friction as the caravan marched for the coast. It was unfortunate for Lugard that Macdonald was the one chosen to inquire into his conduct of affairs in Buganda, the government's terms of reference requiring Macdonald to "explain the causes of the outbreak [of fighting] and the action of British officials". The surveyor's chief qualification for the work, it seems, was being on the spot and therefore cheap.

The following year, when he was in London, Lugard heard of the sad fate that had befallen Selim Bey at Macdonald's hands. The Sudanese commander was accused of treachery by conspiring with Muslim Baganda for the overthrow of the British. Already ill, he died on the way to the coast to answer the charge. Insisting that Selim's loyalty was beyond question and had been repeatedly proved, Lugard commented: "There must have been a strange want of tact to convert a loyalty so sincere into hostility, when Selim was even then a dying man!" Lugard defended the way that he and Williams had treated Selim as a dignitary by pointing out that he held the title of Bey, the highest rank but one in the Egyptian army (the highest being Pasha) and for years had been in command of large districts.

One of the most deeply felt passages in *The Rise of Our East African Empire* is a tribute to Selim, the officer trusted by General Gordon, mistrusted by Stanley, whose remnant force Lugard had brought out of the wilderness that was once Equatoria and resettled in and around Buganda: "To me it is a sad contemplation, that this veteran, selected by Gordon for the command of Mruli; whose valour saved Dufileh; against whom no charge of disloyalty had ever yet been proved amidst all the faithlessness of the Sudan troops; and who had proved at the risk of his life his loyalty to me, – that this man should have been hurried off in a dying state, discredited and disgraced, to succumb on the march, a prisoner and an outcast."

Lugard reached London at a propitious time. The Salisbury government had fallen in the summer of 1892, and the new Liberal Party government under William Gladstone might be expected to be even less inclined than Salisbury's Conservatives to take on Uganda. In fact, it was deadlocked over what to do. The aged premier – 83 that year – was the country's leading opponent of colonial involvements. It was Gladstone who had delayed sending relief to General Gordon in Khartoum until it was too late, so he had redoubled reasons for not tying the country up in another remote and unsuppliable place like Uganda. His foreign secretary, Lord Rosebery, sought the opposite. Under advice from Sir Percy Anderson at the Foreign Office, Rosebery wanted Britain to declare a protectorate over Uganda. It could then move into Equatoria to parry a French threat to the Upper Nile, mounted from their vast north African territories. Gladstone needed to keep Rosebery in the government, which meant that the far younger man was playing his cards from a position of strength.

Lugard, the Church Missionary Society and the Imperial British East Africa Company itself all campaigned strongly that autumn for a Uganda protectorate. Henry Stanley gave his support. Lugard had to combine his campaigning with writing *The Rise of Our East African Empire* to defend himself against the French fathers' claims being investigated by Macdonald. He addressed audiences all over the country. (How unimaginable now for the public to turn out for a talk on a foreign policy topic!) Rosebery may have been moved by the political imperative of blocking the French, others saw the economic potential of Buganda and the surrounding territories, but what interested Lugard's audience most were the plight of the missionaries and the Christian Baganda and the continued scourge of slavery in the region. But as the leaves started to drop in Hyde Park and Kensington Garden, not to mention in Buckingham Palace and the 10 Downing Street garden, it remained unclear who would win this battle for Uganda.

15

Settlement and Strife

*CMS and retention campaign * Sir G. Portal's inquiry * Bishops'
Agreement * Martyr's crown denied * John Bull takes in the baby *
Baganda adapt and survive * Catholicism's English face * Bunyoro
invaded * Mwanga flees * Sudanese mutiny * The two kings fight on *
The country remade*

The Imperial British East Africa Company's stay in Buganda had
been extended by a year, to the end of 1892, thanks to the
Church Missionary Society's hugely successful public appeal for
funds. The CMS now played a leading part in the campaign for
Britain to stay permanently. This became a cliff-hanger. It took
three months to reach Buganda from the East African coast, so any
instruction for the Kampala administration to stay put would have
to be sent from the coast by October 1 at the latest.

Lugard was on his way to England to campaign for retention, but
he had not yet arrived. A CMS deputation visited the foreign secretary, Lord Rosebery, a week before the cut-off date. With Rosebery
it was pushing at an open door, but he had to get retention through
a divided cabinet. A cable from Sir Gerald Portal, the British
consul-general in Zanzibar, did the trick. It warned of anarchy and
bloodshed in Buganda if the Company left. On September 30, 1892,
with barely a day to spare, the cabinet agreed to pay for a three-
month extension.

This was presented as allowing the Company time to wind up its
affairs tidily, although every deferral made it more likely that the
stay would be permanent. The retention campaign began in earnest.
Lugard wrote to The Times and addressed meetings up and down
the country. Henry Stanley spoke out for retention; so did Lord
Salisbury, who had shown little interest in Buganda when he was
prime minister only months earlier. Resolutions in favour of Britain
staying in Buganda poured into the Foreign Office. Somehow, in
November and December, the Uganda Question caught fire.

The big issue for the public was slavery. Professor D.A. Low, in *Buganda in Modern History*, comments: "The British public knew very little about Africa, but the preachings of Wilberforce, Buxton and Livingstone had sunk deep into the national mind, and any reverse in Africa instantly recalled the horror of slavery which was the one thing that most of them knew about Africa."

In a careful analysis of these resolutions, held in the Foreign Office archives, Low found that 104 out of 174 submissions mentioned slavery. Religious and commercial arguments were intermingled: 75 resolutions mentioned trade or commerce. The Victorian era did not see any conflict between the two. The Good Doctor himself (Livingstone) had proclaimed that commerce and Christianity went together as the way to develop civilisation. The leading politician Joseph Chamberlain, in a remark that now sounds ironical but presumably did not at the time, commented: "What is wanted for Uganda, is what Birmingham has got – an improvement scheme."

The (Anglican) Bishop of Chichester stressed the argument was a big fuss about very little when he pointed out that the cost of administering Uganda was "about the cost of a single picture in the National Gallery". More than half of the resolutions came from church sources, including 18 from CMS branches and seven from branches of another Anglican body, the Society for the Propagation of the Gospel. There was a noteworthy joint submission from the three heads of Scotland's disunited presbyterian churches. Few resolutions emerged from Ireland, underlining the inevitable connection between politics and religion. Britain's colonial policy was officially secular, but she was seen as, and in a real sense was, a Protestant power; overwhelmingly Roman Catholic Ireland – at the height of her own home-rule struggle – was unlikely to summon much enthusiasm for Britain staying in Buganda.

Church people, with the fate of the missionaries and Baganda converts in mind, had the strongest motivation for demanding retention. Chambers of commerce were well aware of the trade possibilities of Buganda and the surrounding kingdoms. Much of the publicly voiced support came from Conservatives, not Liberals. But Lugard also addressed many crowded public meetings and the signatures on the resolutions came from all over the political spectrum. Low makes clear that the Uganda Question was not one just for the religious and right-wingers; it was a mass reaction that the government had to attend to.

The campaign was at its height after the cabinet had announced – on November 11 – a commission of inquiry into the retention issue. Sir Gerald Portal, who was to conduct the inquiry, could under his terms of reference recommend evacuation, but as a known enthusiast for retention he was hardly likely to. The campaigners might also have saved their energies if they had known about Rosebery's private directions to the consul (quoted by Low): "... I consider it as settled that your main duty will be to arrange the best means of administering Uganda ... There may, of course, be indicated to you the possibility that should the difficulty of retention be found insuperable, or at any rate too vast, you should so report. But as a rather one horse company has been able to administer I suppose the empire will be equal to it, and therefore that saving clause is mainly one of form." A week later he told Portal: "... I may say this as my confident though not my official opinion, that public sentiment here [in Britain] will expect and support the maintenance of the British sphere of influence."

During Portal's short visit to Buganda, he made a new allocation of land between the Catholics and the Protestants. The Catholics had never come to terms with receiving only the province of Budu. Even Williams, his deputy and successor, thought Lugard's allocation was too restrictive for the Catholics. The Bishops' Agreement was so called because it was signed by Bishop Hirth for the Catholics and Bishop Tucker for the Protestants plus leading chiefs from both groups. As well as keeping Budu, the Catholics received two more mainland provinces (out of the total of 10) and also the Sese Islands. They were given shambas (estates) on the route to the capital so that Catholic travellers did not have to camp on hostile territory.

The agreement, ingeniously but as it turned out transiently, doubled up between the faith groups three of the key posts in the kingdom. There was a Protestant katikiro and a Catholic katikiro; likewise for the mujasi (chief of soldiers) and the gabunga (chief of canoes). To the Kiganda equivalent of the question "whose finger on the button?" the answer was "bitter rivals". It did not last, being abolished seven years later.

In the months that Portal was making his trip north of the lake,

the Uganda Question stayed before the British public. The retention campaign died away, but in the following year (1893) came the
sensational reports of alleged British atrocities during the Battle of
Mengo and its aftermath on Bulingugwe Island (described in the
previous chapter, THE BATTLE OF MENGO). Both sides sent
accounts of the fighting to Europe, but the French ones arrived several weeks before the English ones. In May, while there was no word
from the English, a letter from the Roman Catholic bishop, Mgr
Hirth, was published in France (and republished in the Tablet in
the UK). Bishop Hirth allowed his emotions to get the better of
him, and his language throughout the crisis showed a hatred of
Protestantism. His letter concluded: "It is not to the English officers
that blame principally attaches: they have only the blame of allowing themselves to be blinded by the Baganda, themselves persuaded
by the 'Reverends'. We regret one thing – not to have been held
worthy of the crown of martyrdom."

The Mengo/Bulingugwe episode became a major Anglo–French
international incident. The two governments got into a considerable
flap, and the British prime minister had the affair investigated by the
man on the spot – who was Captain Macdonald, Lugard's adversary. Macdonald's report was highly critical of Lugard, but the
latter won support from his former deputy and successor, Captain
Williams, Bishop Tucker – and the British public. Eventually the
affair fizzled out, although the issue of compensation for the White
Fathers' buildings at Rubaga dragged on for several years.

The uproar had kept Uganda before the British public, which
paved the way for the eventual success of the retention campaign.
Sir Gerald Portal, his own views and his superior's expectations
happily coinciding, duly reported in favour of keeping Uganda. On
April 12, 1894, Britain announced a protectorate over Buganda and
surrounding territories. Punch magazine published a famous car-
toon showing a black foundling labelled Uganda on John Bull's
doorstep. Doughty old John Bull had no choice but to take the baby
in.

For Buganda it was like the Norman Conquest without the Battle
of Hastings. Instead, Mwanga had signed Lugard's piece of paper,
the implications of which he and the chiefs cannot have known. The
Europeans quickly re-made the country, and the other kingdoms

and nations of the Uganda Protectorate – usually with the best of intentions but without of course asking the "natives" whether they wanted it re-made. The question would not have occurred to the Uganda incomers; only the most extreme of radicals in England thought such a thing at the time!

Low wondered why the Kiganda elites seemed to accept British rule so readily. His *Buganda in Modern History*, in the language of its time – it was published in 1971, in the first glow of African independence – asks who were the collaborators and who were the resisters. His answer is that they were often the same people. The politically adroit Baganda had "a dual concern to preserve one's own cultural and political integrity while seeking to ensure that the advantages which could be gained from contact with the wider world were secured as well: a brilliantly constructed ideology, which has the chief claim to being Buganda's greatest achievement". Apolo Kagwa, for instance, was the katikiro (chief minister) of Buganda from 1889, before the coming of the British, until 1926, which was 32 years after the declaration of the Uganda protectorate.

Colonialism impinged less heavily in Buganda than it did in other British African territories. The "native administration" (in the contemporary phrase) enjoyed substantial autonomy formalised by treaty relations, and was willing to take on the colonial government when it needed to. Low believes Buganda was in this relatively favourable position not for the most immediately obvious reasons: because there were few white settlers or because it had been a powerful traditional kingdom; it was because the country "made a quite unusually positive response to the western impact when it came, which earned it a quite unusual reward". This meant among other things that the British rulers saw working with the chiefs and local administrations as the best way to develop the country.

Low's rather comfortable thesis that the Kiganda elites willingly embraced colonialism would be unlikely to appeal to an African writer like Kiwanuka. In his *History of Buganda*, coincidentally published in the same year (1971) as Low's book, he argues it was specifically the Protestant elite that co-operated with the British, for the purpose of entrenching the victory of their faction. Kiwanuka brands the ba-Ingleza chiefs as collaborators, no-one more so than the Protestant katikiro, Apolo Kagwa.

For Kiwanuka, Lugard's victory at the Battle of Mengo – which he believes was provoked by Lugard – was the defining moment for all that came after in Buganda and Uganda as a whole. It meant that Buganda was to be not only a British colony but also an emphatically Protestant state. The events of 1892 intertwined politics and religion to the destruction of former structures of the Buganda state. Kiwanuka points out: "Families had been divided and clans were no longer a source of protection." These processes are sadly common in history, as for example with family members finding themselves on opposite sides in the American Civil War and the forced dispersal of the Scottish clans after the 1745 Jacobite rebellion.

For the Kiganda public, Catholicism was the French party and Protestantism was the English party. Now that Britain had taken over Uganda, this association was very damaging to the Catholic cause. Nor were the terms wa-Fransa and wa-Ingleza, as used in the world beyond, at all helpful. The obvious solution was to send missionaries who were both Catholic and English. This was the inspiration behind the arrival of the Mill Hill Fathers in 1895. The fathers were named after the headquarters of their order, St Joseph's Foreign Missionary Society of the Sacred Heart, at Mill Hill, at that time a village to the north of (now a suburb of) London.

The Vatican agreed to split up the vast Nyanza Vicariate. The north-eastern part was renamed the Vicariate of the Upper Nile and was given to the Mill Hill Fathers. It comprised the eastern part of Uganda and part of Kenya. An Italian missionary group, the Verona Fathers, took the north-western portion, including a small part of Uganda above Lake Albert and much of the Sudan. The name Nyanza Vicariate was kept for the area including western Uganda and German territory south and west of Lake Victoria. The White Fathers retrenched their activities to this vicariate.

After some disputes between the Catholic brethren, the boundary in the Mengo area between the Nyanza and the Upper Nile vicariates was drawn between Rubaga and Namirembe hills – through the Battle of Mengo fighting ground, in fact. This kept the White Fathers in possession of their Rubaga headquarters while leaving the town of Kampala, growing to the east of Lugard's fort, to the Mill Hill Fathers. They were allocated land and built their headquarters on Nsambya hill.

The first party of Mill Hill missionaries consisted of Bishop Henry Hanlon and four other priests. After a difficult trek up-country they arrived at Kampala on September 6, 1895. They found themselves caught up with much ceremony among the Catholic faithful and the small European community. Among their visitors were Archdeacon Walker of the Church Missionary Society and two colleagues, the fathers' neighbours-to-be at Namirembe.

Under the Uganda protectorate, the Roman Catholic missionaries knuckled down to the new order and concentrated on education. The CMS missionaries with Bishop Tucker at their head were another matter. They were proud of the fact that the CMS had been the first in the field in Buganda, and proud too that the society's campaigning had produced the money for the British to stay on in 1892. CMS personnel continued to be highly involved in the politics of the new protectorate, not always to the pleasure of the administration. "Difficult to satisfy, the CMS developed an extraordinary capacity for generating unpleasantness [says Kiwanuka] by writing direct to the Foreign Office, by appealing to their headquarters for support, by writing to influential friends and to newspapers." Bishop Tucker was to be remembered "for claiming a special position for his co-religionists, although the issue had really been decided long before by Lugard's actions".

Even so, the political settlement of Uganda had a long tail. Barely a year after Lugard's accord with Mbogo, the authorities put down an attempted rising by the Muslims.

Next came Kabarega. While Ankole and Toro had been in treaty relations with the British since Lugard's time, Bunyoro remained fully independent and defiant. Kabarega saw no merit in becoming another piece of the imperial jigsaw. From the British point of view, however, Bunyoro was part of the area ceded to them by international agreement (not of course that the country itself had been invited to give an opinion), so to make the claim a reality Bunyoro was invaded in the same year that the protectorate was declared (1894). Kabarega could not withstand the firepower of the colonial forces, but he escaped capture for several years and his followers kept up guerrilla attacks.

Mwanga continued in his royal compound at Mengo, theoretically a Protestant now but unreconciled to the new order. Whatever his shortcomings as a human being and a ruler, it is impossible not to sympathise with the reduced state of the former absolute monarch. He was in office because Buganda had to have a kabaka to provide legitimacy for the regime, but his only power was devolved to him at someone else's pleasure. Mwanga's client status was dramatically underlined when he was fined for exporting ivory without British permission. This was the son of Mutesa, whose single word meant life or death!

In July 1897 Mwanga slipped away from Mengo and went to Budu, the Catholic province that was his main source of support. There he declared his rebellion. After the Battle of Kabuwoko he fled to German East Africa (now Tanzania), where he was detained. He soon escaped and back in Uganda fought another losing battle – Nyendo – before retreating to the bush. He linked up with Kaberega, and the two kings with Mwanga's general, Gabriel Kintu, gave the authorities a lot of trouble with their hit-and-run resistance.

In Kampala Mwanga had long since been deposed. His one-year-old son, Daudi Chwa, was proclaimed kabaka. Kiwanuka makes the telling point that of the 21 Baganda chiefs who formed the deposition council, just one was a Roman Catholic. That was the Catholics' katikiro, Stanislaus Mugwanya.

In 1898 Equatoria cast its final shadow over the affairs of Uganda when part of the Sudanese troops – Emin Pasha's soldiers, whom Lugard had brought out – mutinied and killed their British officers. The authorities managed to keep the Sudanese mutineers apart from the nationalists following Mwanga and Kabarega. The mutiny was suppressed with the help of Baganda leaders. George Pilkington, the CMS missionary and translator of the bible into Luganda, was killed while observing an action against the rebel-held fort. He was there at the request of the Protestant Baganda, but a newspaper letter from an army officer underlined how ambiguous a missionary's situation could become. Captain C.H. Villiers told readers of The Times: "It is owing to the attachment of the Protestant Waganda to men like Mr Pilkington that we have been able to hold Uganda so easily up to the present time. In Mr Pilkington's death the cause of civilization in Africa has received a severe blow and England has lost a devoted servant."

Pilkington was one of the most creative of the early CMS missionaries. His death was a great loss. He gave the Baganda the complete bible in their language, building on Mackay's work. With another CMS missionary, A.B. Fisher, he channelled a revival of religious interest among the Baganda into evangelical achievement. He called for evangelists to operate from "reading houses" (country churches). The result, says William Anderson in *The Church in East Africa, 1840-1974*, was "like magic". In January 1894 there were 20 reading houses outside the Mengo centre; by December there were at least 200.

In the final year of the century, Mwanga and Kabarega were at last captured. They were run to ground by Colonel Evatt on April 9, 1899. In the fight that led to his capture, Kabarega was shot in the arm, which later had be amputated. Mwanga's able general, Gabriel Kintu, gave himself up to the Germans.

Frederick Jackson (*Early Days in East Africa*) related the surgeon's anecdote about Kabarega in hospital. The king was displeased at the attention given to the patient in an opposite bed rather than to himself. While the surgeon, Haig, was stooped over his patient, Kabarega wriggled himself into a position where he could kick the surgeon on the backside. "I didn't mind," said Haig. "It is not everyone who can claim to have had his bottom kicked by a king."

In May the two ex-kings were marched through Kampala on their way to exile in the inaccessible Seychelle Islands. Mwanga no longer had his retinue of pages: with him were a few boys and women. Even Baganda who had no love for the former kabaka must have pondered over his humiliation, the raw display of who were the masters now. Character flaws he had in plenty, but his misfortune was to be born at the wrong time so he spent his whole life as a ruler seeking ways to resist the inevitable.

Mwanga did not survive long in the Seychelles. He died in 1902, only in his middle thirties. Kabarega lived on until 1923. As an old man he was allowed back in Uganda. He died at Jinja while preparing to return to Bunyoro.

After the declaration of the Uganda Protectorate in 1894, Bunyoro had been gradually pacified and was treated as conquered territory. The British did not usually see themselves as conquerors, preferring the more comfortable idea of treaty partners, but Bunyoro was the exception. One expression of this was the Uganda Agreement of 1900 between the British Commissioner, Sir Harry Johnston, and the regents ruling Buganda on behalf of the child kabaka, Daudi Chwa. Bunyoro's counties south of the River Kafu were given to Buganda, leaving 40 per cent of the Bunyoro population stranded in Buganda, according to John Beattie in *The Nyoro State*. It was not until 1933 that Bunyoro had a political agreement similar to those in Buganda, Ankole and Toro. The bulk of the "lost counties" was finally returned in 1965 in a process started in the closing moments of colonial rule.

All of this flowed from Kabarega's determined defence of his country's independence. Baker's hostile characterisation of the omukama had proved enduring. The Banyoro also felt that their traditional enemies, the Baganda, had fed the British overlords false information. At the time a few British voices questioned official policy. Beattie quotes a former provincial commissioner in Bunyoro who wrote in his autobiography: "I like the Banyoro, and I do feel that their action in opposing foreign control hardly merited the consequences which have followed it". Lugard himself wrote, in *The Story of the Uganda Protectorate* (1900): "Kabarega seems to have had some good points, and Emin speaks highly of him, but Mwanga was in every way despicable and loose."

Jackson, who became governor of Uganda, acknowledged Kabarega's courage and fighting spirit: "(H)e never once sued for peace, even when hard pressed; and never grovelled when captured. In fact he always kept his end up, and in some ways was at least a man."

Buganda itself experienced a revolution in land tenure. The Uganda Agreement removed from chiefly control more than half the land area of Buganda. Of the total 19,600 square miles (50,765 sq km), 10,500 square miles (27,195 sq km) were to be held by government and 8,958 square miles (23,200 sq km) were for the kabaka, chiefs and other land occupiers. The balance was made up by allocations to the three regents and the three religious missions. Since even one square mile is a big chunk of land, the agreement gave the missions, "as private property, and in trust for the native churches", significant landholdings. The Church Missionary Society received

40 square miles (104 sq km), the White Fathers 35 square miles (91 sq km) and the Mill Hill Fathers (who had been in the country only since 1895) 17 square miles (44 sq km). Although H.P. Gale, writing (in *Uganda and the Mill Hill Fathers*) in the closing period of colonial rule, says the agreement "has stood the test of half a century, and carried the Kingdom of Buganda safely into the complex currents of the present day", upending the system of land tenure remains the classic action of conquerors. The victorious Normans did the same in England after 1066.

By now Buganda had new forms of land control, the Muslims had been neutralised and the Catholics had seen the king sidelined and then removed. Uganda was ruled by the British and a largely Protestant indigenous elite. It was only a quarter of a century since Henry Morton Stanley visited the unknown and exotic country beyond the Great Lake ruled by the famous prince, Mutesa.

16

Someone Else's House

*Expatriate life * Touring * Medicine in God's name * Evangelising the
north * Uganda Railway * Birth of Nairobi * The lake at last *
Protestants gain ground * Irrelevant school subjects * The 'cultural
cringe'*

For the ordinary people of Uganda, especially in the rural areas,
the change of rulers was not too noticeable except at taxation
time. The British ruled indirectly through the local chiefs. They
had to, because men and resources were too few to do otherwise. As
an old Africa hand told Charles Allen for a BBC radio series later
made into the book, *Tales from the Dark Continent*: "We couldn't
possibly administer all these people and these vast territories closely.
So our policy always was to leave as much as possible to the people
themselves and not to interfere with their lives unless it was obvious
that what they were doing was wrong. If they could settle their own
quarrels, so much the better."

The situation in one district of Nyasaland (now Malawi) was typical of Britain's African colonies: four Europeans (the district commissioner, his two assistants and a policeman), an African sub-
inspector, two sergeants and a dozen police administered a population of 100,000.

The white officials were visible from time to time throughout
their districts through the hallowed institution of "the tour". An
officer might spend as much as half his time in the rural areas for the
purposes of collecting taxes, hearing complaints or just showing the
flag. Former African administrators and their wives who talked to
Allen for the programmes made clear that for many these tours were
what Africa was all about. Safaris into some of the world's most
exotic areas, or the Sanders of the River-style of venturing forth into
the interior, all underpinned with the comfort of being in command
of the country, could hardly fail to enter the bloodstream.

Uganda-born Mavis Stone, who returned to live there for 14 years up to 1962, wove vivid word pictures of Africa: "... long khaki-coloured plains with the flat-topped thorn trees and scrub bushes ... the rather attractive little villages with woven fences ... chicken houses made up like little mud huts with thatched roofs and stuck up on stilts ... the children that were half-grown, all legs and smiles ... the women always graceful, always carrying loads on their heads – even a matchbox I've seen them carrying on their heads – never anything in their hands ... (the camp fire) was usually lit at sunset which we would sit and watch and there was supposed to be a blue flash which you did just see as the sun disappeared ... you had to swat at the mosquitoes while you were having your bath ... then you got into your trousers and mosquito boots and a long-sleeved shirt and you went and sat by the camp fire and had your drink."

Mavis Stone's husband, Richard, who spent his Colonial Service career in Uganda, retiring in 1962 as the Resident of Buganda, remembered the baraza, that institution taken over from the African chiefs, as the main way for the touring official to meet the people. It was an opportunity both to explain government policies and to hear complaints. Mutual leg-pulling was often the style. Villagers would try to bait the bwana by saying something outrageous. "If they succeeded in making the DC [district commissioner] turn a little pink in the face or stutter with rage then this was their day and they all roared with laughter. But of course the DC was also able to pull their legs a bit, and so we carried on these proceedings with the greatest of friendship and enjoyment."

The picture was painted in darker colours by Patrick Mullins, who served in Nyasaland from 1952 to 1964: "It was a tradition of the country that they were hospitable to visitors and this went for the white bwana as much as it did for anyone else. Much of what the DC was always on about cannot have been particularly welcome to them, particularly the enforcement of agricultural rules or the collection of taxes, and I think behind it all most of the village Africans rather wanted to be left alone and not bothered on these subjects. But there was no active resentment; I think this was mostly town-bred. The villagers were polite and attentive and one always felt a little that they weren't too sorry when you went away again."

As late as the 1930s, even at the topmost level, touring parties in

Uganda operated very much as the caravans from the coast of half a century before. Violet Bourdillon, wife of the then-governor, recalled: "I marched every bit of Uganda; we had two fly-tents that we slept under and everything was portered and done on the march." Yet timelessness was an illusion: already in that decade it was possible to fly from Britain to Uganda. A flying boat service starting from Poole in Dorset made several night-stops on its way to Lake Victoria. After the Second World War two other innovations changed Africa forever for the Europeans. The drug Paludrine removed the risk of malaria while the four-wheel-drive Land Rover meant for the administrator that "your people were always accessible", as one official told Charles Allen, adding: "You might have an exciting time getting to them, but you did get there. And it really altered things for us." As no doubt it did for the Africans being visited.

The extraordinary tenure of the medical missionary Albert Cook gives us a series of snapshots of the changes to Uganda society. He came out with a Church Missionary Society party in 1896 and 37 years later was still working in the country at the CMS hospital in Kampala. He did not die until 1951, by which time the simple mission doctor was Sir Albert Cook KCMG. His life has been described in *The Church Missionary Society and Modern Medicine in Uganda*, written and privately published in 1978 by Professor W.D. Foster of Makerere University, Kampala.

Cook's party reached Uganda by the established caravan safari route from Mombasa except that the first seven miles (11km) were accomplished along the fledgling Uganda Railway in a truck pushed by the engine. Then the railway ran out, and it was trekking for three months to cover more than 600 miles (970km) to Mengo.

In the Buganda capital Cook was given a typical missionary house, made of muli (bundles of bamboo) with the windows and doorways also framed with muli. Curtains of bark cloth gave privacy. At night shutters also made of bamboo were used. A "certain Spartan level of comfort", in Professor Foster's phrase, could be achieved; an 1898 photo shows an interior with pictures hanging from the muli walls and serviceable camp furniture. The simplicity of this housing contrasts with the solidity of Alexander Mackay's mission station at Usambiro several years earlier, which had 2ft

(0.6m) thick clay walls. But by the mid-Nineties there were many CMS missionaries in Uganda. The count in 1897 was 38 throughout the protectorate – far more men than women – which was almost the same number of Europeans as the government (40).

Cook was evidently a capable as well as enthusiastic doctor. He performed an appendectomy a year before that on King Edward VII, which was itself hailed as a pioneering operation. He also removed a disfiguring growth from a patient's face against the advice of a medical colleague. That patient became a dedicated hospital assistant at a time when it was hard to persuade local people to do the work.

The CMS soon found there was a culture clash between its desire to recruit hospital assistants and the willingness of the Baganda to take these jobs. A vital practical consideration was that hospital work meant soiling hands. For a people who ate with their fingers, that meant they could not use the communal bowl of matoke – cooked, unripe bananas, producing a staple food with the texture of mashed potato – at home. It was like being a leper in one's own house.

Mengo Hospital, where Cook was based, charged fees to those who could afford to pay. The scale of charges was:

OUT-PATIENTS. One to five cents or if wearing European coats, 10 cents; chiefs and Indians, one rupee including four days' supply of medicine; Europeans and Goanese, three rupees, or five rupees for a home visit.

IN-PATIENTS. Five rupees a day. Operation fees ranged from five to 300 rupees. Africans were not charged fees as in-patients except for circumcision operations in venereal cases.

It is saddening that this church-based hospital used a racially based fee scale, including charging Europeans more than African chiefs. It is a short step, if it is a step at all, from paying more to thinking one is worth more. Whatever the intentions at the time, it was the sort of practice that in the colonial environment ossified into feelings of European racial superiority.

Cook was often called away from the hospital, sometimes over many miles, to treat sick colleagues or their families, which meant disregarding his African patients with their endless burden of ailments big and small. As well as the problem of allocating time between colleagues and local people, the medical missionary was part-doctor and part-evangelist, and had to decide what the proportions were. Care of the body was a way of winning the soul for Christ, but should medicine become the missionary's preoccupation?

Mengo Hospital was open to all but attendance at religious instruction was a condition of treatment. Cook recorded that "at first this led to some little demur on the part of the Roman Catholics, who came and protested, but I said they must either have our Gospel-preaching and medicine, or go without the latter. They chose to attend".

This attitude was fully reciprocated by the Catholics, and had been present in Buganda from the start. Matters continued fraught: in 1904 a CMS caravan to Acholi in the north of the protectorate, beyond the Blue Nile, discharged three porters at Hoima – two Muslims and a Catholic – to avoid the risk of competing doctrines in the mission field. Cook, who was with the party, reported that the terrifying Acholi, who were naked and villainous-looking to European eyes, were most friendly; "not a spear has been raised, or a bow bent against us and we are to all intents and purposes as safe here as say, on Hampstead Heath [in London]".

Cook's facility with languages meant he was often given assignments away from the hospital. He could pick up in a few weeks enough of a language to preach and be understoood in when many of his colleagues struggled for years with Luganda or Swahili. In 1905 Cook was chosen to lead a caravan into the southern Sudan to link up with missionaries sent from Khartoum by the British governor there. The caravan had more than 50 porters – and a bicycle, which Cook was able to use some of the way. He intended to ride from Hoima back to Mengo in two days. This was more than 120 miles (190km), which if achieved is an interesting illustration of the improving condition of the roads.

The outward journey took them through or close to places that proclaimed the memory of vanished Equatoria: Dufile, Rejaf, Gondokoro itself, the former headquarters of Sir Samuel Baker, General Gordon, Emin Pasha ... Crossing into the Sudan (the border was later moved back to near Dufile), the party at first based itself in Mongalla where the local tribe was the Bari, sparse in numbers, unsophisticated and reputedly hostile. Remarkably, Cook did not have any firearms in his caravan. He did "*not* feel naturally drawn to" the Bari but he remembered they had "souls which are just as precious to God as our own" and he was sure "God will implant in my heart a real desire for their salvation". Their time was not yet, however, because the party moved downriver to Bor, still within the borders of Emin Pasha's old province. This was decided by the Khartoum group because the Dinka around Bor were seen as more promising mission subjects than the Bari. In only four months Cook learnt the Dinka language well enough to translate the Anglican morning and evening services (leaving out the prayers for the Royal Family) and 12 hymns.

Professor Foster remarks: "The rapid growth of the Anglican Church in Buganda owed much to the conviction of the pioneer missionaries that the translation of the Bible was a necessary part of their proclamation of the gospel." Among Cook's language contributions in Luganda was a book of Kiganda proverbs with Christian parallels, a medical phrase book and a revision of George Pilkington's Luganda-English grammar. Pilkington, who was responsible for completing the translation of the entire bible, had previously worked with Alexander Mackay on the New Testament, and Mackay alone had even earlier translated St Matthew's gospel. The United Bible Societies still follow this sequence of book (known as a portion), testament and bible in their ongoing work among the world's languages.

In 1931, three years before he retired from Mengo Hospital although not completely from medical work, Cook met one of the historic figures in the Uganda story. This was Lord Lugard, who in 1891-92 had secured the country for Britain with a handful of soldiers and who went on to become Britain's greatest African proconsul. Cook and his wife Katharine were on furlough in England. Lugard, by then in his seventies, invited them to his house in Surrey. Cook recorded: "Lord Lugard was *charming*, with his delicate clear-cut voice, his old-fashioned courtesy, his scholarly habits and pentrating mind. It was an education to be in his company and learn from him."

The best lived lives cannot guarantee a smooth landing at the end, and so it was with the widowed Albert Cook. His final years were shadowed by increasing dependence on morphine. What had started as mild therapeutic doses turned into addiction to a drug that as a doctor he had only too easy access to. A disappointment was that the world seemed uninterested in the memoirs that summed up his life of work and worship. Cook like many another writer showed that an interesting life does not of itself make an interesting book. Professor Foster acknowledges that Cook's *Forty Years in Uganda* is "dull". Failing to find a commercial publisher who would issue it in the form he wanted, Cook offered the manuscript to the CMS editorial department. "We have, as it were, laid it at His feet to be used in His service as He thinks best," said Cook. The CMS too found they could manage without it. Eventually it was published by the Uganda Society as *Uganda Memories*.

For almost all of their time in Uganda, the Cooks were able to enjoy furloughs in England with speedy and painless journeys by the standards of the day. From 1901 the journey from Kampala to the coast, and vice versa, took a few days sitting down rather than three months walking. What brought about this transformation was the Uganda Railway.

The line was driven across almost 600 miles (970km) of often fearsome terrain in the quick time of five years. The chief engineer, George Whitehead, with his railhead chief Ronald Preston, directed an indentured Indian labour force which over the duration of the project totalled more than 30,000. Many of these coolies did not go home after the line was completed; they were the founders of today's East African Asian population. The death toll would be quite unacceptable by modern standards (a single death was news when the Channel Tunnel was being built); nevertheless, Whitehead and his force successfully bridged the strait between Mombasa Island and the mainland, crossed the Taru Desert, spanned the Tsavo River, crossed the Athi Swamps, found a way onto the floor of the Great Rift Valley and out again, cut a way over the mountains on the far side of the valley before bringing the 1m gauge rails to a place beside Lake Victoria that the engineer named Port Florence (later Kisumu). From here steamers crossed the lake to the port for Kampala. From sea level at Mombasa the line climbed to 8,300ft (2,500m) at the Mau Summit (beyond the Rift) before dropping more than 5,000ft (1,500m) to the lake.

Driving a great railway forward mile by determined mile is a romatic undertaking anywhere, but seldom can builders have had such an inspiring goal as that legendary inland sea. Ronald Hardy in *The Iron Snake* imagines Whitehead's feelings when, from far away atop the Mau Escarpment, he glimpsed Lake Victoria for the first time: "On the crest of the hill they waited for the light to strengthen, for the sun to suck mists from the plateau and the plains of the west. It was very cold. Below, the forest ended abruptly and the grass, greening now in sunlight, ran in immense meadows, into purple, into distance. There, behind the mist and perhaps one hundred miles [160 km] distant, Rashedi said, lay the north-east tip of the Lake. The mist dissolved. Something bright at the limit of vision, like a platter of translucent white glass, spread undefined between land and sky. It was a radiance; no more than that. But this was the Nyanza. 'I could have wept,' Whitehouse wrote later. 'It was as if it had never really existed until then … '

"Five years had passed since he had learned that his was to be the task of bringing rail to the greatest of the African lakes. During those years his mind had encompassed nothing else. The Lake was too large, too steeped in history and the myth of exploration to admit of other things. The Lake occupied him, overflowed, it seemed, from the spring of his own ambition. He was of course in bondage to it. Failure of the railroad meant failure as a man: for him nothing would lie beyond. He, and others, would drown in the enormity of the failure. Conversely, success meant professional and public honour."

The city of Nairobi, Kenya's capital, previously nothing more than a collection of huts at a river crossing, was born out of Whitehead's decision to site the headquarters of the railway at a midway point along the line. The colonial administration, which had been nearby at Machakos, could not afford to be off the line of rail and so the new capital was decided upon.

In the building of the Uganda Railway, many coolies lost their lives to man-eating lions, stealing into the fragile tents at nights. Europeans died too. More deaths occurred from hostile tribesmen. With smallpox and other diseases that ran through the coolie camps, the overall death toll was 2,493 Asians – a fearful 8 per cent of all who built the railway – and five Europeans. Tribal resistance came not from the Masai despite their ferocious reputation. Although the line ran right across their territory, they had enough sense not to run onto the guns of the work parties. It was the Nandi who put up the stiffest resistance to the railway line and the British rule that came with it. They continued to resist until 1905 when they were broken by the authorities' overwhelming firepower.

From the start it was realised that effective administration in Uganda, and the opening up of its trade, depended on the railway and the telegraph. Railway activity was present from the start: Captain James Macdonald was conducting a railway survey even while Captain Frederick Lugard was conquering the Buganda state on behalf of the Imperial British East Africa Company. The railway was an intensely political creation. Whitehead had to have one eye on the construction and the other on the British House of Commons. He was under constant pressure to cut costs. His problems were compounded by attacks from the radicals led by Henry Labouchere, for whom the project was an exercise in colonial adventurism. Macdonald's projected route over the mountains beyond the Rift was abandoned when one of Whitehead's engineers discovered a lower – and shorter – route to the lake. The saving was many miles, although shallow Port Florence (now Kisumu) was arguably less suitable than Port Victoria where Macdonald's line would have ended.

The telegraph was laid along the railway track but went ahead of the track-laying (it was a favourite target of the Nandi). It also went to Kampala, not just to Port Florence. When any point on the globe's surface can be reached by satellite-linked mobile phones, it is hard for us to imagine the effect this end of isolation must have had on the European residents of Kampala. Where before it took several months to send a message and get a reply (the time needed to take a message to the nearest telegraph station and bring back the answer), the same could now be accomplished in minutes. The world was becoming a global village even then. The railway also abolished time and distance, or so it seemed to those used to the trek to the coast taking three months: that journey could now be done in comfort in easily less than a week, including the steamer crossing.

All glory fades. Despite the hard-won triumph of making a way to the lake, despite the elation of bringing the rails to the water's edge, the last part of Whitehead's route, including some of the most challenging engineering on the line, was to become a branch when the railway was extended around the lake. An extension to Jinja was completed in 1928, and the opening of the Nile railway bridge in 1931 finally brought the railway to the Uganda capital.

As with medicine, so with schools: it was the Christian missions that founded the formal education system in Uganda, especially after the declaration of the protectorate in 1894. Bishop Tucker reported that in 1898 enrolment in Church Missionary Society (CMS) schools was still only a few hundred but by 1903 the number had grown to 22,000. Growth continued to be rapid: the total primary school enrolment in 1911-12 for all Christian missions in the country was 80,482.

The religious make-up of Uganda changed, reflecting the fact that it was ruled by a Protestant power. Although the Roman Catholics had been more numerous than the Protestants in pre-colonial times, the (Anglican) CMS became the chief beneficiary of government policy. Of those 80,482 primary school pupils in 1911-12 (according to figures cited by Ado K. Tiberondwa in *Missionary Teachers As Agents of Colonialism*), the CMS accounted for 56,482, dwarfing the efforts of the (Roman Catholic) White Fathers and Mill Hill Fathers. In the early 1920s, government financial support for CMS mission activities was broadly the same as for the Roman Catholic missions combined. But the Protestants' success also came from their own efforts. The government stated in 1909 that they had been quicker than the Catholics to recognise that the growth of the educational system depended on the supply of trained African teachers.

An official analysis of Buganda (not the whole of Uganda) by faith illustrated how Protestantism overhauled Catholicism in the early years of the 20th century:

	CMS missions	RC missions	Muslims	Animists*
1911	140,144	181,141	58,401	325,929
1915	186,672	187,592	55,262	252,267
1916	200,308	186,298	51,783	238,544

(The Handbook of Uganda 1920, cited by Tiberondwa)
*The actual term used was "non-readers"

The policy of the British Empire was religious toleration and neutrality, but inevitably much of the African elite took on the religious colouration of the rulers. Mwanga's son, Daudi Chwa, who was declared kabaka of Buganda as a child, was baptised a Protestant. By 1924, 38 out of the 50 senior chiefs in the country were Protestant. Only in Buganda, the scene of the original Protestant-Roman Catholic competition, did the numbers approach parity: 10 Protestants and eight Catholics, with two Muslims.

Until the end of the colonial administration in the 1960s, it was common for the main Protestant church in each district to place a reserved chair for the British district commissioner, with next to that a chair for the chief. For Tiberondwa, this tended to lock the chiefs into the religion of the rulers. The point cannot be pressed too far, however, because some DCs were not Protestant. The Empire was officially secular and did not recruit only Protestants.

The irrelevance of much missionary teaching to African daily experience even shocked secular observers at the time. Simple village children who could barely read and write their own language were taught to worship in the Roman Catholic Church using meaningless Latin; other children learnt exhaustively about the Rivers Thames and Severn or how the Vikings invaded England and Hannibal crossed the Alps.

The Phelps–Stokes Commission, which reported in 1922 and 1924 on Ugandan education, commented eloquently: "The music you hear will not be a native song but the parody of a familiar European hymn. None of the acute problems of village housing, sanitation, water or food preparation are present either in theory or practice ... The chorus of unintelligible sounds is the sing-song of the syllables as they follow one another in meaningless succession. You will hear reading, but it will not describe, explain or appreciate any of the hundred and one real things and actions of the village ... In fact you will wonder if the schools belong to the village world at all." [Quoted by Tiberondwa, see bibliography]

Writing in 1978, Tiberondwa offers a mixed assessment of missionary-based education in colonial Uganda: "Missionaries have been praised and praised again for bringing education and Christianity to Africa. Indeed the missionaries deserve these praises because, despite its limitations and failures here and there, Western education definitely contibuted to African development ... When education enslaves one to foreign values as colonial education has done to the Africans, then that education cannot be regarded as successful because, instead of providing freedom to the Africans, that education has taken African freedom away."

In the immediate sense pinpointed by the Phelps-Stokes Commission, that concentration on foreign values was plainly wrong. Colonialism also produced the "cultural cringe" whereby the foreign values were simply assumed to be superior. Perhaps we should say colonialism accelerated the cultural cringe. In any situation human beings tend to copy the leaders, whether countries, cultures, products or personal role models. However, a further question lies beyond Tiberondwa's valid remarks: was it ever possible to have the pluses of missionary education without the minuses? Everyone, after all, teaches out of his or her own background. Indeed, in a Christian context what are foreign values and what are universal ones?

Certainly knowledge and technology are universal. When well meaning Western consultants in post-independence Africa have tried to introduce "intermediate" technology and "appropriate" education, these have often been spurned as patronising and second-class. In the age of computer-controlled electric motors, who wants a hand-pump? The same body of knowledge is demanded whether delivered under a tree or in a concrete and glass education factory.

17

Bodies and Souls

*Stanley's iron will * A paradoxical character * Mackay the practical Christian * Flying the flag * Lugard: confidence and diplomacy * Land settlement too severe * Sudan might-have-been * Anglicans in force * Religion and traditions * Catholics and Protestants stay divided * Indirect rule*

The characters upon whom this book is focused – Henry Morton Stanley, explorer; Alexander Mackay, missionary; Frederick Lugard, soldier – shared a key quality: toughness. In the circumstances of 19th century Africa, perhaps it is why theirs are among the names that resonate most strongly with us more than a century later. Stanley three times crossed the fearsome Ituri Forest where his colleagues of the rear column managed a single journey of less than 100 miles (160km). Mackay was 14 years in Africa without a break while colleagues came and went, sometimes alone and often with the activity hostility of Mwanga, the king of Buganda. Lugard, with just 50 soldiers, imposed his settlement on the Kiganda state after an earlier representative of the Imperial British East Africa Company, Frederick Jackson, had left empty-handed despite his 400 soldiers.

This quality of toughness is most visible in Stanley. Practically every contemporary and subsequent writer has remarked on his iron will. This willpower was forged in the Welsh workhouse of his childhood and the America of his young manhood, where he survived as a solitary runaway. But tough circumstances by themselves do not produce tough people: there has to be innate material for them to work on.

It was the same will that took Stanley across the Ituri Forest and enabled him to produce his massive two-volume *In Darkest Africa* in just 50 days while sitting in a Cairo hotel room. To produce a book of that scale – it is about 400,000 words, or three to four times the length of a typical modern book – in that time is above all a feat of willpower and physical energy. No matter what documents or diary entries were tipped into the book wholesale, it is a staggering achievement.

Beyond his most obvious quality of willpower, Stanley has always puzzled biographers because he was a bundle of characteristics that it is not easy to resolve into a unified personality. Or is that the point? The Bible-quoting Christian who knew the Good Book well enough to satisfy the kabaka Mutesa on the subject of angels is also the person whose brutal methods were remembered two generations later by the ba-Mbuti pigmies, who hanged several men for punishment and as examples and who engaged in the unattractive practice of abducting women in order to ransom them for food.

Few other African travellers carried on in this violent way. A.J. Mounteney-Jephson in his diary gave an example of Stanley's methods when obtaining a canoe: "All day long we could see canoes ahead crossing and re-crossing the river, the natives were very much terrified and hardly seemed to know what to do. We harassed them all day long and Stanley pursued a canoe with four men in it, he shot one of the men and the other jumped ashore and got off. We towed the canoe to the other side of the river with the wounded native in it, but he bled to death before we reached the bank and the men threw him overboard … " [Quoted by Smith, see bibliography]

Yet as perceptive an observer as Alexander Mackay could comment that Stanley only used violence when he had no alternative and was notably considerate towards Africans. Perhaps Stanley's methods and his achievements were inseparable. He arguably achieved more than any other African explorer, and without the brutal methods there would not have been the achievements. The lion at rest is a peaceable creature. Hungry or threatened, he is dangerous. For Stanley the survival of the expedition and the meeting of its objectives justified the actions necessary to bring these about. Where the expedition was not threatened, he became the resting lion that Mackay saw at Usambiro.

Emin Pasha's associate, Gaetano Casati, praised Stanley's "brilliant conversation and gentlemanly courtesy". These were rarely on display for European colleagues on his expeditions for the leader held himself aloof, often taking his meals alone. He felt separateness to be a necessary attribute of leadership. On the Emin Pasha Relief Expedition, his relations with the other officers were poor, except for Mounteney-Jephson. Throughout his travels, he felt he had found only one equal: David Livingstone. One can see in all this the traces of the workhouse boy and auto-didact, born into the lowest social class and illegitimate as an added burden; ultimately unsure of his place in society and the skills and graces that society demands.

Stanley was the only person who did not see the funny side of his most famous remark: "Dr Livingstone, I presume?" What else, after all, did one say when meeting a stranger? Years later Stanley was being invested with an honorary degree. At a key moment in this dignified ceremony an undergraduate called out "Mr Stanley, I presume?" Everyone laughed except Stanley.

It is possible to see Stanley as an unprincipled opportunist, but the reality seems more complex. Even so, this is a man who started British, became American and ended up British again (and a knight of the realm). He fought on both sides of the American Civil War, which some have seen as a portent for his ambiguous position on the Emin Pasha Expedition. He remained under contract to King Leopold of Belgium while leading the expedition (although unpaid) for William Mackinnon of the Imperial British East Africa Company. The two men's ambitions in Equatoria were mutually exclusive, yet Stanley had propositions for Emin from both.

As well as his iron will, the quality in Stanley most often mentioned is his economy with the truth. He may have been one of those people who, not knowingly lying, are so imbued with self-belief that any setback is overwritten and ceases to exist. *In Darkest Africa* presents an account of the disaster of the rear column in which no blame attaches to the leader. It is patently a selective presentation of the facts designed to exonerate Stanley. For instance, he emphasises that the tragedy occurred because the rear column stayed at Yambuya and rotted away, but on the documentary evidence (actually in Stanley's book) it is clear that he initially expected Barttelot to wait for him to come back, and that moving forward was always just one option. Iain R. Smith, in *The Emin Pasha Relief Expedition, 1886-1890*, says Stanley's inability to make good his promises to Tippu Tip, the Arab trader and ruler, was a key reason for Tippu not supplying enough carriers, which in turn was the reason why the rear column could not move.

Stanley can claim to be the greatest of all the 19th century African explorers, although the failure of the Emin Pasha Relief Expedition dents this reputation. His achievement is the more remarkable because he turned to African travel only after several years as a journalist and foreign correspondent. Ujiji was his Damascus Road; it was the meeting with Livingstone that turned his thoughts to becoming an explorer. In fact, Stanley remained a journalist. His books still read fast and colourfully, if by today's ideas the writing style is long-winded. He donated his newspaper fees for writing about the Emin Pasha expedition to the expedition funds: at £2,200 they were 6.9 per cent of overall income – a vast amount given the size of the project. That was the measure of the world's interest in Emin Pasha and Henry Stanley.

Writing, lectures and his years with King Leopold of Belgium building the Congo State made Stanley a rich man. He cheated death from fever many times on his travels, although ever afterwards he suffered from shaking spasms, which he described as "the Africa in me". Unlike most of the actors in this story, he lived to see his 60th birthday and died in bed. For his closing years he built a handsome house at Pirbright, Surrey. It had been completed just a few weeeks when he died in his early sixties.

Alexander Mackay embodied as much as any one man could Stanley's call for "practical Christian tutors" to serve as missionaries in Buganda. Mackay was an educated and talented engineer, who was never ordained. He was equally at home mending a boat, improvising a coffin without the proper materials, operating a printing press, translating Scripture into Luganda, proclaiming the faith and even unravelling the structure of Kiganda theology, which he discovered had two supreme gods.

His amazing versatility was the key to his survival for so long in the always wary and often hostile environment of Mengo. He was simply too useful to the kabaka and the chiefs. Most of them were not after his message but his hands, a fact that he recognised himself in his letters. He believed that practical help built friendship and confidence, from which acceptance of the gospel would naturally flow.

He also possessed physical courage and a stern devotion to duty drawn from the Scottish presbyterianism of his upbringing. He rejected repeated appeals from headquarters to return home on leave; with the journeys it would mean a year away, and that time he would not spare. In 1887, during Mwanga's persecution of the Christians, Mackay wrote: "I have not the slightest desire to 'escape', if I can do a particle of good by staying." It was clear that if he had wanted to escape he could have done. The mission's boat, the Eleanor, was lying nearby. He was on his own at the Protestant mission and under continual threat of his life. Even he was driven out in the end as the kabaka became increasing desperate and set in motion a series of events that resulted in his own undoing. Mackay went only as far as Usambiro on the other side of Lake Victoria, where he kept busy preparing scripture texts and other materials for Buganda.

Mackay was lionised in his own time. Bishop Hannington, when outside Buganda, found that Mackay's was the name that everyone knew – "But of the others I scarce ever hear a word" – and after his premature death in 1890, aged 40, a book by his sister, *Mackay of Uganda*, quickly ran through several editions. Mackay, unlike his colleague, Robert Ashe, did not write any books, but he did not need to. He wrote many articles. His letters are voluminous and often very long. Many are reprinted in *Mackay of Uganda*, which uses so much verbatim material that it is in effect Mackay's autobiography – an impression heightened by his sister not using her own name as the author. The title page simply reads "By his sister".

Mackay was described by Stanley, without exaggeration, as "the best missionary since Livingstone", but while Livingstone remains a household name Mackay does not. It is curious that he has been forgotten by the public at large. Livingstone himself has his debunkers, but two aspects of Mackay's life seem to present particular difficulties.

Mackay's anti-Catholicism does not play well in our own ecumenically minded age. He loathed their "Mary worship" and perceived that Rome had moved too far from Scripture with its "salvation by sacraments"; he abhorred (in Ashe's phrase) the Catholics' "hocus-pocus mock-miracle-working formulae". Mackay (even disregarding the different age in which he lived) seems to be outside the parameters of Christian unity. Ecumenism, in the sense of re-creating that unity, is not merely a worthy goal, it is a gospel imperative. Yet the vigorous expression and discussion of differences is the first stage of ecumenical progress. Beyond that, though, Mackay's robust defence of Protestant truth cannot properly be faulted when he was faced with an intransigent church convinced of the uniqueness of its revelation and grace-giving powers.

The second way in which Mackay seems to be out of tune with our own times is his vocal participation in the "forward school" of politico-diplomacy. As such he can be seen as an active agent of colonialism. He was a highly efficient "postmaster" for Emin Pasha, facilitating the flow of letters between Equatoria and the coast, but his role with Emin was more than instrumental. He wanted a British occupation of Equatoria as well as Buganda. He saw this as the best means to a desirable end. The end was civilisation in a modern sense. The Baganda were civilised but not in the sense that anyone seized with the biblical commmand to go out and preach to all nations could accept. Mackay was confronted with slavery, fetish-worship accompanied by superstition and fear, and human slaughter for ritual or political purposes.

He must often have been lonely, but he was alone only in sometimes not having another European missionary with him. The mission houses, both at Mengo and Usambiro, abounded with life. As Livingstone, travelling with black companions, found years before, friendship soon transcends skin colour. Stanley has left us with a picture of a comfortable establishment full of books. Mackay's letters make clear that he kept up with events in the outside world, although his information was inevitably at least three months in arrears.

Frederick Lugard, who arrived in Buganda the same year that Mackay died south of the lake (1890), possessed an enviable package of attributes: physical and mental toughness, self-confidence and diplomatic skills. With these he turned his uninvited arrival in the country with a handful of soldiers into control of the country within a year and a half. He was able to exploit and channel to his advantage the faction fighting he found, but a mere bone-headed soldier could not have done it. It was a brilliant stroke to see that a remnant of Emin's Equatoria troops could be brought back to Buganda, garrisoning a vital border and adding to the IBEA Company's forces. It took diplomacy to persuade their commander, Selim Bey, to bring them out; it took even more diplomacy to persuade the Baganda Muslims to lay down their arms and acquiesce in a general constitutional settlement.

That settlement was, probably unintentionally, too severe on the Catholics and was amended by Sir Gerald Portal the following year, but it brought peace to the country for the first time in several years. It was not diplomacy that brought on side the Catholics and the kabaka, who backed them, but fighting. The claimed massacre of Catholics at the Battle of Mengo and immediately afterwards on Bulingugwe Island continues to divide writers.

The controversy did Lugard no good in England but no long-term harm. Within a few years he was back in Africa, in what became Nigeria, where he further developed the principles of indirect rule that he had tried out in Buganda. He became governor of Nigeria, a lord and lived to see the dawn of the present era, dying on April 11, 1945, in his late eighties.

His eloquent book, *The Rise of Our East African Empire*, was written, like Stanley's *In Darkest Africa*, partly for self-defence. Lugard had to defend himself and Captain Williams against Catholic charges of atrocities. The book does not reveal much about the man, who comes across as a steely hero admitting at most to a touch of neuralgia or a spot of fever while all around are dropping. He respects the Baganda, but does not believe in equality between the races. Europeans should "unostentatiously assert" their superiority, while the missionaries Ashe and Pilkington are criticised for listening to complaints by Africans against himself, thus setting off "one Englishman against another". Ashe collects another brickbat for kneeling before the king, as Mackay also did.

In Margery Perham's biography, *Lugard: The Years of Adventure*, her subject comes across as decidedly unstuffy. She knew him when he was deep into his still-active retirement, living as a widower in a cottage at Abinger, Surrey. He demanded to be called "Fred", which she managed to do to his face, but she admitted that privately she was unable to think of the great imperial pro-consul as Fred.

Lugard's racial inequality is not that of a conqueror, however; it is the inequality of the parent and the child. His book has no feeling that Africans are congenitally inferior, or that Europeans are in

Africa to rape it. The question is one of social development. The Europeans' duty and value is as role models. This self-belief fuels what for us may seem the most surprising part of Lugard's activities: his evident conviction that he is entitled to walk into someone else's country and, with a treaty whose import is fully understand by only one side, take it over. Buganda and the countries around had been allocated (without their knowledge) to Britain, and that was that.

It was not stupidity that led African rulers to sign these treaties. What Lugard managed credibly to promise was law and order. The Baganda were tired of civil war. Countries like Ankole and Toro were glad to have protection against their enemies. Defeat in war meant death and enslavement. Lugard himself believed that the most significant part of his work was reducing slavery.

Stanley's 1875 appeal for missionaries in Buganda was one of the most influential letters ever written. It produced an immediate response from the British public and the Church Missionary Society, which one year later had a party on its way to Africa. It was the presence of these missionaries, coupled with public appreciation in Britain of their work and lobbying by the CMS, that later drew an initially reluctant British government into taking over the country. That Buganda today, as the largest part of the country of Uganda, is mainly Christian, partly Protestant and a member of the Commonwealth speaks of the permanent effects of that letter. With another set of circumstances, it might have become German or Belgian, or part of a greatly enlarged Sudan.

When Stanley took on the Emin Pasha Relief Expedition in 1886 he committed himself to a roundabout route that destroyed the expedition's chances of success. Under threat from the Mahdists to the north, the government of Equatoria might have survived if Stanley had reached the province earlier. Nor did it help that his party arrived in rags after struggling through the Ituri Forest. Emin's soldiers could not believe that the bedraggled band really represented the khedive of Egypt. The collapse of Equatoria created a vacuum that was eventually filled by re-incorporating most of it into the Sudan. The tragic history of that country in our own time invites a saddening might-have-been.

A continuing Equatorial Province might have evolved as a pragmatic Muslim state. More likely, it would have been absorbed into Leopold's Congo or the Uganda Protectorate created by the British in the 1890s. As it is, a small part of Equatoria, including the last capital, Wadelai, is within the boundaries of Uganda.

The aim of Consul Holmwood in Zanzibar for the relief expedition to settle the affairs of Buganda as well as Equatoria was not fulfilled, or even attempted. In 1889 en route to the coast with Emin, Stanley declined to intervene in the Buganda civil war. His decision might have had the widest consequences because soon afterwards Carl Peters reached Mengo and obtained from the kabaka a German protectorate over Buganda. Peters's coup, however, was overtaken by the Anglo-German agreement of 1890, so the country stayed in the British sphere.

Stanley could and did argue that the expedition was a success: Emin had been rescued after all. Yet only a fragment of the province's expatriate population came out with him. The officers and most of the soldiers stayed behind. In an accidental way, the potentially threatening armed bands produced the final resolution of the Uganda question. It was with the help of these troops that Lugard took over the Buganda state and his successors carved out the larger protectorate.

Certainly the expedition was a success in balancing its accounts. In fact, it did better than break even. Income was £32,367 1s 10d [20 shillings (s) = £1 and 12 pence (d) = one shilling] and expenditure was £27,709 9s 5d. The balance of £4,657 12s 5d was distributed to expedition survivors and relatives or owners of the deceased. Thus the philanthropic sponsors found themselves party not only to using slaves on the expedition but also to rewarding slave owners for lending their property.

An extraordinary number of those involved with the Emin Pasha Relief Expedition, and plenty who were not, published books and articles about it. The diaries of the two dead officers, Major Barttelot and James S. Jameson, are a vital counter-balance to Stanley's own account. Even a French priest who joined the expedition on its closing section to the east coast found he had something to say. Herbert Ward wrote a pleasant and colourful memoir, quoted from earlier, but he barely marched with Stanley. He joined late, left early (not from his choice) and spent much of the time stuck at

Yambuya. Many of the accounts are hostile to Stanley and the controversy refused to die. Equatoria and Buganda, those troubled countries, cast a long shadow over the life's work of the great explorer.

The finest testimonial to the work of Alexander Mackay and the other pioneer missionaries is the fact that modern Uganda is the third most populous country in the world for Anglicans, with around seven million adherents. This is second only to the United Kingdom, the birthplace of Anglicanism, and Nigeria, a far bigger country. The journal Anglican Frontier Missions projected Anglican populations in the year 2000 as follows: United Kingdom 26.0 million; Nigeria 11.3 million; Uganda 7.4 million; India 4.3 million, Australia 4.0 million, Kenya 2.7 million; South Africa 2.4 million; United States 2.4 million, Tanzania 2.3 million, Sudan 2.1 million and Pakistan 1.2 million.

In 1977, the 100th anniversary year of the first Christian missionaries in Buganda, Archbishop Janani Luwum, the Anglican primate of Uganda, was murdered during the rule of Idi Amin. Uganda had offered up yet another martyr. Eleven years later (1998) a statue of Archbishop Luwum joined 11 others placed on the west front of Westminster Abbey in London representing those who died for the Christian faith in the 20th century. Others include Dietrich Bonhoeffer, the German Lutheran pastor and theologian killed by the Nazis in 1945, Martin Luther King, the American Baptist pastor and civil rights campaigner, and another archbishop, the Roman Catholic Oscar Romero of El Salvador.

Just before he died Archbishop Luwum wrote an article for the commemorative volume, *A Century of Christianity in Uganda, 1877-1977* (edited by Tom Tuma and Phares Mutibwa), in which he stressed the continuity between the early missionaries and the present African-led church. "(O)ne cannot fail to see God's hand guiding every worthy effort by numerous sons and daughters of this country and their missionary counterparts," he wrote.

A list of CMS missionaries printed as an appendix to that volume, covering the hundred years, contained 693 names, some representing couples. Extensive lists could also be produced by the White Fathers and the Mill Hill Fathers.

Luwum tackles head-on the thorny issue of Christianity and

indigenous religion. Noting that Europe itself received Christianity from the outside, he says: "Foreign missionaries have been blamed for undermining traditional religious practices and beliefs but many of us realise today that they had no option since they were planting and building the Christian Church in what was termed a 'dark continent'. They had to make sure that a proper foundation was laid and a complete break with evil practices made lest the Master Builder should test their work now and at the end of time and find it lacking in the spirit of Paul's Letter to the Corinthians when he said:

"'According to the commission of God given to me, like a skilled master builder I laid a foundation, and another man is building upon it. For no other foundation can anyone lay than that which is laid, which is Jesus Christ ... '"

The archbishop praises the government's land allocation to the three main missions (under the 1900 Uganda Agreement, described earlier), which he writes helped to quell the "warring spirit" among the missions. The land grants "allowed the religious groups to operate freely and prove their worth. The people were able to choose for themselves without any repressive measures ... "

That "warring spirit" greatly impeded the work of the Christian evangelists in Buganda in the early days. The main sufferers were the potential converts. A growing awareness of the damage caused by such divisions within Christendom led to the 1910 Edinburgh conference of worldwide missionary organisations, from which the present ecumenical movement has grown.

The original land settlement, by Frederick Lugard, was the least enduring part of his work in Uganda. The resettlement of the Catholics in Budu was immediately modified by his successors as unfair. Even though Lugard was specific that the restriction to Budu applied only to Catholics bearing arms, in the unsettled state of the country the possibility of settling elsewhere unarmed was no great attraction. Sir Gerald Portal, encouraged by Captain Williams, extended the Catholic area with the Bishops' Agreement, but this in turn was superseded two years later, after the Vatican had assigned to the Mill Hill Fathers the eastern part of Uganda, where many of the Anglican mission stations were located. The Uganda Agreement of 1900 entrenched the missions' ability to evangelise throughout the Protectorate. It was not a case of living together happily ever afterwards, however. Uganda continued to suffer religious polarisation, as the final chapter illustrates.

Lugard's main achievement was in a short time to construct the framework of the Uganda state. He solved the problem of the large body of Sudanese soldiers marooned in the interior by bringing them out and finding work for them in Uganda. He brought not only Buganda but also Ankole and Toro into treaty relations with the IBEA Company. The history of Bunyoro within the Protectorate would have been happier if it too had been included by treaty rather than military conquest. With hindsight, it appears that Lugard did not make enough efforts to win over Kabarega, listening too much to the Baganda, who were the traditional enemies of the Banyoro.

His high profile on the Uganda Question, much against the instincts of a typical soldier, and his willingness to address meetings up and down Britain in the autumn of 1892 were important factors in moving the British Cabinet behind retention. But Lugard was never the typical army officer. The exuberant walrus moustache, lavish even for those hairy times, testified to an altogether more creative character.

It is thanks to Lugard that the traditional rulers kept substantial areas of autonomy. The principle of Indirect Rule that is so much associated with his name helped the Baganda and the other kingdoms of the Protectorate come to terms with colonialism. Here were no primitive tribes lacking a civic culture. Although the rulers could not forget that the last word was a British one, the colonial administration worked with and through the rulers and chiefs.

18

Souring of the Vision

*Livingstone's vision half-realised * Christianity an African religion *
Commerce and colonialism * Growth of racism * Rich still make the rules
* Controversial baby formula * Debt writeoff campaign * Suffering from
structural adjustment * Fairness in a coffee cup * The West unreformed*

Livingstone's vision of a benign coming together of "commerce and Christianity" has been only half-realised. That half is Christianity, which whatever the false turns along the way has mutated into an indigenous religion in equal partnerships with churches around the world. A notable case of Africa making its view prevail occurred in 1998 at the Lambeth Conference of Anglican bishops from around the world. The conference, which is held every 10 years, has no binding powers but is highly influential in setting policies for the 70 million Anglicans worldwide. The hot subject of homosexuality, particularly the ordination of practising gays, was widely expected to result in a fudge, perhaps an "international commission" to investigate further and report back. Instead, Third World bishops, of whom those from Africa were the largest group, persuaded their brother bishops to declare that homosexuality cannot be reconciled with scripture and that gay marriage and the ordination of practising homosexuals were not acceptable to the church.

A bishop from Uganda reminded the conference that the king's pageboys had been martyred for refusing, as Christians, exactly the practice that they, as bishops, were being asked to condone. The powerful contribution no doubt weighed in the balance of the result, which approved the declaration by 526 votes to 70, with 45 abstentions.

Commerce in Africa, on the hand, quickly turned into colonialism, which in all but name has lasted to this day as the Western nations continue to make their own rules for trade and aid with Africa.

Perhaps the flaw in the vision was that commerce between continents of such unequal power and development as Europe and Africa could be separated from political control and the arrogance of conquest that comes with it. In Africa, the colonialist mentality grew out of the experience of control; it was not there from the start.

In Alexander Mackay's writings, for instance, there is no sense of Africans as inferior human beings. Indeed, he and the other pioneer Uganda missionaries would hardly have risked their lives except for those with a common humanity under God. The same sense of common humanity runs through the books of early secular figures like Frederick Lugard, the soldier, and Frederick Jackson, the administrator. All three believed that African societies were less developed than – and therefore inferior to – those of Europe, but that is quite a separate matter from holding that one race is inherently superior to others.

By the closing years of colonialism, however, racial attitudes had become entrenched among the whites. F. Spencer Chapman (in another setting a Second World War hero and the author of a famous war book, *The Jungle Is Neutral*) took his family on a motor tour of southern and central Africa in 1953. He wrote about the journey in *Lightest Africa*. Spencer Chapman's chapter Into Uganda, which is 12 pages long, uses the term "native" 15 times. Among the references are "native villages" and "natives [who] paddled dugout canoes" – as if anyone else might be expected in the heart of Africa! At a resthouse a "native" did the family's washing, and other "natives" tried to dig the author's vehicle out of a swamp. Here is a man who does not see just human beings but people who must be instantly put into racial categories.

The same chapter describes Spencer Chapman's excitement at getting permission "to go to remote Karamoja, which is not normally opened to tourists, to see the really primitive African" – language which half a century later we might use about the Rwanda gorillas.

Political control from the outside subverted the lofty and defensible goal of speeding a country into the modern world – the aim of the modern development movement. The Baganda never asked for the country to be eaten. Land tenure was upended and kin structures were eroded for all that British rule was supposed to be indirect. Colonialism bred a sense of inferiority to which, sadly, religious organisations were party. The church-run Mengo Hospital, admittedly with the best intentions as noted in the previous chapter, charged fees based on race. Missionary schools taught children about the Thames and the Seine, the Alps and the Pyrennees, rather than the Nile and the Ruwenzori.

The attitudes bred by colonialism remain with us today, both as a lingering sense of inferiority or its opposite in reaction among former subject peoples, and an exaggerated sense of shame among former colonisers.

In 19th century Africa the alternatives were not European colonialism or stable indigenous rule. If the Europeans had not come, the continent might have seen Arab colonisation instead. Tippu Tip, for instance, had a large area of the Congo under his rule. The introduction of firearms escalated the constant warfare that plagued the continent, creating more opportunities for one African people to colonise another.

When Stanley in 1875 appealed for missionaries to go to Buganda, he set in motion a series of events that led with the inevitability of stars in their courses to the colonisation of the country. There were uncertainties around the edges. In other circumstances more of Equatoria would have ended up in Uganda. Nor was it a foregone conclusion that the British government would take over Buganda from the IBEA Company, but if it had not, another European power would have stepped in.

Yet Stanley and the earliest missionaries had commerce and Christianity, not colonisation, in mind. Colonisation became inevitable partly because a section of the missionary community, the Anglicans, came to believe that externally imposed order and stability provided the best soil for Christianity to grow in, and had the political clout to promote their ends. The White Fathers can be commended for wanting to leave indigenous rule untouched, but Lugard made the realistic point that this would have produced an arms free-for-all and continued turmoil in Buganda.

Despite the Church Missionary Society's formidable lobbying abilities, it would be fanciful to think that religious groups could single-handedly determine major political outcomes. The other factor that made colonisation inevitable was trade. The Great Lakes region was rich in elephants. Stanley's *In Darkest Africa* acknowledged the importance of ivory when it spoke of "every tusk, piece and scrap" being "steeped and dyed in blood", of "the rich heart of Africa" laid waste for ornaments and billiard games.

Uganda in the beginning was worth trading with, provided it could be reached by railway; Kenya initially was not, although the fact of the Uganda Railway passing through it triggered trade and development. The railway proved to be so expensive to build – more than twice the projected costs of the first surveyor, Captain James Macdonald – that trade had to be found quickly to justify the outlay. This forced the emergence of cash crops in Uganda and Kenya, and with the plantations, particularly in Kenya, came white settlers. The Uganda Railway offers a curious circularity: it was built to allow trade, and trade had to be created to allow the railway. Cotton, coffee, tea, sugar, maize, wheat and livestock were among the commodities to emerge.

Land conflicts in Africa between the settlers and the indigenous peoples, which continue to this day in southern Africa, were a consequence of opening up the continent to trade. Behind trade lies capital. As with the Anglo-Egyptian War of 1882, so perhaps with African interventions generally. The British reacted to an army coup d'etat by bombarding Alexandria and eventually taking over the country. At the time, some saw this war as "having been foisted on the government by a clique of investors", notes Lawrence James in *The Rise and Fall of the British Empire*. He adds: "Interestingly, traditionalist Tories and left-wing radicals both identified the manifestations of the new imperialism of the 1880s and 1890s with the backstairs influence of capital."

The new elements in European colonialism were its global nature and its all-pervasiveness on the ground. Where earlier imperialisms were intermittent, perhaps requiring nothing more than the annual payment of tribute, European colonial administrations were never far away from the administered. Technology compounded the practice so that after the introduction of four-wheel-drive vehicles "your people were always accessible", as a British official in Africa remarked, adding: "You might have an exciting time getting to them, but you did get there."

Otherwise, colonisation is as old as the human experience.

Buganda when the Europeans arrived was surrounded by tributary states. During the first Christian millennium, the present Bantu-speaking peoples along the northern shores of Lake Victoria drove out or absorbed the Cushites, who were themselves colonisers of the region in the dawn of history. The Bantu speakers came from the south, from what is now Zambia (F.J. Nothling, *Pre-Colonial Africa*). The Bachwezi people's kingdom of Bunyoro-Kitara flourished between 1350 and 1500. Its capital was first Mubende and later Bigo (both in present Uganda). The Kitara kingdom was surrounded by thousands of tiny chiefdoms stretching over modern Buganda, Busoga, the western Rift Valley, eastern Rwanda and north-western Tanzania.

Bunyoro-Kitara remained the formal style for the omukama and his kingdom. Mubende in the 20th century was at the centre of Bunyoro's "lost counties" dispute with Buganda and the Protectorate government. Banyoro saw these counties as having been colonised by the Baganda. John Beattie, in *The Nyoro State*, records that in 1896 the British political officer in Mubende, William Pulteney, resigned when called upon to officiate in the transfer of the "lost counties" to Buganda. A British official called Forster also resigned for similar reasons.

We can glimpse from the few non-Western states around the world that were never colonised what might have happened in Buganda if, as the White Fathers wanted, it had stayed as an independent nation. States that were never colonised include Thailand, Afghanistan, northern Yemen, Liberia and Ethiopia (disregarding the late and short period of Italian occupation). These now are not so very different from adjacent ex-colonies. They are certainly not more developed economically through being able to chart their own course; in fact, the opposite tends to be true because of more restricted access to capital. On the positive side, the non-colonies are justifiably proud of having kept their independence, and this at some level must rub off on individual psyches.

In Africa today, the rich nations of the West continue to make aid and trade available strictly on their terms. It seems that nothing has been genuinely learned from the colonial experience, when the economic power of the strong exploited the weak. Aid, for example, is rarely without strings. When tied to equipment and material purchases, it may have the perverse effect of benefiting the donor more than the recipient. That is certainly true of the billions upon billions that have been spent on armaments to prop up undemocratic African governments or on unnecessary super-highways or high-rise buildings that offer a spurious sense of modernity and little else.

Although the possession of colonies as a way of mopping up excess ouput of European and American factories has been widely deplored, the merry trade continues often with outmoded or inappropriate product lines. Baby formula is a case in point. This has been widely sold into Africa by Nestlé and other international companies. Whether formula is preferable to breast milk at a certain age may be a point for the well-to-do West but it is not the issue in Africa: there mothers, often in rural or shanty areas, are persuaded through a range of selling techniques to buy a product that they can't afford out of guilt of not doing their best for their child. It gets even worse: these mothers often don't have access to a supply of unpolluted water with which to make up the formula, thus putting their babies at risk.

As the Millennium approached, the London-based development charity Christian Aid announced that for every $1 of new aid to Third World countries $3 was being taken out as debt service (repayments relating to previous borrowings). In that way, the West continues to extract resources from Africa. The benefit of the loans, such as it was, may have disappeared long ago while the repayment burden remains. Nor is it enough for hard-liners to argue that just like everyone else Africa must pay her debts. The circumstances in which many of these loans were taken out will not stand up to dispassionate analysis. Often they were pressed on African governments by banks awash with capital looking for a home, while those governments had no processes of democratic evaluation or public transparency with which to justify the borrowing.

The churches-backed Jubilee 2000 coalition in many countries took the lead in seeking the write-off of unpayable Third World debt. Both the Pope and the Archbishop of Canterbury as heads of the Roman Catholic Church and the Anglican Communion respectively also launched debt initiatives to mark the Millennium. Jubilee 2000 moved not a mountain but at least a small hill in improving official attitudes in the West, with much of the change prompted by

British governments, both Conservative and Labour. The debt campaigners did this with dramatic demonstrations like encircling Birmingham, Britain's second city, with a seven-mile (11km) human chain while leaders of the Group of Eight leading industrial nations were meeting there in May 1998. Another human chain was formed along the River Thames in central London to correspond with a G8 summit in Cologne (Germany) in June 1999.

Some estimates put unpayable Third World debt as high as $250 billion – a hiccup rather than a problem for the international monetary system. The amount, relatively small in global terms, represented for individual countries matters of life and death – of diseases untreated, schools unbuilt, affordable food unavailable.

Perhaps even worse than the debt problem, if that is possible, are the conditions under which the rich world provides new capital to the poor world. Uganda is regarded as a model of structural adjustment under international supervision, but the development charity Oxfam has shown how financial stringencies associated with the World Bank and the International Monetary Fund actually perpetuate the rich world/poor world division. (The World Bank softened its stance in 1998, around the time it agreed to a continuing dialogue with the Archbishop of Canterbury's interfaith group on development issues.)

Structural adjustment programmes purport to be putting the Third World to economic rights after the excesses of the post-independence period, but can equally be seen as the First World re-establishing the terms of trade to its advantage. The de-development of Africa is in process.

A common condition of capital aid is no state subsidies for private industry. But without them how is a small, undercapitalised Third World firm going to compete with imports, or with local offshoots of rich multinationals?

Another common condition is for a freely floating currency, finding its true economic level without being propped up by government. (The value outside the country is frequently nil.) But to exchange Third World currencies with the hard currencies of the West on these terms is like asking the butter to hold its own with the knife. If a currency floats down to one-fiftieth of its former level, what are the consequences? One of the worst is that local firms find imported equipment impossibly expensive so they cannot re-equip themselves; this means in turn that they have even less chance of competing with Western rivals inside the country, not to mention developing exports.

Much-vaunted free trade – where Western countries providing capital insist on more from their Third World borrowers than they do from themselves – helps you to the extent that you have something worth trading. This is less likely for Third World countries trading primary products because these tend to be easily substitutable. For the vast majority of cups drunk, coffee is coffee is coffee regardless of where it came from.

The buying power of Western supermarkets is used to drive down the price received by suppliers. The result is that many crops are picked – often by women – in unspeakable conditions or for pitiable rewards. This is another abuse revealed by Christian Aid. As consumers, we in the West should accept blame because it is our obsession with cheap food that drives the supermarkets. Coffee has particularly suffered from this price assault, and yet fairly traded coffee (where growers and pickers receive fair returns) is readily available and affordable.

The West cannot be proud of its behaviour towards Africa since independence. The leopard of economic imperialism remains at large, and it seems unable to change its spots.

19

The Work Goes On

*From missionaries to mission partners * Role of Namugongo principal **
*Catholic:Protestant divisions soften * Martyrs remembered * Children*
*named Hannington * Affording a bible * Praise from the Archbishop **
*CMS vision of equality * Mission a two-way street*

Namugongo, where the Christians were martyred in the great persecution of 1886, is now a place of pilgrimage. Among the features of the site is a Church of Uganda college training men and women for the Anglican ministry. In late 1998 the college principal, the Rev Stephen Coulson, speaks about his work as a Church Mission Society "mission partner".

"They stopped calling us missionaries a few years ago and called us mission partners. There wasn't any embarrassment about the word 'missionary', but they felt the new term 'mission partner' more clearly reflected what we are – working in partnership with and under the authority of the church here. They would say our contribution to the church is not in big donations but in personnel, in the interchange of sending people here and bringing people from Uganda to Britain.

"The CMS role has changed from pioneering and a sort of authoritative controlling work to just humbly being in partnership. You can't find a CMS office in Kampala because it's not an NGO [non-governmental organisation] functioning as an independent society. It's just here to feed into and be a partner under the church. The other side of that is that over the years CMS has brought Ugandans to Britain for study or sometimes for ministry in the Church of England. Occasionally it has been able to provide bursaries for Ugandan clergy to go somewhere else."

Stephen explains that students at the Namugongo college include five from Sudan and three from Rwanda as well as Ugandans. Among the 50 or so CMS personnel in the country, including partners and dependants, are a family working with Sudanese Christians at Arua, near the borders with Sudan and Congo. "They are working at the Bishop Allison Theological College, where students – pastors and lay people – come from southern Sudan really as refugees. An office for the Church of Sudan is being set up in Kampala. A CMS lady is helping in the logistics of that, and in the future she wants to go up to Arua to be of service to the churches in southern Sudan.

"One of CMS's concerns in the last few years has been particularly to try and see how they can help in the whole work of refugees. I think they would like to be doing more at Arua. Here in Uganda we also have quite a lot to do with the mission partners in the neighbouring countries, particularly in Congo. Twice in the last two years they have all had to be evacuated, and they have come to Uganda as the first stop."

The Namugongo college is an offshoot of the former Bishop Tucker Theological College at Mukono, now renamed the Uganda Christian University, where a CMS couple are teaching theology. "Many of the churches here have a university. There's a Catholic university, an Adventist university, a Muslim university. The Anglican Church felt for a number of years that it ought to have its own university, and so Bishop Tucker became a university offering degrees particularly in education and social sciences as well as teaching theology."

He lists some other CMS personnel at work in Uganda – a woman with the education department in Kampala, a couple at a hospital in Luwero, an architect at Fort Portal, a husband and wife team of occupational therapist and hospital engineer in Kampala and a medical family due to take up Aids prevention in Kampala.

Before moving to Namugongo two years ago with his wife and four children, Stephen worked for four years with churches serving slum areas at the base of Namirembe hill, near the original CMS mission site, where the cathedral now stands. Here he saw Aids at first hand. "In the slum areas where I was working the incidence of HIV-positive would be even higher than the official one in three figure, I think. That's the sexually active adult population, say 15 to 30 in particular. It's the future and it's the useful workforce. Old people are not dying of AIDS. Babies are dying of AIDS, being born with HIV from their parents. When I was in Britain I worked for three years as a curate in Birmingham, and only one time did I bury anyone younger than me. Since I came to Uganda I rarely bury people older than me [he became 38 in November 1998].

"The HIV rate in the slum areas seems to me more devastating, but even out here in the villages what I have noticed really is the loss of children. We baptised my daughter with 22 other children one memorable Sunday last year (January 1997). I've buried five or six of her baptismal classmates, which has been very poignant for me remembering that great day when they were baptised together. Children whose mothers have HIV have a 40–50 per cent chance of being infected."

Against this background, one of his worries about Uganda's booming Pentecostal churches is the practice of all-night prayer meetings – "fairly irresponsible in terms of the freedom and opportunity it gives young people to be promiscuous".

He is the CMS representative in Uganda: "It's a very low-key job, just helping out other mission partners, particularly when they arrive, and occasionally acting as a representative of the Society at great events like the consecration of a new bishop. Each mission partner is under the individual diocese or institution with which they're working, but on the rare occasion when the church here needs to communicate something to all mission partners they might come to me and say you're the representative, it's your job to tell the others."

Stephen acknowledges the "huge history of polarisation" between Roman Catholics and Protestants in Uganda, which continued for many years after the hoped-for settlement of the issue with the Uganda Agreement of 1900. But "things have got so much better" in the last few years.

"If you were Protestant you hated the Catholics, and if you were Catholic you hated the Protestants. Many Ugandan adults I can think of will tell me that they lived next door to a Catholic school but walked 12 miles (19km) so they could go to the Anglican school. On the way they would meet the Catholic children walking from next to the Anglican school to go to the Catholic school.

"Yet those very same people now are quite happy to send their children to Catholic schools even though they are Anglicans. I suppose as a huge generalisation the Catholic schools are better in Uganda than the Anglican-founded ones at the moment. So people are saying, well, I might send my children to that Catholic school because of the good education they will get. It reflects an easing of ecumenical relationships."

Many of Uganda's leading politicians and officials went to CMS-founded schools, particularly Gayaza for girls and Budo, mainly for boys. At Gayaza, three women teachers notched up more than 100 years' service between them. "When I meet top Ugandan ladies, I can almost guarantee half of them have gone to Gayaza and they'll say what about Miss Warren, what about Miss Hobday, what about Miss Cutler? They'll say how much they owe to those ladies and their input.

"I preached at Budo last year at one of their founder's days. Several members of the cabinet who had been through that school were there listening to me preach, which took me aback a bit. But many of their teachers were from Britain and many were CMS."

Not only at Namugongo but throughout Uganda the spirit of the Christian martyrs is ever-present. "There are people alive today who remember survivors, who obviously knew the boys who were murdered. It's only been a generation or so ago, and that's why it continues to be celebrated. Their witness gave such life to the church." We who are further away in time from martyrdom in our countries are offered a dramatic modern example of how the blood of martyrs is the seed of the church.

The martyrs include Bishop Hannington on the Buganda road. Hannington is now a popular Christian name in Uganda. "There's a lot of looking back to those first missionaries, and also a great affection for missionaries in living memory. People like Roy Billington at Mengo Hospital, who died last year [1997]." Dr Billington served in Uganda from 1939 until his retirement in 1971.

Just outside Kampala, at Natete – the site of an early CMS mission house – stands "Mackay's church", built by the pioneer missionary. Nearby is a cave where Protestants used to hide during the religious troubles.

Proud of its long and central place in Uganda's social history, the CMS also looks to the future. Rather than always bringing people to Britain, the organisation is developing its "south/south" initiative.

For instance, a clergyman from Namugongo was sponsored to teach at a college in Mombasa, Kenya.

The finite resources of the CMS have to be shared among several mission fields. Stephen explains: "There was a reprioritisation of CMS's aims and the number of mission partners in Uganda was reduced, particularly teachers. CMS have traditionally sent a lot of teachers to schools in Uganda, but a few years ago they thought that some of the priorities in teaching were in other parts of the world. I think they particularly wanted to help south-east Asia and southern Africa."

It is up to individual church leaders to put in their requests for help. The CMS sees itself as a responding organisation – just as it so famously responded to Stanley's call of 1875 for "practical Christian tutors". Stephen says: "Partnership is a key word of CMS's whole philosophy of what it's doing. Each mission partner has come to Uganda because a bishop has made a request to CMS. It sees itself very much as responding to requests from the church in Uganda."

One of the priorities of the early missionaries was to provide Scripture in the local language. Alexander Mackay translated St Matthews's gospel into Luganda, and the entire bible was completed by George Pilkington. Stephen is delighted that the Luganda bible published by the Bible Society of Uganda is "probably the cheapest book you can buy as a big hardback … when people get to sixth form, they have to buy a number of textbooks and the equivalent size is far more expensive". Even so, the bible costs 5,000 shillings, or about $4 – almost one week's earnings based on the average national per capita income. All is not what it seems, however. Villagers who are largely outside the cash economy (and depress the national income statistics) can do things in another way.

"Villagers are basically self-sufficent for all they need to eat. They haven't got money to spend on a bicycle or a car or fine clothes, but in this part of central Uganda you can't imagine them starving if they're willing to dig the land. The climate and the ground are good. The villagers have a very small income on paper, but they may get a few harvests of matoke [cooking bananas]. If I go to a village to preach and I come back with a pick-up loaded with matoke and chicken and pineapples, I'm very grateful. But while I really appreciate it, it hasn't actually cost them so much.

"You can't buy bibles this way but if you want 5,000 shillings, the cost of a bible, you might put two bunches of matoke on the bicycle and cycle them to the road [to sell]. You wouldn't be able to develop a way of raising your income from $200 to $1,000 a year, but you would for a one-off thing be able to make it."

Stephen says: "CMS has been a huge influence in Uganda not just in the church but in schools and hospitals. [A current mission partner is the engineer at Mengo Hospital, founded by the CMS in the 1890s.] Probably a dozen or more big hospitals around the country were church-founded or CMS-founded."

In fact, the CMS is so well known in Uganda that many older people describe themselves as "CMS" rather than Anglican. "I think all primary school children would know what CMS stands for because it's one of the questions they quite often get in history lessons. In exam papers asking what do the following initials stand for, CMS is often there."

In 1999 the Church Mission Society reached its 200th anniversary. The Archbishop of Canterbury, Dr George Carey – the leader of the worldwide Anglican Communion – addressed around 1,500 people gathered in a huge tent on Clapham Common in London for a celebration service on May 29. He spoke about the CMS's radicalism, with its founding vision of a "missionary society which would be truly worldwide, church-based but not enslaved to episcopacy or ordination". In the 1830s and 1840s it was visionary in its belief in Africa "calling out her own resources" to defeat the evil of slavery.

The Archbishop explained: "The mission was not going to be exclusively from north to south, rich to poor, white to black. Africans themselves were to be equippped for ministry. This may seem unsurprising now, but in those times such thinking was overwhelmingly radical."

Dr Carey said the work of mission societies like the CMS was as urgently needed today as ever, but they had had to adapt from being leaders in mission to serving those who lead. "Sometimes this change of emphasis may lead to a loss of nerve, to the suggestion, even, that the days of mission are over; that there is nothing more for missionary societies to contribute. How wrong this assumption is!

"… We need a new generation of missionary strategists, theologians and teachers, doctors and nurses, agriculturalists and experts of all kinds – all backed by parishes and individual Christians."

Mission, however, is no longer a one-way street. The Archbishop said: "Today in the West we are at last beginning to realise the value of the experience of people from other parts of the world as more and more come from different provinces of the [Anglican] Communion to help us in our mission."

Of that Communion, Uganda is one of the most important parts. Truly, Mackay and Ashe and the hundreds of CMS missionaries and mission partners who followed have done "a glorious work here".

Select bibliography

ALLEN Charles (editor). Tales from the Dark Continent. London: Andre Deutsch/British Broadcasting Corporation, 1979.

ANDERSON William B. The Church in East Africa, 1840-1974. Dodoma, Tanzania: Central Tanganyika Press (CTP), 1988 (first published 1977).

ANSTRUTHER Ian. I Presume. London: Geoffrey Bles, 1956 (New English Library, 1974).

ASHE Robert P. Two Kings of Uganda. London: Sampson Low, Marston, Searle and Rivington, 1889.

BEATTIE John. The Nyoro State. Oxford: Oxford University Press, 1971.

CATHOLIC UNION OF GREAT BRITAIN. Notes on Uganda, or An Analysis. London: Waterlow & Sons, 1893.

CHAPMAN F. Spencer, DSO. Lightest Africa. London: Chatto & Windus, 1955.

COMBY Jean. How to Understand the History of Christian Mission. London: SCM Press, 1996 (French edition 1992). Chaps 7 and 8.

FOSTER W.D. The Church Missionary Society and Modern Medicine in Uganda: The Life of Sir Albert Cook, KCMG, 1870-1951. Published by the author, 1978.

FOX BOURNE H.R. The Other Side of the Emin Pasha Relief Expedition. London: Chatto & Windus, 1891.

GALBRAITH John S. Mackinnon and East Africa, 1878-1895: A Study in the 'New Imperialism'. Cambridge: Cambridge University Press, 1972.

GALE H.P. Uganda and the Mill Hill Fathers. London: Macmillan & Co, 1959

HALL Richard. Lovers on the Nile [biography of Sir S. Baker]. London: Collins, 1980.

HARDY Ronald. The Iron Snake [story of the Uganda Railway]. London: Collins, 1965.

HIRD Frank. H.M. Stanley, the Authorized Life. London: Stanley Paul, 1935.

HOCHSCHILD Adam. King Leopold's Ghost. London: Macmillan 1999 (first published in USA 1998 by Houghton Mifflin Company).

INGHAM Kenneth. A History of East Africa. London: Longmans, Green & Co, 3rd edition 1965 (first published 1962).

JACKSON Sir Frederick, KCMG, CB. Early Days in East Africa. London: Edward Arnold & Co, 1930 (posthumous).

JAMES Lawrence. The Rise and Fall of the British Empire. London: Little, Brown & Co, 1994.

KINGSTON Vera. An Army With Banners: The Romance of Missionary Adventure. London: Sampson Low, Marston and Co. Undated, c 1931. Chaps 3 and 7.

KIWANUKA Malumba S.M.S. A History of Buganda: From the Foundation of the Kingdom to 1900. London: Longman, 1971.

LIVINGSTONE David. Missionary Travels and Researches in South Africa. London: John Murray, 1857.

LOW D. A. Buganda in Modern History. London: Weidenfeld & Nicolson, 1971.

LUCK Anne. African Saint: The Story of Apolo Kivebulaya. London: SCM Press, 1963.

LUGARD Capt F.D., DSO. The Rise of Our East African Empire, Vol 2. Edinburgh and London: Wm Blackwood & Sons, 1893.

MACKAY. A.M. Mackay of Uganda (Mackay, Pioneer Missionary of the Church Missionary Society to Uganda). By his sister. London: Hodder & Stoughton, 9th thousand 1891.

McLYNN Frank. Hearts of Darkness: The European Exploration of Africa. London: Hutchinson, 1992.

MATHESON Elizabeth Mary. An Enterprise So Perilous (history of the White Fathers). London: Mellifont, undated (believed 1970s).

MATHEWS Basil. Livingstone the Pathfinder. London: Livingstone Press, 1943 (first edition 1912).

MURRAY Jocelyn. Proclaim the Good News: A Short History of the Church Missionary Society. London: Hodder & Stoughton, 1985. Partic Chap 7.

NEILL Stephen. A History of Christian Missions (Vol 6 of the Penguin History of the Church), London: Penguin Books, second edition revised by Owen Chadwick, 1986 (first published 1964). Chaps 10 and 11.

NOTHLING F.J. Pre-Colonial Africa: Her Civilisations and Foreign Contacts. South Africa: Southern Book Publishers, 1989 (second impression 1995).

OLIVER Roland. The Missionary Factor in East Africa. London: Longmans, Green & Co, 1952.

PADWICK C. Mackay of the Great Lake. London: Kingsway, 1948 (revised edition).

PAKENHAM Thomas. The Scramble for Africa. London: Abacus, 1992 (first published in UK by Weidenfeld and Nicolson, 1991). Partic Chaps 17, 19 and 23.

PERHAM Margery, CBE. Lugard: The Years of Adventure, 1858-1898. London: Collins, 1956. Partic Part 3.

SMITH Iain R. The Emin Pasha Relief Expedition, 1886-1890. Oxford: Oxford University Press, 1972.

STANLEY Henry M. Through the Dark Continent, Vol 1. London: Sampson Low, Marston, Searle and Rivington, 1878.

STANLEY Henry M. In Darkest Africa, Vols 1 and 2. London: Sampson Low, Marston, Searle and Rivington, 1890.

STIGAND Major C.H., CBE. Equatoria: The Lado Enclave. London: Constable, 1923. Chap 14.

STOCK Eugene. The History of the Church Missionary Society. London: CMS, 1899 (all three volumes). Supplementary volume 1916.

TIBERONDWA Ado K. Missionary Teachers as Agents of Colonialism: A Study of Their Activities in Uganda, 1877-1925. Lusaka: Kenneth Kaunda Foundation, 1978.

TUMA Tom and MUTIBWA Phares (editors). A Century of Christianity in Uganda, 1877-1977. Nairobi: Uzima Press for the Church of Uganda, 1978.

TURNBULL Colin. The Forest People. London: Jonathan Cape, 1961 (Pimlico edition 1993).

VARIOUS AUTHORS. David Livingstone and the Victorian Encounter with Africa. London: National Portrait Gallery Publications, 1996.

WARD Herbert. My Life With Stanley's Rear Guard. London: Chatto & Windus, 1891.

WHITE Stanhope. Lost Empire on the Nile. London: Robert Hale, 1969.

Index

About the author

Cedric Pulford is a journalist with more than 25 years' experience of Africa. His many reports and articles have appeared in outlets as varied as the Guardian and the Daily Telegraph (both London), Ecumenical News International, Gemini News Service and the World Association for Christian Communication's Media Development. He has two degrees in political subjects.